Government and the News Media:
Comparative Dimensions

Government and the News Media: Comparative Dimensions

by

Dan Nimmo and Michael W. Mansfield

PREFACE

In June 1977 the International Communication Association conducted its 27th Annual Conference in Berlin, Germany, in conjunction with the Institut für Publizistik Der Freien Universität Berlin. One of the co-editors of this volume was responsible for organizing programs for the Political Communication Division of ICA at that conference. One such program consisted of a symposium, "Government-Press Relations: A Cross-National Examination." It quickly became apparent from the quality of the papers presented at that symposium, the level of discussion, and the surprisingly large attendance, that scholars in a variety of nations were intensely interested in questions of how governments and the news media relate to one another. It was out of a desire to confront that interest and to stimulate it even more that the idea for this anthology originated. As a result we set about contacting students of government-press relations throughout the world, inquiring about their current research activities and their thoughts about organizing a volume that would provide a comparative analysis of the key aspects of relationships between government and the news media in diverse continental and national settings. The results of that effort are reflected in the essays that comprise this volume.

Because the 1977 Berlin symposium provided a strong impetus for this project, we feel indebted to the scholars who took part in that initial effort to provide cross-national perspectives on government-press relations. Recognition should go first to L. John Martin, University of Maryland, who chaired that symposium. Three participants in that Berlin discussion agreed to contribute to this volume: Rozann Rothman, Dina Goren, and Young C. Kim. It should be noted, however, that their contributions to this anthology were written specifically for the work and are not mere revisions of their earlier papers. Other participants in the symposium provided useful insights regarding what this volume should contain as well as suggestions for potential contributors. They include Jeremy Tunstall, City University of London, Svennik Hoyer, University of Oslo, and John C. Merrill, University of Maryland.

Naturally, the editors of any volume of the scope and variety of this one incur a large number of obligations to numerous people. There are, for example, the contributors not previously acknowledged: David Boyce, Francis Balle, Jean Marie Cotteret, Roberto Petrognani, Osmo

Wiio, Anthony Westell, Carman Cummings, Marvin Alisky, Delmer Dunn, John Western, and Allan Brown. We firmly believe that through their efforts the authors of this volume's selections provide rare insights that readers will find valuable to ponder and compare.

Standing behind the visible contributions to this anthology, however, are a host of unseen efforts no less vital to the publication of such a work. Among these are, first, Anthony Pansini and Normand Grenier who faithfully translated several manuscripts into English. We are grateful to Dorothy Hitt, Priscilla Machabo Bishop, and Paula Hertzler for their help in typing and preparing the essay drafts. We also thank Frances Stanford, Paula Tanner, Carole Smith, Carolyn Pettey, and Helen Badley for their skills in preparing the manuscripts for publication. Lowell Browne provided artistic and creative ideas while Bob Bright gave most helpful advice. Special thanks to Beth Mansfield for her helpful proofing of the manuscript. Two individuals deserve special acknowledgment, for without their support and patience this book would never have come to fruition. First, Herbert H. Reynolds for his faith in the project and his willingness to make a commitment to it. And Marvin Goebel for his understanding and dedication to quality publishing. Finally and foremost, this book is dedicated to Michelle, Renée, and Stephanie Mansfield, daughters of one of the authors.

CONTENTS

Government and the News Media:
Comparative Dimensions

I.
Government and the News Media: Cross National Comparisons

Dan Nimmo and Michael W. Mansfield

If the noted American journalist, Walter Lippman, were alive in the post-Vietnam and post-Watergate era of this decade, he might rue the day that he remarked how "inexplicable" it was that no American student of government placed sufficient importance on the "study of the press and the sources of popular information" to write a book on the subject (1922, p. 320). Indeed, only two decades ago another influential Washington correspondent, in what was almost lamenting tones, observed how "increasingly of late those of us who report from Washington find ourselves the object of curious scrutiny by the political scientists" (Cater, 1959, p. vii).

Everybody it seems, not just political scientists, have at least one book in them about government-press relations in the United States. Journalists write them (Reston, 1966; Wicker, 1978) along with social critics (Leibling, 1961; Cirino, 1971), social historians (Schudson, 1979), and social scientists from a variety of academic disciplines (Krieghbaum, 1972; Sigal, 1973; Epstein, 1973). Whether this surfeit of published interest in government-news media relations substantially contributes to our understanding is problematical. What is apparent, however, is that the explosion of published materials about government-press linkages in this nation has not as yet been matched by comparable analyses of those relations as conducted in other nations of the world.

This is not to say that no studies exist of the transactions involving government and its "fourth branch" outside those with a focus upon the United States. Excellent works, such as those pertaining to Great Britain (Tunstall, 1970, 1971; Seymour-Ure, 1974) and France (Grosser, 1976) demonstrate otherwise. What is lacking are studies that compare and contrast government-news media relations across a variety of political systems by using a common set of categories to detect common patterns and highlight crucial differences. It is the purpose of this anthology to provide such cross-national comparisons, both in order to

permit perspectives on total systems of political information and to add
to those relatively few analyses of a partial, although comparative,
nature (Smith, 1979).

Alternative Modes of Comparison

John Merrill (1974) has stated what he believes may well be a truism,
i.e., a nation's press or media system is closely tied to its governmental
arrangement. Since there are many different philosophies and structures of government, there are a variety of corresponding relationships
between journalism and politics. Indeed, there are so many that one
struggles to come up with a satisfactory set of categories permitting
cross-national comparisons. Two approaches to such categorization
have been used to derive comparisons of news media-governmental
systems. The first is philosophical in its origins, the second functionalist. Although neither provides the basis for the less structured approach
employed in the chapters comprising this anthology, a brief description
of each is in order to highlight the features of the scheme our authors
have accepted.

PHILOSOPHICAL DERIVATIVES

What is surely the standard typology of government-press relationships was published in 1956 in the slim volume *Four Theories of the
Press* (Siebert, Peterson, and Schramm, 1956). The four theories the
authors describe are the authoritarian, libertarian, communist, and
social responsibility perspectives. Although offered as distinctive sets
of relationships, the basic distinction is between authoritarian and
libertarian views and the remaining two are variations and/or compromises along this fundamental dichotomy.

For Siebert et al. in an *authoritarian* system the governing regime is
paramount. It directs the citizenry, a collectivity of people not in themselves competent to make self-governing decisions. The role of mass
communication, and certainly of the news media, is to support the
governing regime and the elite who make the rules. Since the national
government decides who can and cannot exercise the journalistic privilege, press freedom extends only so far as the regime is willing to
permit. In contrast, a *libertarian* system is open, nondirective, and
pluralist in character. The assumption is of a citizenry of rational
beings, possessed with individual rights, and competent for self-
government. The role of the press is to provide a free marketplace of

ideas where through competiton truth can be discovered. As Merrill notes (1974) the libertarian viewpoint has evolved over the years to include the general notion of the news media as "fourth branch of government," that is, as an independent, free institution informing the public about government whether or not such reporting is supportive of rulers' policies.

As critics of the "four-theories" approach have argued (Merrill, 1974), the *communist* viewpoint described by Siebert, Peterson, and Schramm is actually a variant of the authoritarian. The governing regime in such a political system is the Communist Party. The news media are tools of that party. Rather than provide a free and unfettered flow of information, the press supports governing ideology, the state, and the party. "Approved" criticism of party leaders and governors may appear in the press, but only in the name of advancing "true" party interests and ideas.

Finally, the *social responsibility* viewpoint in the "four-theories" model is a variant also, but one with roots in libertarian rather than authoritarian doctrine. It holds that matching liberty of the press is news media responsibility to serve the "public interest," "public good," or "social welfare." Ideally the press should meet its social responsibilities in a purely self-regulatory fashion. If it does not, however, the implication is that government, in the name of the larger public good, may take measures to guarantee that the media are in accord with generally recognized responsibilities. Hence, for example, in the U.S. government steps in via the Federal Communications Commission to regulate use of radio and television frequencies in "the public interest."

The Siebert et al. model has a number of problems that raise questions about its utility for comparing political-journalistic systems. One is that the boundaries between the four systems are ambiguous. It is no easy matter to classify government-press arrangements into one of the four categories. An overly active governing regime may well move the news media from "social responsibility" to lacky of an authoritarian system. Or, an unresponsive press may, in the name of social responsibility and the public interest, assume a de facto libertarian posture. That systems can so easily shade into one another results in numerous efforts to tidy up the four-system categories. Thus Merrill and Lowenstein (1971) replace communist theory with "social-centralist" to include nations of the Eastern European bloc and a variety of developing nations that are neither clearly authoritarian nor communist in the four-theories sense. And, Merrill and Lowenstein substitute "social libertarianism" for social responsibility, apparently to remind that the latter should not be permitted to negate the public interest by evolving into an authoritarian arrangement.

Perhaps the key difficulty, however, in adapting a four-theories framework to a cross-national description of government-news media relations is that it is philosophic in derivation. As a result it provides little guidance to the practical, everyday operations of either government or the press that should be explored in comparing systems. Should the focus be upon formal, legal relationships, informal give-and-take, institutional arrangements, or what? The four-theories implies a legal-institutional emphasis that does not alone yield comprehensive comparisons. Finally, given the nature of the eight national systems represented in this volume—all purporting to be socially responsible democracies in character—to employ a four-theories framework would be inadequate. The framework fails to specify the features in each of the four patterns that are most important when making comparisons *within* rather than *between* government-press systems. Since the government-news media systems explored in this volume are variations on a single type (i.e., social responsibility with shadings either toward authoritarian or libertarian hues), we must search for a more detailed set of categories to examine.

FUNCTIONALIST DERIVATIVES

In a highly influential introductory essay to their volume on the politics of developing areas, Almond and Coleman (1960) generated a framework for the analysis and comparison of political systems. The authors argued that all political systems, be they "modern" or "developing" have four common characteristics: (1) political structures performing a (2) mulitiplicity of (3) political functions and (4) a mixture of rational and traditional characteristics. The key to comparative analysis is to examine the political functions basic to all systems, then identify and compare the structures performing them.

Almond and Coleman identified a variety of input and output functions. Among the latter were the now familiar rule-making, rule application, and rule adjudication. Among input functions were political socialization and recruitment, interest articulation, interest aggregation, and—important for our purposes—political communication. In modern systems, the authors noted, differentiated media of communication perform the "crucial boundary-maintenance function" (p. 46) of political communication. To compare the performance of the political communication function across systems investigators need to examine both political (e.g., the press, political parties, etc.) and social (e.g., face-to-face groups, etc.) structures. Comparison then focuses upon four key areas and the part played by such structures in them—the homogeneity of political information, the mobility of information, the volume of information, and the direction and flow of information.

The Almond and Coleman framework has been utilized primarily to examine political communication in developing nations (Almond and Powell, 1966), although Fagan (1966) modified and extended portions of the mode of analysis to include modern systems as well. In the study of comparative development and the government-press relationship it now stands as but one possible framework, however, as illustrated by the work of Hyer, Hadenius, and Weibull (1975). Nor is it the most current framework for comparing communication systems in more modernized political arrangements. Wiio (1977), for example, offers a four-fold typology based upon two key variables: (1) whether any message reaches a limited portion of the possible audience or any member of it and (2) if there is any constraint on the volume and content of messages themselves. Thus, *controlled (mass) communication* is a system type wherein the audience is open to receive messages relatively constrained in number and content. *Mass communication* involves openness of both audiences to receive messages and openness in the messages themselves. *Private communication* implies relatively closed/limited audiences and messages. And, *directed (mass) communication* consists of a restricted audience for freely transmitted messages—as where economic considerations limit the number of color televisions.

Functionalist paradigms are instructive. They remind investigators that "the press" or "the news media" differ considerably in character across political systems, yet perform a multiplicity of functions. Moreover, like philosophic models, they take into account the open or closed nature of political message selection and content—i.e., whether the press is supportive of government, neutral, adversarial, investigative, etc. As yet, however, functionalist typologies are generalized and suggestive rather than specialized and sufficiently descriptive. They provide relatively few specific categories of relationships between political and journalistic systems that permit cross-national accounts. Hence, although many of the chapters in this volume have implicit perspectives that derive from possible philosophic or functionalist models of government-press relations, readers will note that the

authors of the essays in this anthology (with varying degrees of speci-
ficity as permitted by the information available to them) incorporate a
limited number of explicit descriptive categories instead. These categories have been borrowed from yet another published effort to assess the
state of our knowledge about government-news media transactions.

Categories for Cross-National Descriptions

In a useful essay Rivers, Miller, and Gandy (1975) reviewed the
major studies that had been undertaken into government-news media
relations in the United States. Although derived from a critique of
studies in but one nation, the authors' categorization scheme can easily
be extended to cover what Siebert, Peterson, and Schramm would
include as libertarian and/or socially responsible systems and Almond
and Coleman would consider as modernized polities. For that reason
the authors of this volume's chapters were requested, in so far as
possible, to look specifically at each of the items in the Rivers et al.
framework and to describe them if relevant to the national government-
press in question.

Briefly, Rivers et al. suggest four areas for investigation. The first,
government impact on media includes governmental mechanisms for
control of communication—including laws, statutes, court actions, regulatory agencies, and informal mechanisms, how control is exercised,
and the impact of that control economically, on newsgathering, and on
the news product. Second, *government information systems* refers to
the nature of formal and informal information channels; the characteristics and attitudes of government information personnel; and how
information personnel perform their jobs. Third, *media impact on
government* includes how officials use and regard the news media
(their reading and viewing habits, attitudes about news coverage, and
utilization of news media in policymaking) and how the news media
influence officials at various levels of government. Finally, *the nature of
the news media* incorporates the setting in which the media operate (as
members of the overall social setting, their structures, institutional
norms, ownership, audiences, economic and technological factors,
degree of professionalism, and the nature of news sources); how the
news media obtain information; the characteristics of journalists
(demographic, attitudinal, etc.); and the nature of news content including the volume of news content, overlap between media, subject matter,
and variations over time.

Given variations in national political systems, and how the news media relate to government in each, it is not surprising that in some of the government-press systems represented in this volume, not all of the above categories appear. Nonetheless authors have made a concerted effort to incorporate them where possible and they afford opportunities for useful comparisons across anthology chapters.

Plan of the Volume

The volume begins with an examination of government-news media relations in Europe. After focusing on France and Italy attention shifts to Scandinavia. The selection on the British experience begins a discussion of parliamentary systems which includes Australia and Canada. The articles on the United States and Mexico complete the comparison of North American countries. The final two chapters focus upon the transactions involving government and the "fourth branch" in the nation states of Israel and Japan.

References

Almond, G. A., and Coleman, J. S. *The Politics Of Developing Nations*. Princeton: Princeton University Press, 1960.

Almond, G. A., and Powell, G. B., Jr. *Comparative Politics: A Developmental Approach*. Boston: Little, Brown and Co., 1966.

Cater, D. *The Fourth Branch Of Government*. Boston: Houghton Mifflin, 1959.

Cirino, R. *Don't Blame the People*. Los Angeles: Diversity Press, 1971.

Epstein, E. J. *News From Nowhere*. New York: Random House, 1973.

Fagen, R. R. *Politics And Communication*. Boston: Little, Brown and Co., 1966.

Grosser, A. "Information on French Politics." In L. Maisel (Ed.), *Changing Campaign Techniques*. Beverly Hills: Sage Publications, 1976.

Hyer, S., Hadenius, S., and Weibull, L. "The Politics and Economics of the Press: A Developmental Perspective." *Sage Professional Papers in Contemporary Sociology*, 1975, *1*, 5-42.

Krieghbaum, H. *Pressures on the Press*. New York: Thomas Y. Crowell, 1972.

Liebling, A. J. *The Press*. New York: Random House, 1961.

Lippman, W. *Public Opinion*. New York: Macmillan, 1922.

Merrill, J. C. *The Imperative of Freedom*. New York: Hastings House, Publishers, 1974.

Merrill, J. C., and Lowenstein, R. L. *Media, Messages, and Men: New Perspectives in Communication*. New York: David McKay Co., 1971.

Reston, J. *The Artillery of the Press*. New York: Harper and Row, 1966.

Rivers, W. L., Miller, S., and Gandy, O. "Government and the Media." In S. Chaffee (Ed.), *Political Communication*. Beverly Hills: Sage Publications, 1975.

Schudson, M. *Discovering the News*. New York: Basic Books, 1979.

Seymour-Ure, C. *The Political Impact of Mass Media*. Beverly Hills: Sage Publications, 1974.

Siebert, F. S., Peterson, T., and Schramm, W. *Four Theories of the Press*. Urbana: University of Illinois Press, 1956.

Sigal, L. *Reporters and Officials*. Lexington, Mass.: D. C. Heath, 1973.

Smith, A. (Ed.) *Television and Political Life*. New York: St. Martin's Press, 1979.

Tunstall, J. *Journalists at Work*. Beverly Hills: Sage Publications, 1971.

Tunstall, J. *The Westminster Lobby Correspondents*. London: Routledge & Kegan Paul, 1970.

Wicker, T. *On Press*. New York: The Viking Press, 1978.

Wiio, O. A. "Open and Closed Mass Media Systems and Problems of International Communication Policy." *Studies of Broadcasting*, 1977, *13*, 67-90.

II.
Government and the Media in France

Francis Balle and Jean Marie Cotteret

This study will deal with the press, radio, and television as principal media channels of information. After having studied the legal context and status of press, radio, and television under the state, we examine the government information system and its impact upon the media.

Legal Status of the Media

THE PRESS

This principle was formulated in Article 11 of the Declaration of the Rights of Man and Citizen of 1789:

> The communication of thoughts and opinions is one of the most precious rights of man: every citizen may talk, write, and print freely, subject only to an accounting for abuse of that freedom as determined by the law.

This liberty was in effect the corollary of the freedom of opinion established by Article 10 of the Declaration ("Nobody will be worried for his opinions, even religious ones, as long as their protests do not cause public disorder").

In effect, freedom of the press was established quite later, more precisely under the law of July 29, 1881, which not only affirms freedom of print and of publishing (1st Article) and suppresses the previous authorization of newspapers and periodicals (5th Article) but also organizes these liberties so as to insure their effectiveness.

Except for unusual periods, this liberty has not been questioned since. But we must remember that often-formulated remark to the effect that freedom is real only if the beneficiaries have the material means to exercise it. So, even if anyone may legally enter the newspaper business, the enormous cost of such operations drastically limits the applicability of this freedom.

The limits. Limits on the press stem from administrative regulation. First are rules concerning the publisher, the newspaper business, the status of journalists, etc. And there is a special agency for publications directed towards youth. These are subject to the commission in charge of supervision and control of publications directed to infants and adolescents. Created by the law of 1949, organized by Decree No. 50-143 of February 1, 1950, this commission is a body designed to help the agency in its duty. It is comprised of persons from the administration (representing different interested ministries), the education sector, youth organizations, parliamentarians, editors, authors, and, finally, representatives of family associations and former juvenile judges. These members are named for three-year terms—always renewable—and constitute a permanent body of the Justice Ministry. Each is named, based on qualifications—and ceases to belong to the commission if he ceases the functions (i.e., education, representative, parliamentary, etc.) which initially had him so designated.

Many roles are assigned to the commission. It is charged with advising competent authorities of infractions of the law of 1949, as well as any wrongdoing which would hurt youth by way of the press. It may also warn the Minister of the Interior of publications which seem to justify "forbidding" sale to minors of less than 18 or prohibition of public exposure. It must also give its opinion on the importation of foreign publications destined for youth. And it may propose any measure concerning the administration of publications destined for youth. Finally, the Ministry of the Interior has controlling power over foreign publications.

RADIO AND TELEVISION

In France, the system defining programs broadcast to the public, broadcasting these programs, and organizing and managing the network insuring broadcasting is monopolistic. The two public institutions are: Telediffusion de France (TV broadcasting of France) and the Institut National de l'Audiovisuel (the National Institute of Audiovisual). The role of Telediffusion de France (T.D.F.) is to insure the broadcasting of radio and television programs throughout France and abroad, and to organize, manage, and maintain the networks for broadcasting installations (transmitters, retransmitters, relays, etc.). It is a creature of public creation, formed as a public industrial and commercial business of limited financial autonomy, since its budget is subject to governmental appropriation.

The organization of Telediffusion is as follows: the board of directors is comprised of 16 members, including 8 representatives of the state, 2 parliamentarians designated respectively by the appropriate permanent commission of the National Assembly of the Senate, 1 representative from each of the 4 national societies for programming designated by a proposal of the society's president, and 2 representatives of the personnel of the institution chosen from lists of at least 3 names set out by each of the representative labor unions. The nomination, made by decree, is for three years. The board defines the general lines of action of the institution, based on specific stipulations. It votes the budget and checks its execution. Its deliberations are supposedly final, but some decisions require approval of trusteeship or are susceptible to opposition.

The I.N.A. takes care of archives, research, and professional formation. It is a public institution of an industrial and commercial nature. Its organization resulted from the Decree of 14 November 1974. The board of directors is comprised of 21 members including 10 representatives from the state (representatives of the Prime Minister and of the different interested ministers), 2 representatives from Labor chosen from lists of at least 3 names made by each of the most representative unions, 1 representative of the public institution of broadcasting designated by proposal of the chairman of the board of directors of that organization, 4 representatives (1 per firm) from the national companies and from the production companies, 4 persons designated because of their competence—two of which are proposed by the High Council of Audiovisual. Nomination is made for three years by decree (renewable). The president of the board of directors is named for three years by decree from the minister's council among the members of the board of directors. The director is named by decree, but, unlike the broadcasting institution, by proposal of the chairman of the board of directors.

The four national companies for programming (Radio-France, T.F.1, Antenne 2, and F.R.3) are private beings, subject to the laws of corporations. The only shareholder of these firms' capital is the state. The judicial form adopted divulges the intent to introduce "the methods of private management within the public sector" and to "develop rivalry and introduce competition in the public sector itself." However, since these national firms are subject to the requirements of public service, their structure on many points deviates from public right. In this way, the powers normally exercised by the General Assembly, notably the drawing up of the status of these firms, are here given to the board of directors (the composition of which is also original).

Mostly, the programming companies must conform to the requirements of stipulations set up annually by the Prime Minister. These stipulations, which under the terms of the law of 7 August 1974, fix "the objectives to be reached for the achievement of its mission to public service," have revealed themselves through use to be fairly precise guides concerning the minimal obligations of the networks in various areas (from news to publicity, through musical shows, documentaries, or report programs). We have therefore a system which intends to marry the control of the state with private administration.

On the board of directors of these companies, we find two representatives of the state, one parliamentarian, a person from the written press, a person from the cultural world (necessarily from cinema or F.T.3), and a labor representative. It must be strongly underlined that, if the state appears here as a minority partner, reality makes of the government— which directs the nomination of all members of the board of directors by decree—the master of the composition of these boards. Government names, in effect, at its discretion, the two representatives of the state and the representative of the written press. The parliamentarian is designated after agreement with the appropriate competent commissions of the National Assembly and of the Senate (which allows the majority to choose the board of directors of the companies it prefers to control). The representative of Labor is chosen by the government from a list of suggested candidates submitted by the representative unions. As to the person from the cultural world, that member is chosen by the government from a list of five names proposed by the other members of the Administration Council (of which we have just seen three of five, at the least, are favorable to the government). The government is thus insured of having, if it so desires, a majority within each of these councils despite the minority character theoretically of state representation. The president of each society, chosen from among the members of the Administration Council, is named for three years by the cabinet. Finally, the S.F.P. is a semipublic firm. Article 13 of the law indicates that the shares of controlling character can be held only by the state, the public capital investment having to remain in majority.

This society is responsible for film and video production, and for commercial activity which does not enter public service. It is subject to the laws of the corporations with no exceptions other than those prescribed by the law of 1974 (statutes approved by decree and by the Prime Minister or the minister delegated by the nomination of the President and eventually by the general manager, including increase and decrease of capital and transfer of shares). However, a decree of 30 December 1974, has subjected the firm to an economic and financial control of the state.

Governmental Action and the Media

Within this legal/judicial framework, it is appropriate to examine certain types of governmental action that affect media operations.

DIRECT AND INDIRECT CONTROL

First, we must note the process of selecting the highest ranking persons of the television networks, a process the government in power influences. But more interesting is the exercise of the government's power to control the media. The control is exercised first a priori by the aforementioned stipulations imposed upon the organizations in question. These conditions are decreed by the Prime Minister (or his delegated minister) after advice of a parliamentary delegation and possible consultation with the High Council of the Audiovisual.

The Prime Minister, or the appropriate delegated minister, introduces the stipulations each year in Parliament accompanied by additional clauses anticipated for the following year. These stipulations in no way constitute contractual acts: they are unilateral acts adopted by the Prime Minister or his delegate. The texts concerning the six conditions (Decree 25 April 1975) demonstrate this clearly by stating that the organization "is subject to the conditions of the stipulations annexed to the present decree."

Administrative control is different, depending on whether it concerns public businesses or national firms. For the two public firms subject to the trusteeship of the Prime Minister or one of his delegated ministers (Degree 24 September 1974, for the public broadcasting firm; Decree 14 November 1974, for the Institute of Audiovisual), the powers of trusteeship consist of the right to require a meeting of the Board of Directors, of receiving reports, and of approving certain important deliberations (the opposition suspends the execution until the decision—which must come within the month—of the Minister of Trusteeship).

The control exercised on the national companies concerns merely the approval of the statutes by decree. This rule also applies to the production company. In addition, the Prime Minister or a delegated member of the government approves the nomination of the president and eventually of the general manager, the increase or decrease of capital, and the transfer of shares.

Finally, the public firms are subjected to budgetary control: the budget and the modifying decisions must receive the approval of the Prime Minister or a delegated member of the government. The accounts of public firms are subject to the approval of the Finance Minister: those made by the accountant are under the jurisdiction of the Audit Office. For the national programming firms, the provisional statement of revenues and expenses is simply transmitted for observation to the government.

We must add that the state provides a budgetary donation to Agence France-Presse, as well as direct and indirect help to the press. Also, SOFIRAD is a company whose capital is owned by the French state and which administers participation in a number of television and broadcasting organizations (Europe No. 1, Radio Monte Carlo, Sud-Radio, and Lebanese Company of Television). Finally, the National Company of Press Enterprises manages a participation in French printing houses.

The right to broadcast. The law of 1974 contains four aspects of the right to broadcast: (a) restating comparable provisions of the laws of 27 June 1964, and of 3 July 1972, it presumes (Article [16]) that the government may at any time have programmed and broadcast any declarations or communications which it judges "necessary." *This right,* recognized in all countries, allows the *government to explain* its policies and to address the nation for urgent messages. It is even less debatable since it's the holder of this right to intervene "with open face" in special shows which are expressly announced.

(b) In addition, the new text confirms indirectly the existence of a right to the airwaves during electoral times since, according to Article 16, "the national societies are held responsible for producing and programming, and the public firms for broadcasting shows corresponding to electoral campaigns." But, in this matter, rules are fixed by some special provisions: there is, for the presidential election, a decree of 14 March 1964, which states the principle of the equality of the candidates during the duration of the campaign and, for the election of the deputies, a law of 24 December 1966, which splits the time of speech in an equal manner between the political parties of the majority and those of the opposition.

(c) As had been done by the statutes of 1964 and 1972, the 1974 statute recognizes the right of expression of parliamentary representation in the framework of the broadcasting of the debates; this right is under the control of a bureau of each parliamentary assembly. Some air time must be given to the parliamentary groups of the majority and to those of the opposition.

(d) Finally, and most important, the law of 1974 is innovative by placing on the national public service of French broadcasting the responsibility of insuring "an equal access to the expression of the principal ideological tendencies and of the great trends of opinion" and specifying that "air time is regularly put at its disposal" (1st Article). This right to air time is sanctioned by Article 15: the stipulations of the public broadcasting firm and of the national programming businesses state "a minimum of air time permitting the political parties and the representing professional organizations to express themselves freely." It is now being considered to modify the provisions contained in the stipulations by giving opposition parties the possibility of responding to a governmental declaration: despite its name, this institution would liken itself more closely to the right of air time (conceived as a method of realizing a global equilibrium in the expression of opinions) than to the right of response. Let us add also that, under Article 10 of the 1974 law, it belongs to one of the programming companies (it is, in effect, France-Region 3) to reserve "a privileged place . . . to the organization of programs dealing with the direct expression of the diverse families of faith and thought": the choice of this society as "network of free speech" has sometimes been contested because of its relatively small audience.

The right to respond. The strength of the written press has rendered necessary the protection of individual persons, not only when attack is made upon their honor or reputation (penal rule of defamation) but, in a greater and more automatic manner, when they are put in cause ("named or designated") by a news article. Article 13 of the law of 29 July 1881, opens to them in this case a right of response. But until recently this institution was not recognized in radio and television matters. Official interpretation held that the law of 1881 was directed only to written publications and that its application could not be extended beyond it. Considering the impact of audiovisual techniques, such a situation was not very satisfactory.

Article 8 of the law of 3 July 1972, is maintained in effect by Article 34 of the law of 7 August 1974, which has introduced a right of response on the airwaves of radio and television. In this manner, the new text establishes a fundamental guarantee of the rights of the individual if threatened by the abusive exploitation of the modern methods of information: by protecting those who have been victimized by imputations during a television or radio show, it marks sensible progress in the area traditionally excepted from the application of the law of 1881.

However, the 1972 legislation has adapted the rules of the written press to the imperatives of audiovisual communication without qualification. The conception which inspired the 1972 statute is clearly more restrictive than that which had motivated the authors of the law of 1881. Two series of provisions limit, in effect, the exercise of the right of response on the air: first, this right does not belong to all persons involved. The text requires an attack upon honor, reputation, or interest. The respondent must thus establish the existence of a moral or material prejudice in a way as to allow the system to represent, in a certain measure, a method of reparation for the defamation. Second, to prevent the overcrowding of the airwaves and political deviations from institutions, the law reserves the right of response to physical persons, to the exclusion of corporate persons. More precisely, it gives the right only if it involves safeguarding honor, reputation, or interests of a physical person.

The conditions of exercise of the right of response on radio or television were fixed by the 13 May 1975, decree. This text determines the procedure to be followed in inviting the victim of an imputation to solicit, within eight days, from the president of the programming company involved, the broadcasting of a response. When this demand is accepted, the response must be broadcast in listening conditions similar to those of the contested show. When the demand is rejected, the interested party may go to the National Commission on the Right of Response, an administrative authority whose decisions are susceptible to appeal for abuse of discretion before the state council (A body of administrative law is beginning to develop in this matter: C.E. 16 June 1976, Germes). The advantage of Article 8 of the law of 1972 could not be given to the director of a commercial firm who believes that the remarks made during a radio broadcast have hurt the interests of its business. The judicial form of the latter (a corporate person) prevents opening of a right of response.

THE GOVERNMENT INFORMATION SERVICES

A variety of activities carried on under government auspices exert a modest influence upon the news media. But that influence increases steadily and warrants brief mention.

The High Council of Audiovisual. Created by the law of 1972, this organization has been retained by the Statute of 1974 (Article 16). Under the leadership of the Prime Minister or of his delegate, it comprises representatives of parliamentary assemblies and qualified personalities from the cultural, artistic, scientific, technical, judicial, professional, familial, and labor world. Its role is purely that of a consultant. It gives advice on the problems concerning the orientations and development of audiovisual techniques as well as all other questions posed by the government.

The judicial and technical information service. It is responsible for monitoring overall problems of the written press and of the audiovisual world.

The information and broadcasting service. The S.I.D., which was reorganized in 1976, employs 64 contractual agents to whom are added 11 civil servants at its disposition who continue to be paid by their original administration. S.I.D.'s activities include several aspects, informing users of proper operations and coordinating actions conducted by the ministries.

1. *Publications.* These include the Actualités service (37 publications between 1 January 1976, and 31 July 1977), Actualités Documents (24 publications), and Dossiers de Travail (17 publications). These documents are addressed to the national and local elected officials and to the press.

2. *Campaigns.* The S.I.D. plays the role of advising and assisting agencies on undertaking advertising campaigns. In addition, it administers and controls, together with the French advertising commission, television advertising campaigns as requested by agencies. Thus, it insures the proper adherence to conditions of official stipulations in matters of advertisement of the public services.

3. *Public relations and dealings with the press.* The role of this service is to bring technical help to the ministers, notably those who do not have an information service, as well as to the prefectures. This action is oriented both towards the national and regional press and to foreign journalists residing in Paris or temporarily in France.

Governmental and prefectural information. The S.I.D. provides to government members, to their collaborators, and to the prefects elements of explanation on different aspects of governmental policies (fight against inflation, reform in housing financing, etc.).

Analysis of opinion studies. This service involves helping public agencies to command and exploit public opinion polls.

CONCLUSION

Beyond what has been said, it is very difficult to fix the exact influence of government intervention on the media. We cite two opinions: one is concerned with journalists, the other with the public. A survey conducted in 1976-1977 (see Table 1) with a sample of 120 journalists, representative of the Parisian editorial staffs, of the audiovisual (national and peripheral networks) shows that—asked about the existence of government pressure—numerous journalists stated it, mentioning in rank order the source for pressures.

TABLE 1
Sources of Pressure on Journalists

Source	% All Journalists	%National Networks Only Radio-France, TF1, A2, F3
		Journalists
The business world	43	39
The ministers	40	44
Political parties	39	37
Unions	38	42
Administrations	35	37
President of the Republic	30	24
Police	27	19
Embassies	22	19
Army	18	12

The other opinion (see Table 2) has to do with public sentiment towards political information. Question: if you view, regularly or not, the four listed channels, how do you judge them politically?

TABLE 2
Public Sentiment Towards
Political Information

Sentiment	%TF1 13h	%TF1 20h	% A2 20h	%PR3 22h
		Papers		
Impartial	16	17	3	10
Most oriented towards:				
the majority	5	5	1	3
the opposition	1	4	5	1
no opinion	5	5	2	3

The television viewers judge their news shows as mostly impartial. Notably, T.F.1, where the percentage of those who estimated it was oriented towards the majority is almost equal to those who think the contrary. But the viewers believe A2 to be more favorable to the left.

Media Influence on the Government

The increase in political communication, from the governed to the governing, takes many forms. Except for properly "administrative" information and police reports, certain institutional mechanisms permit those governing to take the pulse of public opinion, i.e., through electoral consultations. Presidential, legislative, cantonal, or municipal elections always permit the voter to judge policy—policy in the English sense of the term.

The increase in political communication also derives from unofficial, less institutionalized or organized channels. These informal means together constitute a sort of "supplementing" democracy. New sites of this democracy are representative public opinion unions, associations, societies of thought, and clubs. New locations develop essential deliberations for knowledge of public opinion by governing bodies: symposiums organized by clubs or societies for thoughts, union meetings, press conferences, and opinion guides. The increased importance of these concurrent circuits of information is at the same time cause and effect of Parliament's decline, a characteristic of most occidental societies.

Between these official and unofficial channels of communication are public opinion polls. Employed in France in 1938, therefore a few years later than in the United States, they have known a strong growth in the period since 1965. The hostility campaign, of which they were the target in 1977, orchestrated by a few senators and followed by numerous deputies, has not really stopped their growth.

In the flow of information the media assuredly occupy a place of their own. They constitute for the governing body a privileged instrument to know the citizen's opinion. Without doubt, the dailies have "depoliticized" themselves during the last two decades, not because they talk less of politics but because they are "making" much less of politics; political columns occupy in the absolute more space, but they are now less often carriers of clearly expressed partisan choices. However, the dailies (in the foreground of which must be cited le Monde) are largely stripped by the bureaus of the diverse ministries. In this respect, the paper constitutes an information vehicle for those governing.

Assuredly, it would be difficult to evaluate the respective part and influence of these different forms of political communication in today's France. The crucial factor which marks these last years is the conjunction of two phenomena: (1) a kind of desocialization of direct institutional mechanisms, i.e., elections, both by use and wear; (2) a credibility crisis of which newspapers are victims, principally those whose reputation for seriousness and objectivity was best established. This conjunction is at the base of the growth of polls; at the same time it explains the increased attention given by those governing to the new informal means of reflecting opinions, those expressed elsewhere than in Parliament or at party reunions.

Since 1973, the national political life has been dominated by elections: legislative in 1973, presidential in 1974, cantonal in 1976, municipal in 1977, again legislative in 1978, and—for the first time—European in 1979. France has never really ceased, in recent years, to live in electoral campaigns. Paradoxically, this situation has stopped neither parliamentary decline nor that of parties. The general feeling of dissatisfaction towards Parliament was noted for the first time in 1973: of the deputies interviewed, 59.8 percent judged the Parliament's role was not "important enough" and 90 percent estimated that this decline operated to the "technocrats" benefit. And at least 80 percent of each group in the Assembly answered affirmatively to the question, "Are the country's affairs more and more often settled by technocrats?" It is true that parliamentarism has been "rationalized" by the Constitution of the 5th Republic, but mostly, the majority factor—that is, the possibility for a government permanently relying on a majority of deputies—takes away from the Parliament some significance from its usual role of censor for the government and initiator of laws.

The parties' decline also accelerated during this period. Key factors of social change work against the "mass" parties which are centralized, numerous, and disciplined: principally the opposition of a heterogeneous middle class with uncertain ways, as the French lifestyle is "becoming middle-class respectable" with new leisure activities. Just as in other industrial democracies, France sees the beginning of great "parties of electors," or "catchall parties" as a joint result of the citizens' depoliticization and of the deideologization of political debate. From now on, the political parties, the Socialist party, the Reunion for the Republic, the Union for the French Democracy and also, up to a certain point, the Communist party, will be dominated, not by their members and their elected representatives but by outside experts, nourished elsewhere than in the seraglio of the political politics. It is the end of the "apparatchiks."

Far from rehabilitating the Parliament and the parties, the frequency of elections has precipitated their decline. The quantity, in one sense, has hindered quality because the period separating the two elections was always too short to permit the parties to conclude new alliances and to interpret the opinion of the electorate. However, because of the impression of shock produced by electoral outcomes and felt by both the citizens and those governing, both governed and governors have become "immunized" to politics, which bars political communication, whatever its direction. So, the election has suddenly ceased to be a privileged or perfect moment of dialogue between governing and governed.

Next to the elections becoming less sacred, another phenomenon dampens political communication: the decline of the press, at least the written press, as a method for those governing knowing the latent feelings or the expressed opinion of the governed. This decline is due, firstly, to the political parties themselves, which are more and more electoral or demagogical and less and less able at the same time to express the aspirations of citizens. After having benefited from a certain revival on the morning of the 1944 liberation, the parties' press has not ceased to decline since the 50s. L'Aube, the great daily of the MRP, disappeared in 1951; Le Populaire, daily of the SFIO, managed to destroy itself. Both newspapers closely identified with the radical party, the Progrès de Lyon and the Dépêche du Midi, have continuously steered away from the party since 1950. La Nation, daily for the old Fifth Republic, is nowadays only a bulletin destined to RPR militants. As to the press of the extreme left, it is very diverse, but its circulation numbers are quite limited. Practically, the lone survivors among the information organs which are representative of public opinion trends are the Communist party papers and those claiming Catholic ideology.

Now, only the weeklies with a circulation of over one million (le Nouvel Observateur, le Point, and l'Express) are a refuge for purely political stands and for substantial files to which public opinion is sensitive and responsive. In some way these weeklies now fill the void left by the decline of the great illustrated magazines such as Match and the dailies now too preoccupied by day-to-day happenings. The weeklies' method of covering current events permits a certain grasp of political controversy.

The second reason for the decline of newspapers as indicators of public opinion is found in the decrease of their "credibility." Relatively recent, this crisis affects inevitably the triangular relationship between those governing, the press, and its readers. Press institutions are criticized at all times, from all parts and from very diverse viewpoints. After le Figaro, le Monde itself has recently been severely and sometimes appropriately criticized in books that obtained a relative but sure success. From absolute rejection of the press by those who consider it (rightly or wrongly) as the instrument of a dominating culture and of ruling interests which they serve to the simple rejection of newspapers—either reading them occasionally, or only paying attention to their most inconsequential headings, or finally guarding against the press as one would use an antidote against poison—the press has lost prestige. The accusations are numerous: conformism, playing Pontius Pilate, and complacently accentuating what is going wrong (ruptures, conflicts, minorities). Still others believe the press is "objectively" the ally of old "establishment."

The increased incapacity of large political parties of expressing public opinion, the diminished capacity of papers of expressing in political terms the diverse concerns of the citizens—the conjunction of these two phenomena explains simultaneously the recent rise of polls and transfer of politics to other sites than parties.

The Characteristics of Information Channels

The channels of information in France are principally the newspapers, daily or weekly. Not that radio or television is less widespread than in comparable countries, or that these newcomers do not exercise, as everywhere else, an influence on the actions or opinions of one and all; rather, the print press, in the country of Girardin and Millaud, continues to play the role of an uncontested guide for other information organs.

The essential thing, however, about the French newspapers is that three-quarters of a century after the first dailies, with millions of circulation, the French press remains in effect that which it has never ceased to be: it presents more difference than similarity with its homologues of occidental countries. The particularities which evolved, common to the press of those different countries, are far from the prevailing characteristics of the French, due to traditions and the judicial system.

AN AUTOMATED MARKET

With the audiovisual challenge, the invasion of the current events book, and with the increasing diversification of the written press, in less than 15 years, between 1960 and 1975, the great French dailies have lost their double monopoly over information and over the written press. Till the 1960s, the golden rule for information media was that of complementation: radio devotes itself to music, television is dedicated to entertainment, and the press alone broadcasts the news. By force of belief that the vocations which they were assigned were unavoidable, the media became what it was believed they were. Competition appears only at the turn of the 60s. Radio, first, puts it in gear, favored by circumstances. The role which it played following the events of the war in Algeria takes on symbolic value. Both journalists and readers discover its extraordinary versatility: due to transistors and the miniaturization of receivers, radio obtained a monopoly of omnipresence. Of all information channels, it was first to accumulate the advantages of great "accessibility" for the user and of an uninterrupted contact with current events.

Television's conversion to information programming was no less spectacular. As far as ubiquity, its performance was far from equaling that of its radio predecessor. And miniaturization of reception cannot go much further than the reasonable size of picture. But since 1960, "magazine" programs did multiply, presenting advantageously the condensed and superficial information constituting televised news.

The same era is marked by the French market for supplying political information: the book. Due to considerable decrease in manufacturing delays, the book ceased to be a durable consumption good, a depository of cultural reference, to become a throwaway good just as any other periodical. At the same time, a new vocation for the book evolved as it set foot in interpreting current events previously reserved for coverage by dailies. In book shop windows, the current history, the commentary on current events, and the firsthand documentary compete at the same time with newspapers and traditional literature.

The years 1960-1965 thus mark the end of an era for information media: those of complementarity, absence of competition, and sharing of markets. By the end of the 60s the press, the book, radio, television, and even cinema were all information channels, each speaking of all things and addressing everybody.

The decade 1960-1970 also marks a vast redistribution of roles within the press. In France, as elsewhere during this period, periodicals took a step ahead of dailies. In 1962, all categories of periodicals already represented 46.3 percent of total annual distribution of French publications. In 1970, the 50 percent level was attained. For the first time in the history of French press, there are now each year more periodicals published than dailies. None of the most well-endowed countries escape the relative decline of dailies. An examination proves it: the nondailies progress, both in the absolute and in relative value.

From this evolution, quite brutal and assuredly irreversible, the French press now gets its principal peculiarity: it lies in the juxtaposition of universes quite unlike each other. On one side, a great number of publications represent society's diversity in all its aspects, by choosing to dedicate themselves, separately or simultaneously, to only one public or one subject. This quest provides an opportunity for the press to develop, both in the number of titles and by the circulation of each. Even more, these newcomers on the market create for themselves new publics or new groups by furnishing symbols and elements of a common identity. Overcoming the double obstacle of time and space, they help legitimize in society's eyes the most diverse minorities. No doubt the news magazines, l'Express, le Nouvel Observateur, and le Point, are first among these specialized publications. Despite the eclecticism of their center of interest, they always answer the need of a clearly limited public and sometimes constitute the refuge for party-oriented ideas which are deserted by the great dailies.

On the other side, the great dailies, less numerous from year to year, attempt to conserve a certain control over information diffusion by reserving to themselves the interpretation of events, the consecration of institutional academism and, when applicable, the enhancement or recompense of politicians to whom they are favorable. Accordingly, the daily's universe in France is itself divided. Some attain this objective, i.e., their circulation is on a national scale, even international, and they are assured of the relative faithfulness of their readers. And there are those trying to obtain monopoly over the local and regional information flow, at least while they are still deprived of it.

Since the beginning of this century, the era of dailies with millions of circulation, dailies have declined from 400 to 300 in 1930. Just before the Second World War, there were only 250 left; at the end of 1950, only 150. In 1979, only 90—barely 80 for the "provinces" and only 12 for Paris when you include Rouge and Libération. Expressed in global distribution, the dailies' decline is no less eloquent: 12 million copies daily in

1940, 10.1 million in 1976. Between 1960 and 1976, the total circulation decreased by almost 800,000 copies. Between 1974 and 1975, almost 700,000, a drop of more than 6 percent.

The rise of "regionals" does not compensate for the decline of the capital's newspapers. And the spread between regionals and nationals does not cease to widen. Between 1960 and 1976, dailies with the national circulation have lost almost 950,000 buyers, i.e., 3 times more readers from 3,300,00 to 2,360,000. During the same period, the "provincials" gained from 6,300,000 to 6,600,000. But in 1975, they lost 100,000 buyers from the preceding year.

Without doubt, the regionals still can rely on the loyalty of their readers and advertisers. And they shall keep for a long time the exclusivity of local news. This "micro-information," black and pink, in the half-shades of family reunions and retirements, responds to a permanent need of social communication. Still the regionals are also subject to the erosion of circulation. And they are resigning themselves as poorly as certain Parisian colleagues to the "aging" of their readership, and to the relative disaffiliation of young readers.

For "nationals" and "regionals" this discovery of publishing realities is sour. Since 1950, the press has never exceeded the fateful level of 260 daily copies per 1,000 inhabitants. In 1946, it was 360. But since 1952, the number approaches 230 with a marked downward tendency, mostly after 1970: 257 in 1960, 254 in 1970, and only 220 in 1976.

A PSYCHOSIS CRISIS

After having been the cradle of the great dailies, it appears as if France is resigning itself since the seventies to becoming their tomb. Nothing can spare the morosity of the French press, this feeling of abject confusion of living at the end of an era: neither the perspectives opened by specialization nor the example of some foreign countries (Sweden or Japan), where the progress of the press is everywhere, brightens the outlook.

Should we see in it a national caprice? Or is it rather a historical fatality, joined in France to the advent of new competitors? French peculiarity or Marconi's triumph? In truth, both explanations seem particularly admitted: the first because it offers to the French press the illusion of cultivating its difference; the second because it provides a feeling of being at a rendezvous with history.

Therein lies the prominent trait of the crisis of the press in France: a psychosis of crisis reaches those very people making it. But it is a psychosis which realities alone cannot justify, as unreassuring as they may sometimes be. Not only does the reduction of publications diminish the number of readers, but simultaneously, it gives credence for the idea that the press lives its last hours. The effect of the decline of readership is to discourage innovation in publishing, which in turn lessens readers; interests that are captive or subject to other temptations. The loop is closing, and the crisis of the daily press keeps itself alive. It produces itself. By a perfectly irrational mechanism, it takes the appearance of an uninterrupted spiral.

The consequences of this psychosis are the reciprocal suspicions between the protagonists of the print media. All confusingly search for a scapegoat. Each seems to lead a war of positions, sharing with others the premonition of a final catastrophe. First the journalists: some invoke the conservatism of the newspapers' directors, others the readers' relative indifference—arguments which offer modest explanation of the erosion of circulation. Then the leaders of the "large" press: they often throw the stone at the journalists, too concerned in wanting to "precede" the readers. They also sometimes deplore the propensity of established powers, public and private, towards the systematic withholding of information. Finally the readers: they lend their trust nowadays more easily to television than to newspapers, even if they are faithful readers. And the press is evidently believed less for what it says than for what it is believed it does not say.

Thus, a climate of suspicion prevails. Moreover, press firms sometimes become battlegrounds between routine-minded and prudent managers and the respective bodies of journalists and printers. Media history suggests at least two comparisons to similar situations: American cinema before 1948 and English press of the early seventies. The Hollywood monopoly was broken under the double effect of the strict antitrust laws and the rise of small independent producers, an ordeal proving salutary and permitting American moviemaking to find a second breath. As to English press, it finally realizes that its old privileges risk becoming the cause of tomorrow's hardships. To save it, its directors now give all necessary attention to the growing multiplicity of the reader's interests: the launching of local dailies with small circulation well illustrates their effort, among others.

The Sickness of the French Press

A lack of confidence in its future, the relative or absolute abstention of readers, relations which seem ambiguous with the powers in place: all goes as if the French press could never break the vicious circle of this "enclosure,"—as if a sort of fatality always impeded print news from being up to the expectations set for it. Those expectations have increased again in our era with the discovery that the progress of societies has much to do with their ability to learn about themselves.

Let's talk frankly: compared to comparable countries, France does not have the news and information media it deserves. How else can we explain the admiration for the U.S.A. expressed by our best professionals? Thus, Jean Daniel in 1966: "The U.S.A. have become par excellence the country of the press. . . . In France, journalism has long been the object of politicians needing a stand, of businessmen, of teachers tired of school and of frustrated editors." And this advertisement made by Olivier Todd in *l' Express,* of September 1977: "Media history must push socialists to carefulness and perplexity: it is in capitalist countries, Great Britain, Germany, Japan, U.S.A., that press, radio, and television relatively independent of political power of the state, the government and even of the money which creates them, can progress."

In truth, the sickness of the French press thrusts its roots in the prehistory of our contemporary media, before the end of the last century. That which already characterized journalism of that era was the dislike of reporting in favor of the columnist. Of the "marshall" of the column, as their era had baptized them, the historian Pierre Albert recently wrote this: "(It was expected of them, not) seriously documented and demonstrative articles, but exercises of style and of mind, original viewpoints which were accepted even if paradoxical, critical remarks. . . ."

The surprising fact is that the expansion of multimillionaire dailies, the *Petit Journal,* the *Petit Parisien,* the *Journal* and the *Matin,* before 1914, has not supplanted columnist journalism in favor of reporting. Still today, the news and information universe, in France, has not really overcome its allergy for reporting, its techniques, dogmas and ethics. Except for a few noteworthy concessions, the dominant ideology in the profession draws its principles and rules only from the columnist taken as a model of the genre: the use of personal interpretation, journalism as a vocation rather than a job, the categorical refusal of the distinction between fact and opinion, the questioning of the ideal of objectivity. From such emerges the survival of a brand of journalism more "representative" than "informative," to reuse an already classic distinction. Journalism "á la Francaise" is more of a preindustrial era, a press which has taken up neither with the governments that lead the action nor with the parties that divide public opinion.

There lies the problem of government-news media relations in France, i.e., in the refusal to make of journalism a true discipline, with its categorical imperatives and rules. That refusal will condemn journalism to being only a semiprofession, an institution neither quite distinct, nor really organized.

III.
Freedom of Information in Italy: Restraints and Problems

Roberto Petrognani

After a twenty-year experience of fascist dictatorship, there quickly arose the problem in Italy of assuring freedom of the press, essential for guaranteeing the democratic method and the political, economic, and social organization that in a modern nation is based principally upon the greatest possible active and informed public opinion. It must be said that this laudable intention has not been matched by complete and efficacious legislation regulating in a clear and definitive manner.

Constitutional and Legal Factors

According to Article 21 of the Constitution of the Italian Republic, "Everyone has the right to express his own thought freely by word (of mouth), in writing, or any other means of diffusion. The press cannot be subject to authorization or censorship." The text does not mention radio and television since in 1947 television was not yet present among the Italian information media; on the other hand, radio and television can be included in the wording: "Every other means of diffusion." It is also to be noted that the same text intended to make reference to the press in general, not specifically to the periodic (Note 1) press.

THE PERIODIC PRESS

The Constitution proceeds as follows: "Confiscation can follow only by an act initiated by the judiciary authority in the case of offenses for which the law concerning the press expressly authorizes it, or in the case of violations of the rules which the law itself prescribes for the direction of those responsible." From this text it appears that preventive confiscation is not permitted; however, the article continues thusly:

> In such cases where there is an absolute urgency and intervention in time by the judiciary authority is not possible, confiscation of the periodic press can be carried out by officials of the judiciary police, who must immediately, and never later than twenty-four hours, make the denunciation to the judiciary authority. If this (authority) does not validate it

within the next twenty-four hours, the confiscation is understood to be
revoked and free of any consequences. . . . The law can establish, with
rules of a general character, what means of financing the periodic press
are to be considered.

This rule has not proved practical, because the matter has not yet been
regulated by suitable laws; thus, the financing of the periodic press is
still a much debated subject.

Article 21 of the Constitution ends: "It is forbidden to publish in the
press, spectacles and other manifestations contrary to good customs.
The law establishes adequate provisions to prevent and suppress the
violations." With these affirmations it appears that any restrictions on
the press that were excluded previously in the same article of the
Constitution are reintroduced. For, although "manifestations of thought"
are not covered, spectacles and other manifestations contrary to good
customs—a concept of "good customs" not well defined—are covered.
And then, among the provisions expected to prevent violations, preventive censorship can be included. Thus, in theory, the Constitution of the
Italian Republic also permits, even if only for manifestations contrary
to good customs, preventive censorship of the periodic press; this is in
contrast to the second paragraph of Article 21 that excludes the press
from any "authorization or censorship." As to confiscation, the decision
is left to the legislature to grant in certain cases to the judiciary authority the power to exercise a form of preventive confiscation; in cases of
urgency such confiscation can be carried out also by an officer of the
judiciary police, though within the limits of particular guarantees of the
provision for the citizens involved. Hence, as far as is affirmed in
Article 21 of the Constitution, it is not clear whether, except for a
declaration of principle for an ample freedom of the press, if in Italy
censorship of the press and preventive confiscation can exist.

In general, at least up until recently, the tendency has been to treat in
a privileged manner organs for diffusion of news, for such organs are
considered fundamental to the working of the democratic system. Yet,
while affirming freedom for everyone to express one's own ideas with
respect to the freedom for others, it is also thought that information
diffusion should be in the realm of public service, rather than the sphere
of private initiative. From this stems the problem of controlling the
process, so that equal opportunities for information are guaranteed to
all political forces, to all political parties, beyond differences in communication media, and instruments. This not so much in the sense that
the state should provide anyone who makes a request with the means of

information diffusion, but in the sense that it has the duty of providing instruments capable of guaranteeing a sufficient plurality of ideas, with respect both to the receivers of the information and public opinion in general.

The first thought was that the organ most suitable to exercise control of the information sector could be the Constitutional Court, which would add this to its already numerous duties. But it then seemed inadvisable to transform an organ by nature eminently jurisdictional into an organ of political oversight. Thus the legitimacy of intervention of the Parliament in its lawmaking function was confirmed. Next to the administrative organs introduced for keeping watch over the information section are legislative organs in the form of special parliamentary commissions on which are representatives of different political parties, and not simply those parties that participate in the government.

In Italy legislation concerning the press is based essentially on the law of February 8, 1947, no. 47, which gave direction to the press, on the law of February 6, 1963, no. 69, which instituted the order of journalists, and the regulation for execution of January 13, 1965, completing that order.

The law concerning the press was clearly enacted to eliminate fascist rules that no longer could be reconciled with democratic institutions. The law, in the first place, defines "the press" and "printed matter": "There are considered to be the press or printed matter . . . all those typographic productions or any other obtained by or physico-chemical means, in whatever manner associated with the publication" (Article 1). In the second place, it specified the obligatory indices which every form should report: place and year of publication, name and address of the printer and publisher, the name of the owner and of the director (Article 2). No special authorization is requested for the publication of an organ of the press, while a registration is expected which allows the individualization of those responsible for any offenses that may be committed through them in the future: "No journal or periodical can be published unless it has been registered with the chancery of the tribunal in whose area the publication is to be issued" (Article 5). Instead, it specifically provides that the director and vice-director of a journal (Note 2), daily or periodic, are inscribed in the list of journalists, except the special case of journals or periodicals "that are party organs or political movements or syndical (union) organizations" (Article 47 of the law of February 6, 1963, no. 69). But in this case it is made obligatory to flank the director who is provisionally enrolled in the list of journalists, with a regularly enrolled vice-director.

The law concerning the press also recognizes an important right of the individual citizen: the right of correction and reply. Journals are obliged to publish fully and gratuitously corrections sent by persons who have seen attributed to them "acts or thoughts or affirmations offensive to their dignity or held by them to be contrary to the truth" (Article 8). In accordance with what is provided in the last paragraph of the cited Article 21 of the Constitution, the law concerning the press refers to rules of the penal code as they pertain to publications destined for infants and adolescents, and those thought to be highly impressionable (Articles 14 and 15).

The penal code of 1930, modified by various legal provisions, foresees many offenses that can be committed against the press as: divulgence of confidential news; instigation to disobedience of the military; subversive and antinational apologia; offense against the prestige of the President of the Republic; villification of the republic, of the armed forces, of the national flag; offenses against the honor of the heads of foreign states; defense of crime; villification of the state religion and offenses against cults permitted by the state; instigation to delinquency; istigation to disobey the laws; attempts against family morals; defamations.

Other articles concern the "right of chronicle" and condemn those who make public either complete acts or parts of acts and documents of penal proceedings whose publication is prohibited by law: the rule referred to is that of the code of penal procedure which forbids the divulgence of acts relative to the formal instruction (preliminary arraignment) or summary of an instruction not reported in a public debate, or in other special cases.

Also punished by the penal code, but as minor offenses, are: the publication or spreading of false and tendentious news; abuse of the public's credulity; abusive exercise of the typographic art; publication of the secret discussions or deliberations of one of the Chambers; arbitrary (unauthorized) publication of the acts of a penal procedure; sale of writings, drawings, and other objects contrary to public decency, election propaganda, and commercial advertising.

With the law that establishes the "order of journalists," an institute found abroad only in the example of Egypt, a juridical position has been given to the journalistic profession. Before and after the passage of the law, much discussion took place in Italy in which, opposing the claims of the journalists to attain an actual professional status were those who perceived in the establishment of the order (or journalists) an evident contradiction with respect to the dictates of the constitution. Weiss (1965) writes that the order limits the right of all the citizens to manifest their thoughts freely; it is in contrast with the existing legislation concerning the "orders" and its professional "colleagues"; it confirms, with the provisions contained in the national contract for journalistic labor, the impossibility of entering into a journalistic career except for a limited number of persons; it imposes a very much questionable distinction between journalists who perform identical functions; it establishes an antidemocratic representative system among the regional and national management organs of the "orders."

According to the law cited, to assume the title or to exercise the profession of journalist, one is required to be enrolled in the professional register (as also must be the director and vice-director of a journal, with the exceptions already seen). The journalists belonging to the order are enrolled in the respective lists of the register, thusly distinguished: (1) list of the "professionals," journalists who exercise in an exclusive and continuous way the journalistic profession; and (2) a list of the "publicists," journalists who perform regular and rewarding journalistic activity but who, at the same time, exercise another profession or maintain a connection of employment.

It is evident, therefore, that in Italy a citizen who wishes to publish a daily or periodical, although otherwise responsible, cannot do so unless he is enrolled in the order and in the list of professionals. The prescribed methods for enrollment in such a list are those necessary for undertaking a journalistic career. First it is necessary to be enrolled in the list of apprentices, which requires one to be employed by a daily or other means of information circulated nationally for at least 18 months. Then it is necessary to pass a professional aptitude examination with written proof both of technical capability and skill in journalism including a demonstration of mastering the juridical aspect of the sector of information. The examination is given before a commission composed of five journalists and two judges. At the end of the examinations comes the enrollment into the order of professional journalists.

Finally, according to the national journalistic labor contract, only one apprentice can be taken on for every ten reporters in each journalistic enterprise (Article 35 of the current national journalistic labor contract). It is easy to deduce that legal provisions give to the journalistic profession a corporate structure that restricts to as many as are already employed the legitimate aspirations of many young people who could invigorate the profession.

RADIO AND TELEVISION: THE EARLY YEARS

The broadcast of news, first through radio and later, from 1952, television, merits consideration. In Italy this service is always performed by a monopoly under the strict control of the government. The RD (Royal Decree) of December 14, 1924, no. 2191, approved the "exclusive concession" to the URI society (Note 3)—Unione Radiofonica Italiana—of transmissions via radio. Up to that moment, operation of transmitting stations was at the disposition of the government, a series of notices worked to preserve state secrets, and standards were set up for the construction of transmitting stations and receiving apparatus, neither of which could be sold without the approval of the government.

The RDI of November 17, 1927, no. 2207 (Law of May 17, 1928, no. 1350), opens with the announcement that the radiophonic service for the entire national territory was conceded exclusively for 25 years also to the URI, which for the occasion had changed its name to EIAR—Ente Italiano per le Audizione Radiofonica. In the convention soon adopted, among the conditions of the concession, it was clearly indicated that "four delegates of the government" would become part of the Administrative Council of the Society, that the naming of the president and the appointed administrator would have to be approved by the government, that the Postal Administration would have to approve the transmitting stations and annually receive the balance sheet of the society, and that the Ministry of Communications would have to approve the annual plan of programs modifiable for reasons of public order (need) by the Ministry of Internal Affairs. Lastly, a part of the proceeds derived by the society from the collection of subscription payments prescribed by law would be paid directly to the State. This particular regime (management) perpetuated itself beyond the historical and political era of its creation so that, in practice, it is not very far from the arrangement still in force.

Soon after the war, the D.L.C.P.S. of April 3, 1947, no. 428, among other provisions, established with the Ministry of the Post and Telecommunications (PP.TT.) a "Committee for the best cultural, artistic, educative, etc., management" of programs drawn up for radio broadcasting and for watching over their being carried out (Article 8). It was arranged that the society's concessionaire, which in the meantime had changed its own name to RAI (Radio Audizioni Italia), should prepare a three-month plan of programs subject to the approval of the Ministry of Post and Telecommunications, the ministry having sought the opinion of the subject committee.

At the expiration of the 25-year agreement, the concession was renewed for a period of twenty years with the D.P.R. of January 26, 1952, no. 580, which approved the new accord between the Ministry PP.TT. and the RAI. With this decree, the concession was given exclusively to RAI for radiophonic and circulating television services (with the decree of the Council of Ministers of May 2, 1949, there had been established a "Commission for the study of problems relative to the development and spread of television in Italy"), of telediffusion by wire, and—this time without exclusiveness—of circulating radio photography.

The RAI pledged itself to effectuate services "of a social purpose," to have headquarters in Rome, and to take care of publicity either alone or in a preeminent society, IRI—Instituto per la Ricostruzione Industriale. The administrative council of the RAI would have six members designated by the Presidency of the Council of Ministers, by the Ministries of Foreign Affairs, of Internal Affairs, of the Treasury, of Finance, and of the Post and Telecommunications; the corporative board of the RAI was to be presided over by a functionary of the General Accounting Office of the State; the naming of the President, of the Delegated Counselor (Managing Director), and of the General Director was to be approved by the Ministry of the Post and Telecommunications, with the advice of the Council of Ministers.

The RAI, among other things, declared itself disposed to "lend its aid for the manifestation of general or collective interests" or "gratuitously put at the disposition of the government for up to two or three hours a day, excluding the nightly ones, the radio broadcasting stations for government communications." The control over the society was effectuated by reference to the above mentioned D.L.C.P.S. of April 3, 1947, no. 428, but the general overseeing of the obligations associated with the concession was assigned to the Ministry PP.TT.

RADIO AND TELEVISION: CONTEMPORARY REGULATION

In essence, as also with the legislative acts necessary to guarantee the development of television services and necessary technological changes, this convention remained in force until 1972, the date of expiration. Then there occurred in Italy a vast controversy in the political field, and hence in the legislative field, with the radio-television services at the center. Since the entire 30-year span following the war was dominated by the supremacy of one party only, the Christian Democrat flanked by minor parties in a more or less subordinate position, it is clear that its interposition was felt in massive measures in areas bound closely to the influence and direct control of the government. The information sector in Italy has always been in this condition. Journals (newspapers), which enjoy a relative autonomy, are seldom read, but first radio, then television, which are now in practically all homes, are administered by the State as a government monopoly. This has permitted practically uncontrolled power in shaping veritable spheres of exclusive competence by one party and its allies with the exclusion of any other concrete and effective participation. This obviously places heavy limitations (restraints) on the objectivity of information, as do the procedures of hiring journalists mentioned previously.

The progressive loss of consensus on the part of the Christian Democrats and of the lay parties of the center that had sustained them for long years, the failure of the center-left that had overturned the Italian Socialist party and had placed it in key posts of public administration, the advance of the Communists with the support of young people after '68, and last, but not least, the maturation of Italian citizens in facing values and conventions no longer proposable have, since the beginning of the 70s, placed information at the center of a national debate. Thus was outlined the need for reform of the entire information sector that should begin with a radical renewal of radio-television services, reform that the State was able to intervene in at first with great results.

Meanwhile, private companies attempted to break the monopoly of emitting antennae (broadcasters), but were harassed by the law and saw their transmission studios closed by the authorities. Then, opposing the growing requests on the part of private companies to send messages, the government declared that the law could not permit the "invasion" of the few transmission bands by so many stations. The political parties, all in accord, declared themselves in favor of the State monopoly for the simple reason that the parties of the center had considered it an accomplished fact; the others, given the prohibitive costs of the plant and equipment for transmission, feared that in a free regime only a broadcasting society (company) in the hands of holders of large amounts of capital could be established, to the exclusion of the forces of the middle and popular classes.

The situation is reflected by the convergence of several factors. First, technological progress has placed at the disposal of growing numbers of social groups instruments capable of transmitting messages at very limited costs—television via cable, television via the ether (air) with limited range, and FM radio transmission. Second was the period of uncertainty following the expiration of the 20-year convention between the State and the RAI, a period in which it was not clear who had power, who could make decisions concerning transmissions, etc., and which lasted for more than three years. Lastly was the attitude of the Constitutional Court, to which many magistrates had recourse in judging the legality of the private installations springing up.

With the decisions nos. 225 and 226 of 1974, the Constitutional Court (given the unrestricted radio electric frequencies for noncirculated transmissions, the destination of these to the far reaches of the national territory, and the lack of risk in establishing a monopoly in the private sector) held that reasons existed for voiding every justification of a State monopoly. This ruling, according to the Court's decision, would also favor the greater spread of freedom of expression and thought sanctioned by Article 21 of the Constitution.

An important aspect of the problem was then brought out with the regional elections of 1969, by the actions of the regions operating under ordinary statute. Each region now took part in the management of RAI-TV through the Parliament-Regions axis. All this brought about a rapid diffusion in the entire national territory of radio and television stations of a local character, directed by private companies, by exponents of parties, or by organs of the press, always unopposed by the authorities and in agreement with the decisions of the magistrates charged with controlling and slowing down the phenomenon.

Finally, with the law of April 14, 1975, no. 103, providing new rules in the matter of radiophonic and television diffusion, Parliament decided to regulate. Article 1 of the law textually affirmed:

> The broadcasting of radiophonic programs via the ether or, on a national scale, via wire and of television programs via the ether or, on a national scale, via cable or by whatever means, constitutes, in the sense of Article 43 of the Constitution, an essential public service and of a character of preeminent general interest, in order to amplify the participation of the citizens in the social and cultural development of the Country in conformance with the principles sanctioned by the Constitution. The service is therefore reserved to the State. The independence, objectivity, and the opening to diverse political, social, and cultural tendencies, with respect to the freedom guaranteed by the Constitution, are the fundamental principles of the radio television public service discipline.

To carry out the aforesaid purposes and principles, the same article reaffirms the competence of the commission provided by the D.L.C.P.S. of April 3, 1947, no. 428, with the new name of "Parliamentary Commission for the General Direction and Supervision of the Radio-television Services." This commission is composed of forty members jointly designated by the two Presidents of the Chambers of Parliament, from among the representatives of all the parliamentary groups.

Article 3 established that "The government may provide the radio and television public service with any technical means, through an act granting a concession to a total public participating stock company on the advice of the parliamentary commission for the General Direction and Supervision of the Radio-television Services."

From Article 8 it is perceived that the administrative council of the concessionaire society is composed of 16 members, of whom 6 are elected by the shareholders and 10 by the parliamentary commission by a majority of three-fifths of its members, of whom 4 are chosen from those designated by the regional councils.

Title II of the law regulated the "Installations for broadcasting sound and television via cable." This permitted broadcast via cable limited to individual communities, or to geographic areas of different communities with an overall population not greater than 150,000 inhabitants. Each network could enroll a maximum of 40,000 users. The installation of the plants could come about only with the authorization of the Ministry of the Post and Telecommunications and of the district having competence in that territory.

Lastly, Title II of the same law set out the rule that for matters of "Private repeating installations via the ether for both foreign and national sound and television programs." Such installations, "which do not conform to the purpose of broadcasting programs in the Italian territory," are subject to preventive authorization by the Ministry of the Post and Telecommunications; they should not interfere with the national public service networks; the authorization is to be released by the ministry subject to prior favorable advice by the Ministries of Foreign Affairs, of Internal Affairs, and of Defense. Moreover, the installations should conform to the technical rules established by a suitable regulation provided by the law and considered on the basis of the technical plans of the installations themselves to take care of the demand. Article 6 of the law specified rules in matters of free access.

After a few months, the Decree of the President of the Republic of August 11, 1975, no. 452, granted to RAI, under the new name of RAI, or Radiotelevisione Italiana—a stock society (corporation) under the

terms of the convention with the Ministry of the Post and Telecommunications—exclusive radio and television public service for the entire
national territory and the service of filter radiophotography, not exclusively, for the term of six years to be renewable. According to Article 9,
the RAI in providing this service utilizes three amplitude-modulated
radiophonic networks and three freqency-modulated; five channels for
radiophonic broadcast by wire, with a provision for a sixth for stereo-
phonic broadcast; two television networks for circulation broadcast via
the ether for an equal number of programs. Article 17 sanctions the
obligation of the RAI to complete a third national network, suitable for
broadcasting in regional range. Moreover, it anticipates that RAI will
begin to effectuate transmission in color simultaneously over the two
networks, using the system PAL-Phase Alternation Line.

The advent of color television introduced in Italy a factor also relevant from the social point of view. Indeed, the government delayed its
coming on the market because of the high cost of receiving apparatus, as
it was afraid that the citizens would be exposed to a new object of
consumption at the expense of purchases for more necessary and productive things. Then, after a period of experimental transmission, color
entered officially in nightly television starting in 1977-78, with a notable increase in subscription fees for those who decided to view television in color.

The complex of rules specified by the law of April 15, 1975, no. 103,
came to be commonly known as the law of "reform" of the RAI. The
principal feature was passage of the function of control and supervision
by the government to Parliament, through the institution of the Commission for general direction and supervision. But the realization of the
reform, three years after the enactment of the law, is problematical, for
there now has happened what was foreseeable, i.e., the political forces
present in Parliament have divided areas of influence very precisely
inside the RAI and things are going if not worse, then certainly not
better than before.

Thus, for example, the first television channel and the second radiophonic one are dominated by political forces of the government (by the
Christian Democrats and by the Catholics); the second television channel and the first radiophonic one by the lay forces of the left, Socialists
and Communists mainly; the third radiophonic channel remains essentially for cultural transmissions by groups of lay people of the left and
of the "avantguard." Regarding the third television network, at present
the RAI gives assurance that it will be kept above partisan influences,

but when it becomes functional it, too, will probably suffer partition among spheres of influence.

Meanwhile, the privately owned radio and television stations in Italy prosper. Estimates are that there are more than 3,000 radiophonic and more than 300 television stations located in all the principal cities. Yet there has not been any definitive legislation enacted in matters concerning the regulation of these broadcasters or the supervision of the contents of the programs, and to protect the viewer (and listener), there is only one projected law concerning "the discipline of radio-television installations in local areas" on the table of the Council of Ministers.

In these months of uncertainty the same rules in force for periodicals are valid for radio and television, with the inconvenience that these bring with them. For example, the decision no. 202 of July 15, 1976, of the Constitutional Court that has liberalized the installations of radio-television via the ether of a local character permits the possibility of installing new broadcasters by a simple administrative authorization.

Freedom of Information

After this analysis of the existing legislation regarding information and the diffusion of news, it remains to examine two important questions that exercise a decisive influence upon freedom of information: the question of professional secrecy for journalists and the maintenance of secrecy in instructional (preliminary) penal procedures.

The rights of doctors, lawyers, and priests to maintain confidences in the exercise of their functions is widely acknowledged. But for the journalist the right of professional secrecy, or better, the right not to reveal private sources of information received, is not recognized. The law of February 6, 1963, no. 69, establishing the order of journalists says textually in the third paragraph of Article 2: "Journalists and publishers are expected to respect professional secrecy concerning the source of news when it is called for by the fiduciary character of it. . . ," but the code of penal procedure does not provide for it, so that journalists are forced to testify as to the origin of certain news under penalty of sentence by the tribunal. Cases are frequent, and the journals and organs of information in general join with the journalists on trial while judges threaten penalties, even though minimal. All this occurs in expectation of a modification of Article 351 of the code of penal procedure which would extend to journalists the prerogative of professional secrecy.

According to what is contained in Articles 164 of the code of penal procedure and 684 of the penal code, the publication of instructional (preliminary) acts of penal proceedings is prohibited "even as a summary or in the guise of information." This makes for a specific legal restriction to freedom of judicial information. Despite doubts concerning the constitutionality of such a ruling, the Constitutional Court confirmed it with decision no. 25 of 1965. The fact remains that the existence of such a form of secrecy tends to remove from public view the development of certain judiciary investigations, the control of which on the part of the public would be important for political and social considerations. This contradicts the basic right to information and freedom of the press in an ordered democratic society.

The problem emerged in all its reality in the first half of 1978, in the course of the dramatic kidnapping and killing of Aldo Moro, president of the Christian Democratic party, by a group of terrorists of the Red Brigade. The problem quickly arose whether or not to publish the communications that the terrorists were sending periodically to the editorial staffs of the journals (newspapers), to political figures, and to parliamentary intimates of the kidnapped man. Opinions were conflicting: some dailies published the entire text of the messages, others reported only brief summaries, while all presented with great prominence opinions of many more or less competent persons interviewed concerning the advisability of giving so much publicity to the demands of the terrorists and to the appeals of a man no longer master of his own will. However, except for some letters of a strictly personal character from Moro to his family, publicity was restricted to prevailing events, according to the best recognized canons of the journalistic profession, notwithstanding several interventions by the judiciary authorities.

Several days after the tragic conclusion of the Moro affair there was delivered to the management of the daily *Il Messagero* of Rome a last communication attributed to the Red Brigade—the 10th, to be exact. Informed of the fact, officials of DIGOS (Divisione Indagni Generali ed Operazioni Specials, or General Investigation and Special Operations Division) of the Questura (Police Headquarters) seized the leaflet that contained the communication and the Procurator of the Republic on May 20, 1978, issued the following ordinance that was quickly sent to the management of *Il Messagero*:

> The Procurator General *holds* that in the sense of Article 684 c.p., it is forbidden to sanction the total or partial publication of acts and documents of a penal proceeding; and that any copy that has been handled

before confiscation is, from the time in which the provision came into being, improperly retained since the release or the retention of copies from that time can only be determined by the competent magistrate and, therefore, as regards the subject, cannot be divulged; *holds* that the leaflet, confiscated by personnel of DIGOS on the premises of *Il Messagero*, of today's date, which begins with the words "The Red Brigade to the fighting communist organization" is a criminal item according to Article 306 c.p., which is the subject of penal procedure; *warns* the organs of the press and of television broadcast concerning the making public in any way of the contents of the said leaflet; *orders* the confiscation of every copy of the said leaflet by whomever retained; *assigns* to the management of DIGOS the execution of the present decree. The Substitute Procurator General: Guido Guasco.

All the same, *Il Messagero* of Rome published the communication although incomplete and omitting some lines in code. It held the initiative of the Procurator of the Republic to be a tardy act for, at the time the magistrate learned of it, the leaflet had already been circulated by press agencies. The warning of the Procurator General not to publish and comment adequately on the communication of the Red Brigade constituted "not only a very grave deed without precedent, but an attempt to trample on the free right of information, guaranteed constitutionally and appears to be a device of preventive censorship." In this the Roman daily was supported also by the committee of editors and by the manufacturing council. Expressing solidarity with the management of *Il Messagero*, the dailies *Lotta Continua, Il Manifesto*, and *Vita Sera* also published the text of the communication.

With surprising rapidity, the management of *Il Messagero* was indicted and brought to trial under the accusation of having arbitrarily published a document (a leaflet of the Red Brigade) covered by instructional secrecy. At the same time, the managers of the other dailies which had published the communication were indicted. The case aroused reaction and comment from Italian cultural and journalistic circles that denounced the intervention of the Procurator General as injurious to freedom of the press and the right of information.

The tribunal of Rome, after much debate, during which the Public Minister had demanded the conviction of the defendants on both accusations, fined the journalists for having given to the press a document that should have been protected by instructional (preliminary) secrecy, but at the same time absolved them from the accusation of not having respected the warning of judicial authority not to publish it, inasmuch as such an act does not constitute a crime since in Italy preventive censorship of the press is not permitted.

From all the considerations advanced up to now, it is clear that the situation concerning information in Italy is an anomaly. On the one hand are constant affirmations of absolute freedom of the press and the right of citizens to become informed quickly, completely, and objectively. On the other lies insufficient clarity of constitutional rules which gives rise to often contradictory decisions, the existence of limited forms of censorship and confiscation, offenses specifically covered in the penal code, restrictive and almost corporative regulation of the journalistic profession, lack of recognition of professional secrecy for those responsible for obtaining information, and instructional (preliminary) secrecy. All support the fact that we are still a long way from overcoming the rules inherited from the fascist regime which still too often exercise influence in a nation that should instead have need for a modern, stable, efficient, and a truly free system of information.

The Journalist and Newsgathering

This state of legislative affairs has direct consequences for the structure of information in Italy, indeed for the way news is gathered and circulated. A tight network of rules and regulations is a condition of work for the journalist who must take it into account. A journalist cannot avoid the possibility that his activities may be influenced by them. It is to be noted that both the government and public societies use press services or information offices as filters through which the news must pass before reaching the journalist. Even for incidental everyday information, the journalist depends on what is referred to him by authorities of different areas such as the press offices of hospitals, or those of the police, or of civil (urban) guards.

In these surroundings, the particular bureaucratic character that distinguishes them often makes a law or regulation prevail over the good sense and respect for the right citizens have to be informed. Certain facts must be discarded, certain others can be referred to only within certain limits, or with some degree of suspicion. And noncompliance with explicit legal admonitions may result in the exclusion of the guilty journal from sources of news.

Because of this attitude of authorities, the journalist often must turn elsewhere than government in gathering information. He turns to his friends, to his personal subordinates, to more or less reliable rumors— all to the evident detriment of the credibility of the news. Or, no matter what the risk, he may present partial aspects of the truth in keeping with the interests of the persons who pass on the information. And it is also necessary to consider that in Italy the distinction between actual reporters and journalists does not exist. In Italy the journalist performs diverse functions: a little of the reporter, a little of the chronicler, a little of the commentator, a little of the politician, a littie of the judge. The professional who has not obtained experience in each area will have difficulty in mastering his journalistic work.

As for the subjects that interest journalists, there are some about which it is not permitted to speak freely, such as for example, the problem of prisons. It is often said that the convict is not readily reaccepted into society once the penalty is paid. The journals have a most important role to perform in this matter, if only to maintain a contact between the world closed to the convict and the society that exists around him. But coverage of penal conditions is strictly regulated. To write something in his journal, to pursue inquiries in a matter, etc., the journalist must not only present a formal request to the Ministry of Internal Affairs and to that of Pardons and Justice, but also to the Managements of the local appropriate Penal Institutes. These requests are very rarely granted. The existence of such obstacles results in the press being little concerned with the problem of prisons and their inmates. The same is true for many other aspects of national life on which similar news coverage restrictions are placed.

The lack of a guarantee of professional secrecy constitutes a notable restraint on journalists. It is true that judges are perceptive when faced with an offense not covered by the penal code. Nevertheless, the journalist feels defenseless because of the uncertainty of his rights. Before publishing or reporting news—often important but received in confidence—the journalist faces such an internal conflict that he rarely discloses the information.

Another factor that influences the character of news is the rapport created between employers and workers in journalism. We have already noted the rules governing entry into journalism in Italy. There are no established degrees (diplomas) nor requirements of a special character. More than 40 percent of those who become journalists do so on the recommendation of political headquarters, the rest in various other ways including having relatives as journalists, friendships with publishers, etc., and only a very few by demonstrating personal capability. Hence, newspaper enterprises, as well as the radio and television societies, are full of journalists lacking professionalism whose work leaves much to be desired.

Political Uses of Information and News

All Italian ministries are involved with problems pertinent to news and information. The Presidency of the Council, every Ministry and the Chambers, the Constitutional Court, the Local Societies, the Public Societies, etc., have press offices to assure a continuous flow of news to citizens as is essential to a good democracy. The Presidency of the Council has two distinct services: the information service and the office of literary, artistic, and scientific ownership; the Ministry of External Affairs takes care of cultural relations with foreign countries; the Ministry of Public Instruction has the initiative in the national cultural sector, control of Academies and Libraries, and takes care of the spread of culture; the Ministry of Pardons and Justice presides over the register of journalists; and the Ministry of Post and Telecommunications controls the relation with the RAI-Radiotelevisione Italiana for the diffusion of news over the air (ether).

In Italy there is no overall state regime for dispensing information, at least in an explicit way. Nevertheless, there is a close bond between information flow and government affairs. The state feels its primary task is informing citizens about the objectives of general politics, and the government feels its duty is keeping these same citizens current concerning its own activities. It is also a right that accrues to the government from the fact that it is the direct expression of the consensus of the majority of the electorate. The information sector is so important for the formation of public opinion that the state can do no less than to provide the instruments necessary for it to have a part, in the most correct and objective manner.

But here also lies a weakness: at the moment when technology makes available to citizens sophisticated means of information diffusion and it has finally become possible to learn everything about practically anything as it is happening (or almost so) in all parts of the nation, at the same moment technology has made possible the most refined techniques for manipulating the transformation of truth.

One of the fears most discussed is that of "neutrality" of information—not only *objectivity,* i.e., conforming information to the truthful facts, but also an attitude of *detachment* from partisan motives—a truly auspicious and perhaps utopian view given the Italian situation. This can be better understood if we keep in mind the structure of the Italian political system wherein among the plurality of present parties there are some which are clearly "anti-system" and ready, once they assume power, to overturn democratic institutions.

PARTISANSHIP AND THE NEWS

In Italy there is one daily newspaper for each political party, in addition to a number of other journals not openly partisan but which, obviously, perform important functions in the political field, especially as they have a larger circulation and their proclaimed independence, or neutrality, make them more credible. And, we have seen how the practice of distributing television and radiophonic network channels mirrors with exactness the political and party situation in Italy.

Although for some years the practice has been of deciding actions of the government only after repeated consultations between the President of the Council of Ministers and the secretaries of the parties that support the executive, the nominal responsibility for political management of the nation belongs to the Christian Democratic party. In comparison, on the administrative level, the Communist party has won the majority of seats in a large number of local communes, provinces, and regions. Even where it has left the formal management to the Socialist party, it has a crushing majority.

This has consequences for the public information process. At the governmental level, in the press offices associated with the different ministries, are persons very close to the Christian Democratic party, and often, even where this is not so, the press office is handicapped in being a neutral news source by the presence of persons intimately tied to the secretary of the ministry that governs the department. On the party level the press office is often limited in its function to serving the head of the Political Secretariat speaking in the name of the Political Secretary.

CONTROL OF THE FLOW OF INFORMATION

The most common form of communication to the news media is the press conference at the central headquarters of the different parties rather than at parliamentary or ministerial bodies, except for routine communications concerning expiration of laws issued through the press offices of the ministries. Also much in use in recent years is the interview, prepared with the collaboration of friendly journalists, and granted by the President of the Council, or sometimes by individual ministers, to this or that journal, or to the radio-television, on subjects of particular prominence.

In particularly important moments in the life of the nation, radio and television broadcast direct the sessions of the parliamentary chambers, with comments by appropriate members of Parliament, and the newspapers report the texts of the principal speeches and interviews. Regarding information concerning Parliament, and more particularly political information, there is the "pastone" (a large mass of dough). It is a large article on page one, prepared by the parliamentary reporter of the newspaper, in which are kneaded the speeches of the political leaders, the comments of leading personalities, official communications released by the press offices, opinions gathered in the corridors of Parliament, etc.—all selected to be politically consistent at the moment with the biases of the journal. Today, the "pastone" has almost disappeared, leaving instead comments of "experts" who follow the development of current political events daily through the newspapers and then furnish summaries and judgments based upon their own political convictions.

In local areas, power centers are distributed among the various political groups, according to the more or less legitimate and more or less lasting alliances and coalitions that conform to election results. The press offices associated with the parties and the local information media generally correspond with each other in views. But there are means to reflect different ideological positions such as publishing in the inside pages of local chronicles views agreeable to the majority in power, yet continuing to publish on the first page or in other chronicles views of a different character conforming with those of their readers. Radio stations carry local newscasts that contrast with the general character of the views of the network to which they are affiliated since such newscasts are transmitted from the local headquarters of the RAI-Radiotelevisione with the collaboration of personnel bound strictly to the party that governs the Region.

These remarks concerning press offices and the news organizations associated with the government and the political parties suggest serious problems with completeness and objectivity in information diffusion. These problems are exacerbated by the fact that press offices are not controlled by the National Federation of the Italian Press, but influenced instead by the internal regulations of the different ministers of the local societies, communes, provinces, and regions. Thus, they are dependent on such agencies and as such are subject to the administrative directives provided for all the other areas of labor. In some cases membership in the order of journalists is not even required for employment since the press offices do not enjoy the prerogatives provided for journalists by the laws establishing the order already analyzed. They must subscribe instead to rules provided for those workers designated as "experts in documentation and information." Often these persons, who are mere bureaucrats, are flanked by actual journalists acting as consultants performing the functions of defining problems and disseminating news to the media. In practice they are the ones who write official speeches for the political spokesmen, reports for assemblies, accounts of press conferences, etc.

All of this produces problems for the journalist assigned to cover press conferences but who does not know whom to turn to as the true news source. At times agencies refuse to furnish any information, thus placing them in a position to control, in a certain sense, the flow of information. Or, they often succeed instead in creating situations where the news is not exact, approximate, or even a little objective.

The press conference is often the only access of the journalist to a public agency. But as a newsgathering device it is flawed because it constrains the journalist to the text that he has received which, among other things, is issued in official jargon inappropriate for popular dissemination. Also, the press does not always receive information directly from the responsible official in such conferences (mayor, assessor, etc.) but from other functionaries who interject their interpretations of the news.

All of this could be overcome if the political hiring by press offices could be eliminated, and there be placed in such delicate positions real information professionals, i.e., journalists able to effectuate, personally and for their colleagues more directly involved with the news media, all the investigations essential to verification of news provided by the ministries or by the local societies, in order to guarantee their truthfulness and objectivity—professionals who know how to write press releases in such a way that they could be used directly for the dissemination of the news itself. For some time the problem received the attention of the National Federation of the Italian Press, which attempts to enroll journalists into the order and into regional associations connected to press offices. Regional groups have been established under the heading of GUS (Gruppo Nazionale Giornalisti Uffici Stampa) headquartered in Milan from whom should emerge a specific category of journalists within the compass of the Federazione Nationale della Stampa.

As regards the work of the Associated Press offices, those officials who perform in routines directly dependent on a political party to which they belong do not write text except as to peculiarity of usage, or nonusage, of terms typical of their partisan adherents. Those who perform their activity from a professional point of view, however, comprise a category that merits consideration and whose working procedures are of greater interests.

It is well to clarify that the journalist or head of a press office, of whatever public agency, national or local, is a journalist in every way and so feels—even if he must keep the same hours and customs of the other employees of the agency for which he works and on whose staffs he is included. He does not limit himself to the news given him, but performs an active role as "searcher" of news, thus making himself effectively an important link between the public agencies and the news media.

The press office undertakes the preparation of news, recognizing in the first place the needs of each of the news media. It prepares complete stories, including headlines, for the newspapers and brief, very concise but equally exhaustive notes for radio, television and for "private" radio. Then in order to leave colleagues in the media a greater freedom in the use of stories, these are often composed of short interchangeable paragraphs, so that the message can be cut at pleasure for arrangement in pages, without the necessity of rewriting.

Journalists often publish the entire press release, initialing them directly or signing them with the name of the editor who is interested in the object of the story. Sometimes other information is added to provide original and complete accounts. It is very difficult for official releases to be published incompletely or distorted in content. More frequently they are flanked by a comment in which the editor expresses his own point of view, but communicated in an official way. And, it must be remembered that official accounts are not directed only at the specialized periodic press, but also to the general media either for information or entertainment. In this case, stories are treated in various ways, shortened or interpreted, according to the needs of the periodical that uses them.

The prominence that is given to national political news is almost the same in all of Italy, and in all the news media. But, as regards local agencies or public organizations, news assumes a different prominence according to the importance they hold for the interested public. That is a function of the distance between the issuing organizations and the central headquarters of the news media that publish them.

How does the press office control the use that is made of the releases they send out? As regards the printed press, each journal or periodical that publishes the release is a tangible document preserved over time.

The press office regularly acquires the principal news publications that are issued at local levels and on a national scale, those with which it has continuing relations. Others are provided by *L'Eco della Stampa* (The Echo of the Press), a national service that follows all the Italian press and sends to the appropriate subscribers all the news and stories of interest. For radio and television there are listeners who follow transmissions day by day and monitor broadcasts.

The press associated with such organized interests as political parties monitor accounts of the problems of the groups represented, above all through the specialized press, or by a continuous contact with the general press and information organs. It is associated with the more prominent foreign systems of information that service its area, and it utilizes the internal networks of information on the bureaucratic and diplomatic levels, government documentation services, official publications of the state, regional bulletins, acts of the sessions of the chambers, communal, provincial, and regional councils, the deliberations of commissions, and everything that is usually behind the information that commonly reaches the citizens.

In these ways occur the very important work of updating and summarizing comparisons between the press offices and the news media, a slow and continuous rationalization that produces consequences for the workings of government itself. Indeed, often from the collaboration between the press offices and journalists there arises a series of anticipated situations involving certain subjects and certain problems which reach the executive level where effective information processes are considered essential to sound and correct government action.

Press Influence on Government

The news media play a central role in the formation of public opinion and are essential for proper functioning of the democratic structure of the national community. It is clear, therefore, that, in Italy, where the information process rests predominantly on political bases, everything printed, said, or seen, comes to be attentively followed, studied, and analyzed in a political key. Every beginning comes to fruition, every controversy followed and often channelized with suitable questions and answers, and every criticism evaluated, through the continuous work of the press offices which, in particular cases, act as public relations offices, in the name of the interests they represent, as well as in the name of government and the political order. This is so true that

the press office often is called officially "Press Office and Public Relations," almost as if the two functions were interchangeable. But the
more true intent is certainly that of commanding a class of information
personnel employed in political propaganda for the use and consumption of the interest on which they are dependent.

In this situation, news media exercise little influence over the high
functionaries or associates of press offices. Obviously, there should be
a distinction between the different organized interests upon which
influence can be exercised. For example, one important difference is in
the political as well as administrative areas between large-scale interests on a national level and the smaller groups on a local level.

The government responds in a very limited way to the news media.
The political parties, in addition to their official dailies and periodicals,
can utilize certain times of radio-television programs, or the pages of
political chronicles of dailies and periodicals, especially on occasions of
great election events. But the government—the various ministries, the
responsible politicians in the national field—do not draw great out-
bursts from the press, which, whether it wants to or not, has not made
the political classes aware of its particular independence or particular
prestige. Rather, the press has shown itself, at least up to now, always
very obsequious and respectful, and therefore not certain to merit any
great degree of consideration.

In press offices, some officials (few, to be truthful) review articles of
major importance, disseminating them in circles where they may have
influence. But, for the most part, reading and dissemination of what is
printed occurs in an episodic manner and with poor perception. This is
an indication of the poor credibility the press enjoys in Italy, at least in
those circles that count and where there is a possibility of influencing
the politics of government. Above all, it is to be noted that the press in
general limits itself to chronicles of political happenings, sometimes
with the comment of an editor on a political level, but does not exercise
any form of criticism whatever, either of censorship on what happens
or on what is decided, and often not even on the part of the press
ideologically in opposition to the dominant class or to the party in
power. This is because of the political opportunity of the moment,
characterized by too many tenuous balances that everyone fears upset-
ting. Thus, it is not difficult to understand how little the news media
influence the government.

Where the press does exercise a more decisive influence is at the local
level, especially in rather small communities. Attentive to the forma-

tion of public opinion favorable to them, criticism by the press in the local pages of the journals, remarks, and stories opposed to the workings of the majority (above all, if reinforced by investigations and evidence) is greatly feared. The press thus has the power to move the waters surrounding problems, and very often contributes to solving them.

A most important role at this level is also performed by "private" radio and television which, if they do not enjoy a vast popularity in the national field, are greatly followed in local matters and make a notable contribution to the information process and to the formation of public opinion, and cannot therefore be ignored by local politicians and administrators.

In general terms, the small influence that the press and news media exercise on policymakers in political classes flows in part from the complex and special nature of the political world itself, which in Italy is characterized by a very extensive hinterland, penetrated with difficulty, where information has a predominantly instrumental function and hence is scarcely autonomous.

The Plight of Italian Newspapers

The change in the news media in Italy since the end of World War II has been marked by a progressive drop in leadership of the dailies, the goodly number of copies of weeklies sold, the notable growth of television, and diminished listening to radio.

Each information medium in Italy has its own unique history but there is a common constant to all: the high degree of politicization typical of the entire Italian information system and, at the same time, the often passive character of business (except, obviously, the RAI-TV) observed by everyone. It is clear that the initiative is always of a political nature, that is, the pursuit of a political idea at any price, even beyond the problems of costs and internal organization to the news enterprise.

To have an understandable and clear picture of the news media in Italy, it is necessary to specify their characteristics and the functions performed. First of all, it is essential to remember that until relatively recently the sole instrument that disseminated news, ideas, and attitudes among the public was the journal (newspaper). Heir of the famous "Gazzetta" of Gozzi, the journal provided local information. Indeed, it should not be forgotten that Italy has only recently become one nation, and that at first the sheets of news had perforce a very circumscribed character. There never, however, failed to be an official sheet of economic or diplomatic news, aimed above all at merchants, bankers and politicians who based their actions in great part on them.

The condition of Italy at the time, the economic unbalance and, above all, the different levels of education among the population, greatly limited the dissemination of the journals. Information reached citizens by way of a few learned men almost always having vested interest in what they leaked out, and with considerable delay. There quickly formed a suspicion of newspapers on the part of those not knowing how to read, and often not being understanding of the significance of what was reported, they identified the learned ones with the cultured classes that held power.

The Italian journals had a radical change with the beginning of the Risorgimento, about the second half of the 1800s. Newspapers became the center of attraction in the struggle against foreigners who occupied so many parts of the peninsula, and of the first attempts to achieve independence and to unify the nation. But the people did not always have a great role in these movements, and the information sheets were useful to only a small minority. Some journals founded in those years are still publishing, and are among the more accredited, above all in Turin, then the capitol of the kingdom of Italy, in Florence, Rome and Milan. From their character in those decisive years, they have retained a tendency for political jargon not always understandable by everyone, entire pages dedicated to the subject and problems of high culture, and references and reports on the world of the economy, very often cast in tones appealing to few readers. Above all, in every such journal there is an emphasis on general national and international happenings, leaving little space for the local chronicle readers prefer.

Thus, in Italy journals are little circulated, few are read and few believed—perhaps reflecting the atavistic suspicion that surrounded them in the past that has remained attached to the pages of the dailies, even when earlier problems have been overcome and citizens are more mature and can truly treasure an instrument of such low cost and ready usefulness.

Certainly, the journals themselves carry much of the blame. Very often political motivations of groups in power are much stronger than the economic motivation which could better contribute to a reduction in expenses and better organization. And the fact that in Italy there does not exist a local (citizens', regional, or for a group of regions) press results in a few newspapers monopolizing news transmission in small territories.

Another factor that is a liability of the press is the bad postal service that discourages mail subscriptions that once constituted the great resource of the publishers because they could program new expenses and investments on average per-subscriber terms.

The Popular Media: The Weeklies and TV

As is obvious, the prospect for communicating political information via newspapers in Italy is certainly not bright. Instead, where things are going better is with the entertainment and recreation media including the weeklies and, in very great measure, television. Here are a few figures: according to data drawn from the report of President Giovanni Giovannini to the assembly of FIEG (Federazione Italiana degli Editori de Giornali), the Italian Federation of Newspaper Publishers, on June 13, 1978, in Italy there are 85 daily journals, 350 weekly and 1,445 journals of greater periodicity (fortnightly, monthly, quarterly, etc.). And 4,900,000 copies of dailies are sold (one copy for every 11 inhabitants); 17,000,000 copies of weeklies; 31,500,000 copies of all other publications. In addition, of all these journals, 95 percent are sold on newsstands and only 5 percent by subscription. Even admitting that a single copy of a journal can reach at least three or four persons, it is easy to understand how difficult is the life of a daily newspaper in Italy.

The weeklies enjoy a greater solidity: this is a post-World War II phenomenon, based on publications of a very popular character, greatly illustrated, with coverage of celebrities from show business and television, hence already well known to a great part of the public. The contents of weeklies are of questionable taste, or a low cultural level, and little incisiveness. The greater portion of the weeklies cater predominantly to the female public and therefore treat problems of the home, domestic economy, fashion, babies and photo-romantic proposals, rosy accounts, and much correspondence of the heart. Also there are weekly publications "for men only." There are also radical journals or those carrying the views of particular groups such as in the feminine movements.

The great mass of Italian citizens regularly watch television programs. This addiction has greatly limited radio listening. Since the advent of color TV in these last two or three years, the cinema is also threatened. At the beginning of 1978 there were more than 18 million

TV subscribers, and the average audience was 22-23 million viewers per night, with peaks of 28-30 million. Programs were received in almost all of Italy, excluding marginal areas difficult to reach by electromagnetic waves, but not over 3-4 percent of the total potential broadcasting area.

Listening to radio has been diminishing with the increase in TV viewing and as a function of programs transmitted: the purely spectacular appears on TV and light music prevails on radio, as well as interviews. Radio is an important medium for political communication, truly noteworthy after the "reform" of RAI-TV. The services and news that informed Italians regarding the kidnapping of Aldo Moro reacquired for radio thousands and thousands of faithful listeners.

Private television and radio, springing up in Italy in recent years in impressive numbers, do nothing but repeat programs of RAI-TV without proposing alternative programming. Nevertheless, they have a sizable following because they cover local events that the present structure of RAI-TV does not permit. Nevertheless, RAI-TV is preparing a third television network of a regional and local character, and a fourth radiophonic network, especially to limit the effects of this competitive situation.

The Structure of News Organizations

The internal structure is not the same for all Italian dailies. And, in recent years there has been a modernization of the procedures for editing and printing of newspapers with the intent of reducing costs. Modernization will have consequences for the structure of the newspaper business, perhaps resulting in reductions in personnel and reorganization. It is possible to speak of three basic processes in the publication of the dailies: *editing, administration-circulation,* and *publicity.*

Editing involves the Director (Manager), one or more chief editors who coordinate the activities of a series of services: Internal, Foreign, Pagination, Third Page, Provinces (local headquarters and correspondence offices in important centers), Economics, and Sports. Each of these services employ numerous editors, who are not assigned to fixed areas, but are utilized for different subjects. The director employs a network of special correspondents, a vital area for every daily of a certain importance, which integrates the work of foreign correspondents with that of the principal Italian cities. Especially important for journals that do not have their central headquarters in the capitol is the service provided by the Roman office updating goings-on of national politics. The Chronicle is in care of special editors who divide it into "black," "white," and "judiciary."

The administrative problems of the journals are taken care of by the Administrative Director, who also manages the circulation organization of the journal, maintenance of contacts with retailers (newsstands), and utilization of numerous sales inspectors.

A very delicate area of the daily journal is advertising. Given the precarious situation of the daily press in Italy, advertising often constitutes the needle of the balance scales for the freedom of the press: advertising by large economic and political groups on the pages of large chains of dailies is a powerful and often hidden channel of influence and of conditioning on the press and the news media in general since news organizations are unable to balance the annual budget without it.

Television and radio employ RAI-Radiotelevisione Italiana, a state licensed monopoly that furnishes stories. Therefore, their internal sturctures are very similar. The task of serving the entire Italian society gives their structure a macroscopic character with enormous deficiencies from a professional point of view. Internal operations are filled with people close to the political parties who seldom contribute to program development and thereby represent billions in outlay and almost a total loss. The RAI-TV in the first months of 1978 counted 12,186 employees, not including those employed in recent months to make up the third television network and the fourth radiophonic network, now in preparation. In addition, it has 20,000-25,000 consultants who are paid for services rendered, and another 10,000 intellectuals, plus an imprecise number who furnish RAI-TV indirect personal services.

The more relevant production areas for radio and television are: direction (management) of the programs; journalistic direction (management), which employ all the national information services and coordinate the local ones; technical direction (management), especially engaged with the processes of visualization in television; and lastly administrative direction (management), which occupies itself with regular collections of rents from subscriptions and with the important area of advertising.

The RAI-TV, in addition to central installations in Rome, flanked by large centers of production in Milan and Turin, has 21 regional centers whose roles are still being precisely defined. The production centers nevertheless constitute one intermediate structure that enjoys organizational autonomy in the development of programs.

Ownership and Management of the News Media

From a summary examination of Article 21 of the Constitution of the Italian Republic on freedom of the press, there emerge numerous lingering contradictions or inconsistencies that contribute to confused legislation concerning press freedom in Italy, cloaking the area with obscure and mysterious pockets. Among the more mysterious are the budgets of dailies, their circulation, sales, and above all their ownership. For the most part, owners are hidden behind strange names or behind the names of convenient societies, all of which tell little of how things are.

Article 21 states in the fifth paragraph: "The law may stabilize, with rules of a general nature, that will make known the means of financing the periodical press." *May*, and not *should*. Hence, the matter is at the mercy of groups who succeed in imposing their influence on the press. The wording of Article 21 was the subject of considerable discussion in the session of the Constitutional Assembly, on April 14, 1947, but was issued in the present form notwithstanding the opposition of numerous political figures. Thus, the anonymity surrounding ownership of the dailies, in the last analysis does nothing but increase the distrust which Italians reserve for their journals. Only with the law of June 6, 1975, no. 172, has publicity of budgets been requested, but there is yet lacking an organic provision that regulates the matter.

It is possible to draw a general picture of the ownership of dailies, bearing in mind exceptions flowing from changes in top management co-ownership and in various areas of influence. According to reliable estimates of the actual state of affairs, managements of Italian dailies is as follows: industrial groups, 14 (for about 400,000 copies sold); political parties, 20; Christian Democrat, 9, Communist, 3, Socialist, 2, Republican, 1, MSI party, 1, and other party heads and ethnic minorities (for more than a million copies sold); Catholic Church, 8 (for about 300,000 copies sold); cooperatives, 2 (for about 200,000 copies sold); public industries and banks, 1 (25,000 copies); Monti Group, 6 (for about 700,000 copies); FIAT Agnelli, 2 (for about 600,000 copies); EFI Agnelli, 3 (for about 300,000 copies); publishers, 12 (for over a million copies sold). In addition there are specialized managements of sport and economic journals.

There is lively discussion in Italy about the size of several colossal publishers who are cornering management of dailies, weeklies, and various periodicals, together with their participation in the book publishing world, in cinematographic performances, and in audiovision. The net worth of their fortunes is discussed, as are the political interests they support, and how they influence the decisions of the greater part of the citizens. This management policy is criticized by many parties as annulling freedom of press and rendering a pluralism of ideas a mere affirmation of principle, not a fact.

The problem of ownership of radio and television obviously is not raised, the RAI-TV being, as the organization which manages them, directly bound to the Italian State through the participation of the IRI. The innovations that have been introduced by the so-called "reform" of the RAI, have their origin in the composition of parliamentary oversight commissions.

Given that very recently the monopolistic regime of radio-television in Italy has been broken by the addition of private radio and television broadcasters, the character of the ownership of these new broadcasters is undefined. Many broadcasters are linked to the dailies already mentioned and, hence, their owners. In addition, others are the outlets for cultural and publishing groups. Others, lastly, are commercial enterprises of small groups who invade the ether as a form of investment for modest capital in the hope of being able to multiply it in a few years. It is clear that, in a political climate such as the Italian one, the preeminent character of these broadcasters is ideological and is part of the Italian political struggle. The centers of transmission are the newsmen, journalistic columns, and stories services that keep citizens up to date even in the small centers of the peninsula, with events that interest them most. A law has been proposed by the government to regulate the entire matter and, it has been insinuated, to oppose the proliferation of these "free" voices, feared on the part of the many who love to cloak their own political actions in mysteries and ambiguities of various kinds.

The Economic Maladies

As regards the print media, the biggest problems are again with the dailies. The report of Giovannini to the Assembly of FEIG noted that for every copy of a daily sold by the publishers there is a loss of 75 lire in contrast to an intake of 200 lire from advertising and sales; out of 85 managements only 2 have reported a profit in their balance sheets for 1976. Given that the market for dailies in Italy is weak and the level of sales places Italy in the last place in Europe (together with Turkey) the publishing trade needs a law to systematize as much aid as is needed. For example, in Italy the price of dailies is set by law, and it is thus difficult to balance receipts and costs. At this point the publishers deem it necessary in the sphere of technical innovations to do what must be done to bring the business to a more favorable position.

To the solicitations to which it was subjected from many sides, Parliament replied with the law of June 6, 1975, no. 172, on the subject of provisions for the publishing trade. It constitutes an attempt to coordinate what was prepared at different times by public powers in that area. Nevertheless, the law is limited to charging to the community of citizens a part of the liabilities (losses) of the business instead of attempting to eliminate the deeper causes of those liabilities. The assistance provided in the Act by the State to the publishing trade has only replaced that of private societies which, of course, controlled the information process. And in the last analysis, the law may provide an ulterior from of control exercised by the political powers. Publishers declare themselves in favor of the separation of the information media of whatever form from dependence on public and private aid in the name of freedom of the press. Obviously, independence requires improvement in the balance sheets of the journalistic enterprises—hard to achieve in the face of market rigidity and gigantic costs of employed personnel.

Today, the orientation of the managing class—unable to affect the price of the product itself—is toward the introduction of radical technological innovations that permit rebuilding the profits of the enterprise through the reduction of the costs of production. From this point of view, new technologies do not represent a marvel of progress to be admired and to be introduced only to maintain currency in a publishing competition on a world level, but as the principal investment for a reduction of costs, and hence for the maintenance of a free system of information in Italy.

Between blue and white collar workmen, the dailies in Italy employ 13, 472 people (in 1977) at a cost for labor of 195.3 billion lire; it is clear that introducing new technologies, above all in typography, will permit a reduction to relieve the burden of prohibitive cost in a market of continuing net losses. In 1977, the volume of business of the Italian press, comprising dailies and various periodicals, was about 770 billion lire, net from deliveries and from payments to newsstands. Outlays for dailies were 254 billion, for weeklies 270 billion, for other publications

240 billion. With the data available, relative to 1976, it can be established that dailies registered a loss of 63 billion lire, with an increase of 56% over the previous year's deficit. And if calculations take into account aid from the State, the deficit can be calculated to be 126.3 billion lire.

The introduction of new technologies does not aim only to modernize plants but also to achieve a new solution to business problems, a solution, however, in which unions and political components must collaborate—unions to guarantee a reform of labor, and the State to assure the readjustment of business management for increasing production is made without shocks. Add to this the concern of the Federation of Publishers over the opening of a third television network which could attract the advertising required for sustaining the daily press.

It can be seen there is need of real and proper reform, a provision that is capable of doing away with the aid furnished by the State guaranteeing independence of the press. To accomplish this, the proposals of the law of July 7, 1977, no. 1616, were presented to the Chamber in the name of the group leaders of the parties that support the government. Because of the numerous uncertainties that this proposal has raised, a committee has been formed within the Commission of Internal Affairs to rework the text of the law and propose eventual changes to the commission itself.

The publishers are critics of the proposed law, declaring it completely harmful to freedom of the press and a sanction for meddling by the state into matters concerning information. Meanwhile, the law of June 6, 1975, no. 172, was postponed to June 30, 1978. With this, the government declares itself disposed to remedy in a definitive way the difficulties of the daily press. For example, the law seeks to improve the distribution networks, protecting the rights of the newsstands, and seeking to facilitate the introduction of new technologies, not so much for the goals proposed by the publishers, but to expand the demand for the journals.

News and News Sources

The news sources of the Italian media are those common to all similar media in other countries. Nevertheless, it is of interest to examine in detail the networks that concern themselves with each day's events of the world. A distinction can be made between sources: (1) each medium in fact has its own sources (i.e., its correspondents) used by the internal organization itself; (2) intermedia sources; and (3) external sources, i.e., organizations for the continuous dissemination of news that serve the proper institutional ends of the means of information.

ITALIAN NEWS CORRESPONDENTS

Among the actual sources of news for dailies, there are the chron-iclers (reporters) who have access to primary sources of a specific character. For example, to compile the daily chronicle, the chronicler turns to: (1) For the "black" chronicle's crimes, robberies, etc., to the police, to the commisariat of public security, to the caribineers; for disasters, to ambulance services, to fire fighters, to the city patrolmen, to the obituaries, to the traffic policemen, to the railroad police; as regards the more relevant scandals, to the guardians of finance, to the Procurator of the Republic, to the superintendent of finance, to the customs. (2) For the "judiciary chronicle," to the police court, to the tribunal, to the assizes, to individual lawyers, to the prisons. (3) For the "white chronicle's" news of a political and social character, to the commune, province, prefecture, to the party managers, to the unions, industrial associations, to the Chambers of Commerce, to the sessions of conventions, of conferences.

For much other news of different interest, the chronicler turns to theatres, airports, women police, museums, clinics, and universities. In addition, and it is a relevant component among the various sources of news, the chronicler is in contact with numerous readers, is informed by friends and by acquaintances, who often perform the role of signal-ers of more or less important events. Finally the chronicler can use the different press services.

As usual, the work of the chronicler is not publicly recognized. As far as it appears to the public, he is anonymous, except for the sports chronicler. Lately, it has been sought to personalize the work of the reporter by preceding stories with the neutral inscription, "edited by."

Another source of great importance is correspondents who send news from other locales than the headquarters of the news organization itself. Provincial and regional correspondents who communicate by telephone or by teletype sometimes, use the "outside sack," a kind of express at a reduced rate. In addition, there are lesser correspondents, without a truly professional qualification, who send news irregularly from small provincial centers—usually students or younger employees who transmit by outside sack. Only in exceptional cases do they use the telephone. Some journals accumulate their messages in local offices which then send them to the central editorial staff by means of teletype.

Then there are correspondents who transmit either from foreign capitals or from Rome. The first are really and truly editors of the journals, or of radio-television, who send complete stories on various subjects. At one time it was essential for them to follow the politics of a country and to inform the Italian public. Now the interests of readers have broadened so that foreign correspondents send articles on the politics, customs, economy, or even simply on events—especially on the outlook of life in foreign countries. Italian journals also use special correspondents who follow events of great import, often in localities far distant from the zone of circulation of the journal.

The Roman office is an institution that demonstrates again and again the political character of the Italian journals. It is composed of a dozen informants among politicians, followers of Parliament, Vaticanists, and background and editorial writers as expanders of political notes in general. These comprise the important stories of journals that are signed or at least initialed.

INTERMEDIA SOURCES

The intermedia sources of the Italian journals are of two types, outside collaborators and other journals. The outside collaborators of the journals are not many, and differ from those abroad, where they form a conspicuous part of information services. The collaborators are classified as regular and irregular. They have acquired a certain growth with the introduction in journals of special pages that deal with medicine, ecology, industry, politics, export, economy. Often, however, these specialists to whom is entrusted exposition do not succeed in overcoming a certain professional tone that discourages the reader. Their bylines are much sought after and usually appear weekly. The irregular collaborators, in the last analysis, come from aspirants who do not succeed in joining the journal directly: the actions taken by the union of journalists and of the order of journalists to eliminate work abuses have greatly reduced their number.

In Italy, there is little assignment of services on the part of one journal to other noncompetitive ones. Nevertheless, this is a possible source for information for smaller regions and provinces.

EXTERNAL SOURCES

The foreign sources of the Italian news media are constituted principally of information agencies that transmit daily from every part of the world. Italian journals are furnished news mainly by the agency ANSA (Agenzie Nazionale Stampa Associata) which transmits daily over four channels by teletype. ANSA was founded in 1945 with the object of furnishing news to journals of liberated regions; in July of the same year it was extended to all of Italy.

According to the statute ANSA "has for its object to assure, with complete reciprocity among its associates, in the climate of freedom democratically guaranteed by the Constitution, an extensive service of journalistic communication, providing for the collection of information destined for the Italian and foreign press, and to its dissemination to the publishing enterprises of the Italian journals." ANSA proposes to collect and distribute the information "with criteria of independence, impartiality, and objectivity."

ANSA has 14 regional offices in Italy: Milan, Turin, Genoa, Bolzano, Trent, Venice, Triests, Bologna, Florence, Rome, Naples, Bari, Palermo, Cagliari; 69 offices abroad—24 in Europe, 10 in Africa, 12 in Asia, 4 in North America, 18 in Latin America, and 1 in Australia. ANSA has the exclusive services for Italy of "AFP," "Reuters," and the "UPI."

The news reports of ANSA are, for Italy: (1) Italian news report (daily, 50,000 words); (2) foreign news report (daily, 30,000 words); (3) sports news report (daily, 16,000 words); (4) news reports for the cinema (daily, 3,500 words); (5) news reports for the theatre, radio, and television (daily, 5,000 words); (6) special services of current events in the more important foreign happenings (daily); (7) documentation services; (8) index of the monthly listings of principal events.

From abroad: (1) Italian news report for Europe and North America (daily, 9,000 words); (2) international news report in the Spanish language (daily, 48,000 words); (3) international news report in the Portuguese language (daily, 48,000 words); (4) international news report in the French language (daily, 12,000 words); (5) international news report in the English language for Europe, Africa, the Mid East, the Far East, Oceania (daily, 12,000 words); (6) international news report for shipping (daily, 7,000 words); (7) weekly report of Italian events, in Italian, French and English. In addition, ANSA transmits a weekly religious news report in Italian for Italy and abroad.

Lastly, on the fourth teletype network, ANSA circulates a daily news report that includes a review of the press; a selection of general news; the "regional Bulletin"; the "union Bulletin"; a book news report (weekly) and a news report on fashion (weekly). ANSA also has its own service for circulation of photographs regarding important happenings.

The financing of ANSA is of a triple nature: rents paid by the journals; rents paid by private (individuals and societies); and agreement with the State based on the creation and maintenance of offices abroad that supply foreign news reports.

In addition to ANSA, there are other agencies in Italy, the principal ones of which are ITALIA, financed by ENI; and ASCA (Agenzia Stampa Cattolica Associata).

Other foreign sources are spokesmen agencies and specialized agencies. The first distribute at Rome news of a political nature to journals and to correspondents from foreign capitols, under the form of mimeographed copies. Since 1970-71, there are party agencies broadcasting and, above all, "current topics" even at a regional level. The others furnish particular information, for example, of an economic character, or even texts and pictures or photographs.

Radio and television, in addition to having a structure similar to that of the journals so that they often use the same correspondents, resort more often also on foreign collaborators as experts, arrange interviews with political personalities of prominence, and frequently include participation by the public. One organization also permits radio and television to broadcast local transmissions of the regional centers.

Characteristics of the Italian Journalist

Clearly in Italy as elsewhere, the chroniclers, the reviewers—in sum, the journalists—are an essential component of the entire process of political information. What, then, is the training for the journalistic profession? Consider the code developed by a team from the Superior School for Social Communications of the Catholic University of Milan on behalf of the UCSI (Unione Cattolica Stamp Italiana), in 1972 (Note 4).

The study by the UCSI took into consideration a sample of 42 journalists, 34 from the dailies and 8 from the weeklies; 6 of the dailies had national circulation, 8 local-regional circulation. Of the journalists interviewed, 21 were editors and chroniclers, 13 chief editors and chiefs of services, 2 managers (directors), 6 special and regional correspondents; all were selected because they were particularly representative and experts in their professional world. Among these journalists, 18 had had experience working in the daily press as well as the weekly press, 21 with only dailies, and 3 only with weeklies. With regard to education, 21 were found to have been college graduates (laureates) and 21 had finished studies up to the mid-superior school. Those interviewed had an average age of 43.7 years; the average number of years during which they had performed journalistic work was 20.1 with an average starting age of 23.6 years. On the average, they had waited more than five years before being enrolled in the order of journalists; 17 were under 40 years of age and 25 over; the younger had had to wait longer for the enrollment.

This entry into the journalistic profession has become more difficult and, with the introduction of an examination provided by law, the probability of discretion on the part of the publishers has increased. The hypothesis does not seem to be confirmed that the journalistic profession is transmitted from father to son, even though the circumstance of having the father already associated with a journal can facilitate a career. With regard to the glamor attached to the journalistic profession, for one-half of the journalists interviewed, it had a special attraction since they were children, while for the other half it was an occupation as any other.

In summary, here are the conclusions of the investigation:

(1) Very rarely can the journalist choose the journal where he will work, and this brings to him an uneasiness very near to schizophrenia in political attitude: on the one hand the ideas of the man, on the other that of the journalist who gives his own labor to a definite organ of the press.

(2) Journalists experience heavy censorship within the journal, but more often they employ forms of auto-censorship, usually seeking individual solutions to their problems.

(3) The prevalence of auto-censorship often discourages ideological conflicts, but when these do arise the journalist almost always comes away the loser. Nevertheless, there is a difference between journalists who work for party organs and journalists of non-party dailies: the former support the party on matters of average importance, but avoid vital questions; the latter take sides more often and more at length, considering a defeat a predominantly personal matter.

(4) Advertising plays a great part in every type of press, not only in the sense that the journalist should speak well of certain industries that finance the journal, but also as censorship of certain type of news.

(5) Although not able to arrive at the determination of the degree, there is a clear connection of the institutional spheres of power with the press: undue pressures and even reprisals have been verified as certain. The cause of all this is to be sought in the structure of power connections between capital, press, and political power.

(6) Concerning objectivity of information, one group of the journalists interviewed prefer a clear factionalism to a false objectivity; others are drawn to a personal honesty, to a pluralism of sources of information, to the distinction between news and comment; others invoked respect for the facts.

(7) The majority understand "public opinion" as something positive and manipulated, up to a point of contempt: it is certain that he who feels himself conditioned and not free himself, often dispels his own discomfort toward those who are more manipulated, without at any time exhibiting a conscience.

(8) In connection with the profession, the emerging problems are those of the order of journalists, which many would abolish, those of the schools of journalism, the limitation of the power of the director (manager), more unionization of the category, to regulate the practitioner and combat abuse.

At the conclusion of his work, the investigators attempted to delineate a possible ontological code for the Italian journalist that, within its general lines, can be summarized as follows:

(1) freedom of information is a fundamental right in a democratic society;

(2) the exercise of the right of information must be free;

(3) the exercise of the right of information must be responsible;

(4) the journalist should defend the professional secrecy of the sources of information;

(5) the information must be true, in the sense that it must respect the right of the readers to know and freely form a mature opinion of events;

(6) the right of the human person to his own reputation, and to the defense of his own private sphere, is to be respected.

Conclusion

The political information situation in Italy, which emerges from these considerations, does not appear to favor the application of such a code as that of the USCI report. The conditioning which journalists encounter in their work has been reviewed along with the obstacles which impede freedom of the press and, in general, free manifestation of thought that is sanctioned by Article 21 of the Constitution. If guarantees are to exist to make a concrete ethical ontological code credible for the journalist and applicable through a new "status" for the journalistic profession, a considerable updating of the entire pattern of the political information process is necessary.

Given the relations that connect public powers to the information sector, instead of conditioning journalists' training in accordance with particular goals, rules should condition journalists to carry out the service to which they are called in a society that wishes to label itself free and democratic. In this direction, a decisive element that can really clear the information situation in Italy is the "participation" in these times of the public. That participation enlarges the area of debate between journalists, publishers and the government concerning the real receivers of the dispatches from the news media.

Reference Notes

1. "Periodic" is distinct from "periodical."
2. "Journal" includes any journal, newspaper, gazette, magazine or periodical, leaflet, pamphlet, etc.
3. "Society" includes any society, business, company, corporation, enterprise, or other similar organization.
4. An analogous study undertaken in 1977 by CESDI (Centro di Documentazione e di Studi sull' Informazione), with financing of the National Council of Research, was conducted on the same plan and with the same methodology as that of the UCSI. Notwithstanding some formal subjection on the part of the journalistic class, it added nothing substantially new.

References

Barile, P. & Cheli, E. (Eds.). La Stampa Quotidiana Tra Crisi e Riforma. Bologna: Il Mulino, 1976.

Bini, L.; Del Gross, L.; Garzonio, M.; Melchiorre, B. & Uggeri, I. (Eds.). I Condizionamenti del Gionalista. Milano: Coperative Editrice Donati, 1973.

Biscardi, A. & Liguori, L. L'impero di Vetro, La Prima Grande Indagine Sulla RAI-TV. Torino: SEI, 1978.

Borio, F.; Granata, C. & Ronchetti, S. Giornali Nella Tempestra, Indagine Sulla Liberta di Stampa e Sulla Crisi dell'Editoria in Italia. Tornio: EDA, 1975.

"Conferenza Nazionale Sull'Informazione Per Un'Organica e Democratica Riforma." Recoaro, 21-22 settembre 1973 - Unione Cattolica Stampa Italiana; in: Annuario UCSI, 1974, 33-421.

Giannuzzi, S., Luigi. La Circolazione delle Notizie Nell'Ordinamento Italiano. Napoli: Jovene, 1965.

"Guistizia e Informazion." XV Congresso dell'Associazione Nazionale Magistrati. Torino, 13-16 settembre 1973, in: Quale Giustizia, 1973, 25, Fascicolo speciale, Firenze: La Nuova Italia.

Murialdi, P. La Stampa Italiana nel Dopoguerra, 1943-1972. Bari Laterza, 1974.

Pansa, G. Comprati e Venduti, I Giornali e il Potere Negli Anni '70. Milano: Bompiani, 1977.

Petrognani, R. Il Linguaggio Giornalistico, Un'ipotesi di Studio Sui Mezzi D'informazione. Dissertazione, Universita di Firenze, 1968-69.

Radio e Televisioni Libere, Informazione e Cultura. Convegno Nazionale di Studio del'UCSI, Roma, 25-26 febbraio 1977, Bologna: Edizioni Parma, 1977.

Weiss, I. Il Potere di Carta, Il Giornalismo Ieri e Oggi. Tornio: UTET, 1965.

IV.
Government and Media in Scandinavia

Osmo A. Wiio

Scandinavia is a typical European example of two different approaches to the relationship between government and media: the press and the broadcast media are based on different models. The press is traditionally an open system with private ownership, whereas broadcasting is based on government control. Finland, however, is a case by itself as it also has a private television company in addition to the government company.

Two Basic Models

I suggest that there are two basic models of the "Right to Communicate" (Wiio, 1977). The models are based on the ownership dimension of the right to communicate: does it belong to the government or the individual?

The Society Owner Model is the historically older model and still prevailing in the majority of the countries in the world. It is based on the idea that the society owns the right to communicate freedom of speech, freedom of expression, freedom of publishing, etc. The society may, under certain conditions, allow an individual to use this right. The society has, however, an unconditional right to control the use of the right to communicate by the individual and to take the right back if it is used against the interests of the society.

The Individual Owner Model is historically much younger and in use only in some 30-35 countrites of the world. It grew from the ideological background of the French Revolution and British economic liberalism. According to the model, the right to communicate is owned by the individual citizen. His right cannot be restricted except under certain conditions: mainly to protect the right to communicate of other citizens.

All the countries of the world are somewhere between the ideal types of the two models.

U.S.A.   Japan   Australia   Iran   China
        Western Europe   U.S.S.R. & Eastern Europe

Individual   Scandinavia   Society
Owner Model   Owner Model

The locations of the countries on the continuum are based on several different dimensions; none of the dimensions are decisive alone. One has to consider such factors as freedom of opinion and expression, right to be informed, protection of privacy, right to inform, right of reply, right to publish and broadcast, right to own media, right to control media, etc.

The discussion about the right to communicate tends very much to concentrate on the issue of media ownership. U.S. opinion seems to equate the right to communicate with the freedom to publish and own the press and broadcast media. The socialist countries answer that commercial ownership of the media does not guarantee freedom of speech or expression; these freedoms are dictated by commercial interests according to this view.

Many European countries have accepted a "middle road": there is some government control and ownership to ensure the publication of societal interests such as education, culture, public information, etc. On the other hand there are privately owned and controlled media to allow for freedom of choice, criticism of the government, individual interests, etc. Scandinavia offers a showcase for such a mixed system.

Privately Owned Press

Freedom of the press has long traditions in Scandinavia. The first newspaper, however, was founded in 1645 in Stockholm to explain government policies. In 1766 one of the most liberal press laws in the world was passed in Sweden, and a year after the first daily newspaper was started in Stockholm and around the same time in other Scandinavian countries. Since about that time freedom of the press and the right to publish have been protected by the law in Sweden, Denmark, and Norway.

In Finland the situation was somewhat different as Russia conquered Finland from Sweden in 1809 and Finland was an autonomous Duchy of the Russian Empire until 1917. During the Russian time the press was censored, but private ownership was allowed. When Finland became independent, freedom of expression and the freedom to publish were stated in the constitution.

The newspapers in Scandinavia have been traditionally founded by political parties. Thus most of them have been active in government affairs although the media are owned by private persons, foundations, business companies, etc. Thus *political papers* or *party papers* are very common in Scandinavia. In Norway and Sweden practically all the papers have a political affiliation; in Finland the development has gone in another direction.

In Finland some papers were originally founded purely for commercial reasons, or a party paper lost its political affiliation. The largest newpaper in Finland—*Helsingin Sanomat*—was originally a party paper of the Liberal party but declared itself independent after the Second World War. Presently only about a third of the total circulation of the press in Finland is by the party press. There is very little concentration of ownership of the press in the Scandinavian countries. For instance, in Finland the largest publisher has two papers and about 10% of the total circulation.

Another common feature of the Scandinavian press is that although the press is often political, the affiliation does not directly correspond with the number of seats in the Parliaments. An example is Finland where the socialist parties—Social Democrats and Communists—have about 45 percent of the seats in the Parliament, but their papers have about 10 percent of the total circulation of the press. The recent tendency by the general public has been to prefer nonpersuasive, nonaffiliated media.

The newspapers in Scandinavia usually feel very free to criticize the government—or whatever part or function of the society. The right to obtain information from the authorities is very extensive, all official documents are in the public domain unless specifically declared confidential—and that is difficult. The rights of the individual are well protected and privacy has recently been enhanced by new legislation.

Much of the new legislation about the right to communicate is coordinated in all Scandinavian countries by the Nordic Council. For example, new copyright legislation is presently coordinated in this way.

Subsidies and the Press

Since about 1945 there has been a strong structural change in the Scandinavian press. In Sweden there were 240 papers in 1920 and 146 in 1976. In Finland about 30 percent of papers published in 1946 are now dead, and very few new papers have been started. However, the total circulation of the press has somewhat increased.

The press in general has been in great economic difficulties, and smaller publishers have often perished. Thus freedom of choice has diminished, a familiar development in many other parts of the world as well.

In the Scandinavian countries this has been seen as an undesirable development for a democratic system. The Finnish Government Committee on Communication Policy said in 1974:

> An integral part of a democratic form of government is the right of a citizen to send and receive information without any advance interference. A democratic form of government requires—to function properly—that freedom of speech and freedom of expression are secured also in practice by a pluralistic communication system.
>
> The press—especially the newspapers—has traditionally a central position in the fulfillment of communication needs in a democratic society. The Committee feels that the press continues to be invaluable as an orientation medium for the citizen; as a forum of free discussion which is so essential in a democracy. . . .
>
> It is considered necessary to secure certain economic prerequisites for the functioning of the press in particular, due to its unique social importance; these conditions enable the press to function with maximum efficiency and make it economically viable.

Similar declarations have been made by several other government commissions in other Scandinavian countries. The political system has considered "press morality" as an alarming phenomenom in a democratic society.

As a practical result of this worry there now exists a system of "press subsidies" in all Scandinavian countries. The government is supporting the press in several different ways. Newspapers receive direct government support: they get tax benefits, low-interest loans, postal and telecommunication concessions, transport grants, government advertising, training and research grants, and subsidies for joint distribution and production.

In the fiscal year 1978/79 this subsidy in Sweden was U.S. 60 million dollars and in Norway and Finland about 25 million dollars. In Denmark the press has resisted subsidies, but nevertheless, some 5-10 million dollars are attributed to it, and much more if tax concessions are taken into account. The exact amounts are, in all cases, under dispute as the press usually does not accept government definitions of subsidies.

The idea behind the subsidies is "noble," and subsidies have, in fact, saved many papers and stopped the press mortality in Scandinavia. The coin, however, has another side as well. It is argued—often by representatives of the press—that there are "strings attached" to the government support. By accepting public support the press is selling its independence and becomes dependent on the political system and the political parties.

On the other hand the political system may use the subsidies to influence the structure of the press. Subsidies are granted to papers which are favored by the government and not given to papers which do not support the government. These fears are mainly theoretical, but there are some indications already that they may be at least partly justified. In Finland a part of the subsidy is automatic and comes to all papers. However, some of the subsidy is "selective support," and it is usually given only to party affiliated papers. This tends to enhance their competitive situation against the nonaffiliated press, which may result in a more partisan press. This development is not regarded by many as welcome.

Broadcasting

Broadcasting started in Scandinavia during the 1920s mostly as a private enterprise but was soon controlled by the government. As an example the Finnish broadcasting was started by radio amateurs in 1924, and until 1934 there were several independent stations. Then a "public company" was formed and in 1948 the Parliament took direct control of the Finnish Broadcasting Company by appointing the Board of Governors of 21 persons. The government owns the majority of the shares of the company, although there are some individual owners left.

The system is somewhat similar in other Scandinavian countries. In Sweden the government does not own Sveriges Radio but has complete control, and the company has a broadcasting monopoly. There are government broadcasting monopolies also in Denmark and Norway. In Finland, however, there is no broadcasting monopoly. In fact television was started in 1956 by a private company which was bought eight years later by the Finnish Broadcasting Company. However, there still is another private television company—MTV—which buys program time on the FBC channels (program 1 and 2) each evening. MTV sends about 25 percent of the total TV time, and its programs are often quite popular. The system is somewhat similar to the British system with a government controlled company and a private company.

The reasoning behind the government controlled European model of broadcasting (á la BBC) was that the radio frequencies are a limited natural resource. The electromagnetic spectrum for radio transmissions is traditionally highly congested, and international regulation was necessary at least in such an area as Europe where there are many small countries close to each other. Each country had to be assigned only a few channels to make it possible to obtain broadcasting without interference. This also usually meant concentration in the national broadcasting system.

Concentration became, however, an end itself even after the original reasoning was not valid anymore. Political reasons tended to replace the original technical reasons. The socialist parties in Scandinavia are for centralized control of the broadcast media, and they resist private ownership of the broadcast media for ideological reasons. In Sweden, Denmark, and Norway the Social Democrats have been more or less continuously in power.

The broadcasting monopoly is, however, breaking down in Sweden since the nonsocialist parties came to power for the first time in over 40 years. Already during the last years of the Social Democrats a second TV channel was created to compete with TV1. Then after the change of government in 1978, a new law was passed in Sweden to establish something called "närradio" (neighbor radio), a system of small radio transmitters around the country run by civic groups, schools, etc. Another innovation was to cut the Swedish Broadcasting Company (Sveriges Radio, SR) into five independent companies: SR as a mother organization, television, national radio, local radio, and educational broadcasting. The financing will still be through license fees for the audience to listen to the radio and to watch TV. No commercials are allowed in Sweden, Denmark, and Norway, only in Finland.

Communication Policy

During recent years in all Scandinavian countries communication policy has become a "hot issue." New communication technology has given new opportunities for communication development, and it is heatedly discussed what the role of the government should be in the implementation of the new communication systems.

Cable television is an example. Traditionally telecommunications are controlled and owned in Europe by the government through its Post and Telecommunication Administrations. Thus it has been "natural" that any such communication system as cable television is controlled by the government. Such is the case in Sweden, Denmark, and Norway but not in Finland. In Finland most of the telephone networks are owned by private companies and a cable television network is expanding in Helsinki through the local telephone company cables. This development is heavily criticized by the socialist parties, but they have a minority in the Parliament and cannot change the situation.

A similar discussion is under way about broadcast satellites. The Nordic countries have a common satellite plan called NORDSAT to send a geostationary satellite for radio and television broadcasting to all Scandinavian countries including Iceland. However, the plan is resisted mainly by the socialist parties. They claim that the system is a danger for the national cultures, that the system is too expensive, that the audience would only "slalom" between light entertainment, etc. The proponents of the system say that the satellite would enhance the Nordic community, that it would provide more choice of programs and that the opposition is only afraid to lose political control of the programming. No final decision had been made about the NORDSAT plan in 1979.

Official government commissions and committees have made several reports on communication policy in Scandinavia, and for an outsider it might look all very organized and planned. It is true that the importance of communication policy has been realized in Scandinavia. It is a long way, however, from committee reports to action. In many matters the political ideologies are so far apart when talking about the "right to communicate" or "freedom of expression" that it is very difficult to find viable solutions in the decision making bodies of the government.

References

The Finnish Government Committee on Communication Policy. *Report 1 and 2,* Helsinki, 1974.
Gustafsson, K. E. & Hadenius, S. *Svensk Presspolitik.* Boras, 1976.
Ortmark, A. "Freedom's Boundaries." In A. Smith (Ed.), *Television and Political Life.* New York: MacMillan, 1977.
Smith, A. *Subsidies and the Press in Europe.* PEP, London, 1977.
Wiio, O. A. "Open and Closed Mass Media Systems and Problems of International Communication Policy." *Studies in Broadcasting, NHK.* Tokyo, 1977.

V.
Government and the News Media: The British Experience

David G. Boyce

The British experience is central to any discussion of relations between government and the news media. It was in Britain, after all, that the classic doctrine concerning this relationship was formulated in the late 18th and early 19th centuries; and 20th century developments in the ownership, structure, and control of the media have ensured that the debate is a lively one still. Some half a dozen official reports—of Royal Commissions and Government Committees—plus innumerable pamphlets, Parliamentary debates, and books have examined the role of the press and broadcasting since the Second World War. It might be said that the results of these investigations have hardly been commensurate with the labour; but they have at least provided an important commentary on the difficulties that beset a liberal democracy when it tries to combine its traditions of a free press with a characteristically modern concern for the standards and performance of the "watchdog of the public interest."

Government Impact on Media

As far as the liberal theorists were concerned, the only desirable, indeed admissable, role for government in its relations with the press was to stand aside and let a free press communicate—perhaps even commune— with a free people. "So true is it," wrote James Mill in 1821, "that the discontent of the people is the only means of removing the defects of vicious government, that the freedom of the press, the main instrument of creating discontent, is, in all civilized countries, among all but the advocates of misgovernment, regarded as an indispensable security, and the greatest safeguard of the interests of mankind." The public could only criticise its governors, could only choose them in the first place, if it possessed "the most perfect knowledge relative to the characters of those who present themselves" to its choice; for the governors to impose restraint would be tantamount to the government choosing the directors of the public mind, and such a course of action was despotic (Mill, 1821/1967, pp. 19-21).

Such sentiments corresponded neatly with the economic position of the press in the early 19th century. The respectable and legitimate press, which paid its various taxes and duties to the state, was suffering from what it naturally regarded as the unfair competition of the unstamped, illegal, and radical press which flourished in the political ferment of England after Waterloo. Press reformers argued that, by ending or reducing press taxation, the government would encourage capital investment in an expanding newspaper market, increase the flow of advertising to the "best papers," and thus encourage "more temperate and disinterested friends of the people who would lend themselves to their real instruction." As Mill put it, it was surely not "good policy" to hand the power of teaching the people exclusively to persons violating the law. The free market, therefore, would produce a press that could enlighten public opinion and destroy one that was threatening to pervert public opinion. It was a neat argument, and, to the government, in the end it was a convincing one. With the repeal of the last remaining "tax on knowledge" in 1861 (the paper duties), the way was opened for the press to become big business.

But not only business; it is perhaps tempting to be cynical about the high presumptions of the 19th century press, and to contrast these with its obviously growing commercialism and its self-interested preservation of the status quo. The Times argued that the press was "daily and forever appealing to the enlightened force of public opinion," even described itself as a "perpetual committee of the legislature," at the very time when its competitors were complaining bitterly about its monopolistic position in the world of the news media. W. T. Stead, one of the founders of the "new journalism" of the late 19th century, could argue that "human interest" stories and sensationalism were necessary to arouse the interest of democracy, and that to bring issues to the public notice it was sometimes necessary to "print in capitals." Nevertheless, the idea of a free press in a free society was one that prevailed throughout the 19th century and was one that few journalists would have wanted to deny. Economic well-being meant political independence, or so it was said; and this independence was regarded as the cornerstone of the fourth estate. Without it, wrote Frederick Greenwood, "the country is not best served, nor party neither"; in England, he added, "we may boast of a newspaper press that could always be called independent on the whole and in the main."

Governments could never subscribe fully to such high sounding and lofty ideas; nor, for that matter, could journalists. Governments in the 19th century were prepared to drop legislative control of the press; but there were other means of influencing journalists, by an exchange of information, for example, or by assiduous cultivation of well-disposed editors. And in the early 20th century, as some newspapers ran into increasingly acute financial difficulties under competition from Lord Northcliffe's mass appeal press, there was always the chance to inject sums of money from party funds. Such expedients did not always ensure loyalty, but at least they kept politicians in touch with newspapers; and newspaper editors gratefully received contributions, while at the same time insisting that they were independent political figures. Editors needed information, political gossip, cash, and they could only obtain such precious commodities from what James Mill had called the "governors." Eventually the "Northcliffe revolution," basing a successful mass newspaper on revenue from mass advertising, was to prise the press free from political finance and end the day of what J. L. Garvin called the "party tied daily rag." But in the process, many quality political newspapers, such as the *Globe,* the *Westminster Gazette,* and the *Morning Post,* were to perish; and their fate served to modify the idea that the interests of the fourth estate could best be served by a free market economy news media (Boyce, Curran, & Wingate, 1978, pp. 19-40).

Governments professed to admire the "quality" political press, however much they had tried, like Lloyd George, to suborn it by fair means or foul. "Who," asked one M.P. in 1918, "elects the press? Any rogue with a million of money . . . can get control of the press, or a portion of it, at any minute; and so where is our democracy?" "Men like C. P. Scott . . . A.G. Gardiner," proclaimed Michael Foot in 1946. "Those are the real journalists, the men who maintained the great traditions of British journalism, but they have, in the past 20 or 30 years, been fighting a losing battle against increasing odds. Therefore, it is the business of this House of Commons to come to their support." Chain newspapers had not been built up by the choice of the public; they had been built up by "financial manipulation" (Boyce et al., 1978, pp. 37, 346). It could be argued that such criticisms, which came mainly from the Left in British politics, were the natural response of men whose party could not maintain a successful newspaper in the economic climate of the 20th century "capitalist" British press. Whatever the motive—and to put it thus would be again to oversimplify, and to underestimate the hold that

fourth estate ideas had on public men—such criticisms, such sentiments, had important consequences for relations between government
and the new mass media that were establishing themselves in the 20th
century: radio and television.

THE BROADCASTING MEDIA

Wireless broadcasting began in the United Kingdom in 1920, and two
years later the Marconi company began to provide regular broadcast
services. In 1922 also the Post Office authorised a British Broadcasting
Company to start work, replacing the Marconi company, and consisting of representatives of the major wireless companies, with the smaller
companies invited to join. Until 1926, the BBC was not a public body;
but neither was it an ordinary commercial enterprise. Its dividends
were restricted to 7½ percent by the Post Office, and its first general
manager, J. C. W. Reith, believed that wireless could be an instrument of
public good, upholding standards of taste, integrity, and knowledge
(Smith, 1974a, pp. 37-39, 44-45). Meanwhile the government set up a
committee under the chairmanship of Sir Frederick Sykes to examine
the financial, organizational, and national implications of the new
medium. Its deliberations were shaped by a number of factors: by the
example of the United States, where a free-for-all in the broadcasting
world had quickly produced a "cacophony of the air"; and by the feeling
that to allow financing from advertisements would inevitably lower
standards (Smith, 1974a, pp. 39-40). It was this fear of what wireless
could do to the people, if not properly supervised, that helped shape the
final form of the BBC, a form recommended by the Crawford Committee
in 1926. The BBC was to be a public corporation, "acting as Trustee for
the national interest," led by a board of governors, under a chairman
appointed by the Crown. Its ultimate controller would be a government
official, the Postmaster General, who issued wireless licences and
collected licence fees (Smith, 1974a, pp. 50-55).

This kind of semi-independent monopoly reflected a mixture of libertarian notions about the freedom of the press and government concern
about the potential power of the new medium, summed up in the words
of the House of Commons in 1933: "The position of the Corporation is
thus one of independence in the day-to-day management of its business,
and of ultimate control by His Majesty's Government" (Burns, 1977, p.
12). Moreover, because the popular press appeared to be neglecting its
traditional role as educator of the public and as an instrument of
democracy, the idea of the BBC as trustee for the nation, responsible to

the government for its performance, found many adherents; and since the free market of newspaper competition had produced, not a "republic of letters," but a mélange of trivia, there was little resistance to the plan of a public monopoly of the wireless broadcasting system (Burns, 1977, p. 180; Smith, 1973, p. 33). But the idea of a free press was not set aside, for the BBC received its first Charter under Royal Seal, not legislative enactment, and the charter contained no prohibitions and scarcely any restrictions (Smith, 1974a, pp. 56-59).

But how would this mixture of constitutional dependence and political freedom affect the BBC's treatment of political issues? From the beginning politicians were wary of the new medium, and on several occasions they intervened to warn it off controversial topics. In April 1923, for example, a Labour M.P. objected to a broadcast talk relating to a building strike in London, and the Postmaster General replied that he thought it "undesirable" that the broadcasting service should be used for dissemination of speeches on controversial political problems. On another occasion Reith was refused permission to hold a debate on unemployment. In the general strike of 1926 Winston Churchill, in his readiness to take any measure to put down a strike which he regarded as illegal and unconstitutional, was prepared to take over the BBC and use it as a government mouthpiece. Reith resisted this pressure and tried, on the whole successfully, to steer a middle course, broadcasting messages from the General Council of the TUC as well as the government; but he was greatly assisted by the confidence of the Prime Minister Stanley Baldwin, who resisted attempts in the Cabinet to take over the company, and who even enlisted the help of Reith in preparing an important speech, a speech he broadcast from Reith's own house. Moreover, the government refused permission for the BBC to arrange a broadcast by a trade union or labour spokesman, mainly, Reith believed, because of pressure from Winston Churchill. And when the BBC tried to "editorialise"—to give its own appreciations of the situation—the Postmaster General intervened to point out that such editorials should be submitted to him for approval; eventually they ceased (Briggs, 1961, pp. 360-384).

The BBC, therefore, had to establish itself as a body with certain political rights and as a body that was in the business of giving authoritative news in the face of hostility, not only from government, but also from the newspaper press, which feared the BBC as a competitor in the news producing business (Burns, 1977, p. 181; Smith, 1973, pp. 87-88; Smith, 1974a, pp. 50-53). That it did so was partly because of its own efforts, partly because of the efforts of opposition politicians, and partly because of the luck of circumstances. Broadcasting was, indeed still is, primarily a medium of entertainment, but the sheer speed with which information can be broadcast, compared with the delays of printing presses, inevitably thrust the BBC into the news disseminating field, especially in time of crisis. This was particularly important during the Second World War, when the BBC emphasized the importance of news and, moreover, of truth and consistency. The nine o'clock news reached nearly 50 percent of the total population; experiments were made with news programmes; information was collected through war reporters. Before the war the government had seriously considered shutting down the ordinary broadcasting service in wartime, and the Committee of Imperial Defence had decided that in the event of war the government should assume effective control of broadcasting and the BBC. But the war produced a national hunger for news, and, moreover, news of an authoritative kind, not official government propaganda. In any case Reith, who took over at the Ministry of Information (a body established in 1935 which, it was envisaged, would censor BBC programmes), believed that the theme of the war should be that "this is your war, the nation's war." It was of more value to the war effort and to the government that the BBC should appear to be objective and authoritative than that it should be a mouthpiece of a government propaganda machine, and this prestige stood the BBC in good stead in any future dealing with the government (Briggs, 1970, pp. 6-7, 167-168, 329-345).

Then again the possibility that the BBC might lose its "fourth estate" mantle was hardly likely to occur in a pluralist political system. Opposition parties wanted their share of the air, and from the beginning they pressed for opportunity to use the medium. In 1926, during the general strike, the BBC summarized the opinions of government critics, such as David Lloyd George, and Lord Grey broadcast on behalf of the Asquith Liberals (Briggs, 1964, pp. 372, 376). Eventually the opposition parties managed to win the right to broadcast their own rejoinders to statements made by government ministers which could be construed as "political" (Burns, 1977, p. 182; Smith, 1974a, pp. 69-72). This left an area of uncertainty about what was "political" and what was a nonpolitical national issue, uncertainty which gave rise to controversy in 1956, when the Prime Minister, Sir Anthony Eden, maintained that the British invasion of Suez was a national war, and that the leader of the Opposition, Hugh Gaitskell, had no right to reply to his eve-of-war broadcast. The BBC maintained that British policy was a matter of debate, and that the public had the right to hear the arguments for and against. The BBC won its point (Goldie, 1977, pp. 182, 183). And in the same year it won another important victory when the 14 day rule (under which the BBC was to refrain from comment on issues which were to be debated in Parliament for a period of 14 days before the debate) was reduced to 7 days on the recommendation of a Select Committee of the House of Commons. A year later the rule was formally abandoned (Goldie, 1977, pp. 123-125; Smith, 1974a, pp. 113-117).

Nevertheless, government could not abandon or forget its potential control over the BBC, and a kind of running battle, at times fierce, at times diminishing to a lull, has characterised relations between the state and the corporation. The very permissiveness of the BBC's Charter proved in the end to be more irksome, though not more respective, than any kind of formal controls would have been; as one authority had put it, "The pressure on a man who is free to make decisions in his own way is much greater than that on the man who merely does as he is told" (Burns, 1977, p. 195). This especially applies when the free man knows that in the end, though he is operating on a very long leash, the leash does exist.

The leash not only existed with regard to commercial television, however: it proved to be a much tighter one than was ever fastened to the BBC. The campaign for commercial television was a well-or-chestrated affair, involving a section of the Conservative party, which itself represented the national mood—a mood which sought to turn away from wartime austerity, and open the way to a prosperous, mass-consumption society (Smith, 1974a, pp. 62-63). Advertising was an essential part of this society; and the Conservative government of 1952 spoke also of the need for "some element of competition when the calls on capital resources at present needed for purposes of greater national importance makes this feasible" (Smith, 1974a, pp. 100-103). The 1954 Television Act set up the Independent Television Authority (in 1972 the Independent Broadcasting Authority) in a new public corporation, which would own the transmitters and hire them to a group of new companies; these companies would make programmes, transmit them through the corporation's facilities, and collect revenues from advertising to cover their costs. This was adopted because the government had "decided as a basic principle that there should be no 'sponsoring' and that the responsibility for what goes out on the air shall rest upon the operator of the station, and not on the advertiser" (Goldie, 1977, chap. 8; Smith, 1974a, pp. 106-111). Thus ITV would be in a similar position to the press, who accepted advertisements, but remained responsible for their own news and editorial columns. Thus the twin principles of private enterprise and effective control could be neatly combined.

MEDIA RESPONSIBILITY

But what about political content? The government's proposals referred to the need for "impartiality in the treatment of all controversial issues, and subject to agreement (revised from time to time) between the parties and the BBC on party political matters" and insisted that the new corporation should not be allowed to broadcast its own views (Smith, 1974a, p. 109). This latter restriction applied also to the BBC; but in the Television Act of 1954 the government spelled out its meaning more clearly: the authority was charged with the duty of satisfying itself that, as far as possible, programmes complied with certain requirements. Among these were that "nothing is included in the programmes which offends against good taste, or decency, or is likely to encourage or incite to crime, or lead to disorder, or to be offensive to public feeling, or which contains any offensive representation of or reference to a living person." That the programmes should "maintain a proper balance in their subject matter." That any news given in the programmes was "presented with due accuracy and impartiality." That "due impartiality is preserved on the part of the persons providing the programmes as respects matters of political or industrial controversy, or relating to current public policy." This was a formidable array of controls, and has been taken to exclude ITV from transmitting political satire: "any offensive representation of or reference to a living person" (Smith, 1974a, pp. 109-111).

The attempt to make the BBC and the IBA conform to ideas of the national interest meant that television in contemporary Britain became embroiled in a series of controversies, especially in the 1960s and 1970s, when television broke new ground in political coverage, in political satire, and professional political reporting. Both the BBC and IBA found themselves in the limelight, the BBC over its programme "A Question of Ulster," in which it brought into the studio representatives of the conflict in Northern Ireland (Smith, 1974a, p. 129) and again following the transmission of "Yesterday's Men", a study of some recently unemployed Labour politicians who had just been ousted from office in the general election of 1970 (Tracey, 1977, chap. 10). ITV found itself brought before a court of law for its screening of a programme about the work of Andy Warhol, the American "underground" film maker. These controversies were not without effect on the running of both the BBC and IBA. In the case of the BBC, the protests about "Yesterday's Men" brought forth a Complaints Commission, on the BBC pay roll, which would consider complaints from those who regarded the BBC's replies to their objections as unsatisfactory. The commission consisted of three former public servants of distinction, but there were those who wished to see a full scale broadcasting council outside the BBC and IBA, and governing the standards of both. IBA, for its part, found that its appearance before the courts placed a greater responsibility on the members of the authority for ensuring the "quality" of individual programmes transmitted within the independent system (Smith, 1974a, pp. 129-130, 234-237). These, of course, were not hard and fast rules, for even within the strict charter of the IBA there is much room for debate about contravenes public taste or the public interest, and what does not; and the task of deciding what is tolerable is not an abstract one, but one which each individual controversy helps to evolve and clarify.

Nevertheless, the post-1945 attitude, that there should be some kind of public accountability for broadcasting, that broadcasting had to live up to certain standards in the national interest, had profound repercussions on the other main news media in Britain, the press. Just as the idea of an "irresponsible" press had in the 1920s shaped the structure of broadcasting (which was organized in such a way as to avoid, hopefully, the worst excesses of the popular press), so the idea of responsible broadcasting "helped push back the directions in which press freedom had been driving" (Smith, 1973, p. 45). In short, it helped create the so-called "social responsibility" theory of the press: a theory that might be summed up as holding that journalism was too important to be left to the journalists. The freedom of the press, it was held, was not an unconditional or an absolute thing. It carried obligations to society, and it had to fulfill these obligations in order to merit its privileged position under government. These obligations encompassed the traditional libertarian notions of servicing the political system, enlightening the public, and safeguarding the liberties of the individual by serving as a watchdog over government. In so far as they were not being met, it was the responsibility of some agency to put the matter right (Peterson, 1956/1973, chap. 3). But of what agency? After all, the whole concept of a free press in Britain was based on the economic freedom of the press, its ability to exist based on the free market economy, on selling its product to the people. The dilemma was well put by the 1949 Royal

Commission on the Press, which on the one hand held that "in our opinion the newspapers, with few exceptions, fail to supply the electorate with adequate materials for sound political judgement," yet admitted that "if the press is not aware of its responsibilities to the public it cannot perform its functions adequately; but if it is not free, it cannot perform them at all" (Report, 1949, p. 154).

The solution adopted in Britain was one which Gerbner (1977, p. 263) has described as "normative constraints"—that is, "expectations of political and public service by media organizations for which they may be held socially accountable without falling under the direct control of either state or party machinery." The 1949 Royal Commission on the Press recommended a Press Council to encourage a sense of public responsibility in the press, to condemn and publicize questionable practices on the part of the press, to investigate complaints, to seek redress if the complaints were justified, and to refute them if they were not. The press refused to accept any such body in 1949, viewing it with suspicision as a form of censorship. An attempt to introduce one by statute law failed, but the press at last agreed to set up its own council in 1953. Its chairman was not an independent layman, but in 1963 the Press Council was reconstituted with a lay Chairman, Lord Devlin, and in 1973 it was enlarged to give a bigger lay representation (Levy, 1967; Murray, 1972).

But the problem was how to give such an organization teeth. Its only sanction was publicity, which was hardly likely to worry errant pressmen; journalists were not bound, legally or professionally, to respect it; and even if it adjudicated in favour of a complainant, it could not redress the damage already done. It could draw attention to a transgression of ethical standards; but it could not deter a determined editor from pursuing a particular line. On the contrary: the 1949 Royal Commission on the Press emphasized that a Press Council "would depend for its effectiveness on its moral authority rather than on statutory sanctions" (Report, 1949, p. 173).

This was the crux of the matter. Restrictions on the activity of the press, albiet applied in the interests of a more professional, more socially responsible journalism, might in the event inhibit the very activity that it was intended to promote. Therefore, the Press Council was anxious to stress that part of its brief which aimed at protecting the journalists in their dealings with public institutions; in the words of the 1949 Royal Commission, "to keep under review any developments likely to restrict the supply of information of public interest and importance" (Report, 1949, p. 174). The increasing role of government in people's lives, especially after 1945, and the growth of bureaucracy, laws, and regulations, enabled the press to claim that social responsibility was not a one-sided affair; that the press had its responsibilities, and that these included the right and the duty to ferret out official information if it seemed to be in the public interest. But British government was notoriously secretive and discreet in its operation, fearful and suspicious of publicity, and with its traditions backed up by a whole set of controls—the Official Secrets Act (first introduced in 1889, and designed to deal with a public servant who communicated information "corruptly or contrary to his official duty")—and strengthened in 1911 and again in 1920; Defence ("D") notices were inaugurated in 1912, which amounted to a form of self-censorship at the behest of a government department; and of course the ordinary laws of the land, including contempt of court and libel laws, which, with the heavy damages usually awarded in Britain, deterred the press from taking chances (Seymour-Ure, 1968, chap. 4).

But here again there was a dilemma, epitomised in the fact that the Franks Report on the Official Secrets Act (1973) was produced and debated, with M.P.s in favour of a broader right of publicity; and two weeks later the Younger Committee on Privacy reported, and the debate in the House was characterised by a general wish on the part of the members from all parties that there be more protection of privacy (Smith, 1974b, pp. 183-190, 197-205). Yet at least one modern editor has alleged that the role of the press in the modern state has changed, with the increase of government activity, with the complexity of modern industrial society, and that the disclosure of facts and information is more than ever necessary today. Thus there comes the plea for some overriding principle, setting aside libel or contempt of court, if this is deemed to be in the public interest. The crucial test must be the public good, and the public good must be proportionate to the methods of inquiry and disclosure. Circumstances must determine everything, and there was much to be said for a general defence that publication may be necessary in the public interest. Newspapers had no more rights than had ordinary citizens; but they would "certainly like to be relieved of some of the restraints based on the exercise of an ordinary citizens rights to know" (Evans, 1974, pp. 21-47).

Since Labour has been the governing party in Britain throughout most of the 1960s and the mid-1970s, its opinion on the question of the right of the press to information is significant. In a pamphlet, The

People and the Media (1974), it agreed with journalists that "freedom of publication . . . information and opinion in Britain is hedged about by an excessive number of regulations and restrictions." It committed the party to creating a more open society, and expressed a concern that the amount of censorship must be reduced, and the public's access to information improved. It strongly criticised the Official Secrets Act and the Franks Committee report, especially for retaining ambiguity and the wide range of discretion conferred on it by the executive—the fact that a document was secret if a minister said so. But the Labour party did not specifically acknowledge the public interest as a defence for newspapers charged under any new legislation. However, the press should have greater freedom of comment on the conduct of cases and in the interpretation of the law, providing this did not open the way to "trial by newspaper." And although it warned that the media should not take precedence over other institutions that were rooted in the elective principle, it admitted that the balance had tilted too far away from the interests of public information. At the end it returned to the government's side of the argument concerning social responsibility: the claim of the media to freedom of expression "is a strong one . . . provided that the media themselves are not merely the mouthpieces of a few people" (Labour Party, 1974, pp. 8-11).

Government Information Systems

It cannot be said that the Labour party has lived up to the intention it expressed in *The People and the Media* (1974). The habits of secrecy and discretion proved to be as instinctive to the Labour administration elected in 1974 as they had to any other administration elected before that. In 1974 Sir John Hunt, the Cabinet secretary, acting with the approval of Prime Minister Harold Wilson, sought to stop the *Sunday Times* from publishing extracts from the revealing diaries of the late Richard Crossman, a Cabinet minister in the first and second Wilson governments. In 1976 a vigorous inquiry was instituted into the leaking of Cabinet papers to the *New Society* weekly. And when the government decided to review the whole question of official secrets in November 1976, it was still determined to maintain that "information relative to security and intelligence matters is deserving of the highest protection whether or not it is classified," and even defined military information in a more comprehensive way than Franks had done. Moreover, a week after this statement the government accepted recommendations designed to secure greater confidentiality for Cabinet documents. An attempt had been made earlier, in 1975, to place an embargo on the publication of minister's memoirs like those of Richard Crossman; and government showed no inclination to act to clear up legal perplexities for journalists concerning defamation of character, obscene, libel, or contempt (Whale, 1977, pp. 127-145).

Nevertheless, governments in modern Britain are not only concerned with protecting their secrets from journalists; like it or not, they have to supply at least some information to journalists as part of the process of political communication. Indeed, in an increasingly complex, much governed society, the task of political communication becomes more urgent and at the same time more difficult. A good deal of the art of politics lies in persuasion, and government has two broad methods of persuasion at its disposal: it can use the news media as a means of disseminating information and argument; or it can rely on its own sources for explaining policy and, thus hopefully, gaining consent to policy.

Governments have always found it necessary to communicate with the governed; but this was a relatively easy task when the political public was small, intimate, and easily reached by speeches from the platform or in Parliament. But in an age of mass democracy and mass society, the politician, as Graham Wallas put it, looks out at his public as at a photographic plate on which he must imprint his picture slowly and forcefully; in other words, he must cultivate an "image" of himself, an image easily recognizable to his mass public (Smith, 1973, p. 113). This can be a pipe-smoking Stanley Baldwin or a bell-ringing Quintin Hogg; but, whatever the image, the politician knows he is at the mercy of the news media for its projection to the public. Yet herein lies the dilemma of the politician: in order to create a favourable picture of himself and his policies, he has to rely on news media which in the past—and today—treat him with scepticism, perhaps even derision. The press has always been a great unmaker of political reputations, from Lord Bute in the 18th century to Harold Wilson in the present day, and politicians have approached it with a mixture of dread and fascination. On the one hand they use confidentiality, especially in their dealings with the Lobby correspondents, journalists who have access to the M.P.'s Lobby and who are in daily contact with them. Through their Lobby organization these political journalists have collective conferences with ministers and with representatives of the Opposition, as well as with individual members. Lobby correspondents guarantee the secrecy of such proceedings and write about the information gleaned therein without revealing their sources. Thus ministers can use the Lobby correspondents as unofficial mediators between themselves and the public. Ministers can give background information about a proposed piece of legislation or explain how they intend to deal with a specific problem. But complementing this clandestine activity is the Parliamentary Press Gallery, consisting of journalists who report the proceedings of the House, and thus act as conveyors of information to the public. Which channel a minister will use depends largely on what he is trying to achieve. If a minister wishes to test the temperature of the water before committing himself to a particular course of action, the confidentiality of the Lobby provides an ideal medium; but if he wants to use the more formal methods of a parliamentary announcement, he can use the Press Gallery; or he can use a combination of both Lobby and Gallery (Seymour-Ure, 1968, chaps. 6, 7). For example, in handling publicity for a White paper on defence, the minister presented the paper to the House, but he also saw the Lobby correspondents and answered their questions, then recorded a statement for sound radio and for the BBC and independent Television, and made special recordings for the United States, Australian, Canadian, and Overseas service of the BBC (Ogilvy-Webb, 1965, pp. 26-29).

In their dealings with the press, politicians have always been able to comfort themselves with the fact that they can try to win a section of it over to their side—as Lloyd George did so effectively during the Great War—and by the consideration that, since much of politics is a public activity, then to some extent at least publicity—good or bad—is part of their stock in trade. Better, perhaps, unfavourable publicity than none at all. But in his dealings with the new mass media—radio and television—the politician is faced with a much more formidable task. Because the new media subscribe to the "social responsibility" theory of the media—and indeed because government has insisted that they so subscribe—politicians cannot "win" over these media to their side, since these media must be, by law, neutral. Moreover, politicians can try to win press support by distributing knighthoods and other largesse, as Lloyd George did—"What you can't squash you square" (Margach, 1978, p. 13)—but such tactics cannot be attempted with the BBC or IBA without instant cries of the free media in danger. Government, in short, has been hoist with its own petard; it cannot persuade the media to support its policies, because it has already forbidden the media to do so. Yet government cannot ignore the media, because of the wide audience they reach, and because of the way in which they pervade all classes, all walks of life.

Thus ministers have used, first radio and then television for over half a century, without ever knowing how well the media are putting over their particular skills. In the early days it was different; Lord Reith was quite happy to put the finishing touches to Stanley Baldwin's speech during the General Strike (Burns, 1977, p. 14). But as relations between the BBC, IBA and the government became more formalised, politicians *de jure* debarred themselves from any control over political broadcasting. Party political broadcasts are arranged formally, between the BBC, IBA and the parties; but the government does not have any privileged access to either of the media for presenting its politics, and they are usually seen and heard when their activities are of news value. However the choice of what constitutes news value does of course lie with the media, not the government; and when a minister allows himself to be interviewed on radio or television, he once again finds that he has little control over the instrument by which he is hoping to influence public opinion. And this applies not only to the questions which will be asked of him; it applies also to the question of timing, schedule, the broadcaster's claim to represent the public (as against the politician), the desire of the broadcaster that the politician should appear when it is to his disadvantage as well as when it is to his advantage (Goldie, 1977, pp. 328-330; Smith, 1973, pp. 114-119).

Small wonder, then, that government in its public relations capacity should try to professionalise its own information services. And since the First World War, government information services in Britain have grown from modest beginnings, in such things as the Post Office Annual Report, the Home Office Information Bureau, and the Ministry of Information, to the vast apparatus which modern government deploys in what the official historian has described as the "deliberate, planned, and sustained effort to establish and maintain mutual understanding" between itself and the public (Ogilvy-Webb, 1965, p. 21). Today every major government department has an Information Division; while the Central Office of Information provides common publicity services for the individual departments. The Central Office of Information provides common publicity services for the individual departments. The Central Office of Information has itself a whole range of "divisions," including advertising, exhibitions, films, photographs, publications, and reference divisions. Work for the Central Office of Information and for the government departments is undertaken by Her

Majesty's Stationery Office (Ogilvy-Webb, 1965, pp. 41-46). This new world of public communication has not left untouched even the civil service, which trains its personnel in public relations (Ogilvy-Webb, 1965, chap. 8). More recently, even army officers are given training in media technique. Information officers became career civil servants instead of temporaries who might go back to their original jobs if the minister or the policy changed (Ogilvy-Webb, 1965, pp. 185-187).

This formidable array of government information services helps solve a few at least of ministers' problems in communicating with the public. For while the information services themselves rely to a large extent on the media, with, for example, the Central Office of Information having its News Distribution Service ready to communicate with the press, radio and television, they consider certain kinds of publicity as too important to be left to the "ephemeral pages of the daily press" (Ogilvy-Webb, 1965, p. 199). Recruitment for the armed forces; recruitment for the social services; information about laws and regulations; what to do in an outbreak of foot and mouth disease; telling people their pension rights, or to cash their war bonds, or whatever—all these subjects require the government information services to supplement the press and communicate with the public directly. But the line between routine administration and routine publicity, and the political position of a particular minister is not always clear. An information office might be called upon to defend his minister in public on a matter of controversy; and when a minister opens a new school, or hospital, or when he issues brochures about the armed forces, or the police force, he may very well contribute to the creation of a favourable image of himself (Ogilvy-Webb, 1965, pp. 194-195). John Profumo's advertising campaign for the armed forces in the early 60s, emphasising the valuable training the army offered its recruits, not to mention service in enviable spots such as Hong Kong, helped not only army recruitment but also Profumo's increasingly favourable public image.

Nevertheless, the politician cannot escape from the fact that his best medium for publicity is the press, radio, or television. And it has been admitted that "most information officers would agree that if you can get it, space in the free media is much more effective than paid-for publicity" (Ogilvy-Webb, 1965, p. 113). A good deal of information work consists in inspiring useful comment in the free media. Thus the chief press officer at the Ministry of Labour might talk casually in the press room to a representative of one of the popular Sunday newspapers, and might suggest that there was suitable material for a "human interest" story about the growing number of accidents to young people in industry. The ministry would be glad to see this represented in a dramatic fashion, more especially as the paper's mass circulation would ensure that a substantial part of the working population would read the story. If the newspaper's editor liked the idea then such an article would appear. Suggestions such as this could best be made by journalists, who knew what was "news" and what was not; and it is not surprising that many government press officers were themselves former journalists (Ogilvy-Webb, 1965, p. 110).

Thus, through the Lobby, the Parliamentary Press Gallery, and the government information services, government and the media work in close connection with each other. In a sense, they are both in the same business, and just as journalists cannot exist without hard political news, so government cannot exist without journalism as a medium for disseminating political news to the public. This close harmony is only part of the picture. The difficulty confronting politicians when they try to employ their skills on the uncomfortable medium of television has given rise to frequent clashes between government and the news media. But journalists have their problems as well. If they see their job as that of investigative reporters in the modern, collectivist, bureaucratic state, acting "as a minefield through which authority, great and small and at every level of policy and administration, must step warily" (Williams, 1957, p. 289) then they are more likely to become aware of the constraints, rather than the advantages, which the British political system places on their activities.

In February 1965 the *Sunday Times* published a leading article, "Power and the Press," promising an assault on government secrecy, and it appointed a political correspondent, Anthony Howard, as its "Whitehall Correspondent"—a title chosen to show where the key decisions about policy were being taken, and where Howard would go to discover what they were. Within a year the venture came to an ignominious end, with the "Whitehall Correspondent" whisked off to Washington without comment. Civil servants might be trained in public relations; but they were also trained in using the cloak of anonymity. A circular went out from heads of departments indicating that the Whitehall correspondent was not to be spoken to; government ministers spoke darkly of a journalistic assault on the principle of ministerial responsibility, i.e. that a minister, not a civil servant, was answerable for what went on in his department. With civil service and government

ranks tightly closed, investigative journalism, at least in this form, was
doomed to failure (Seymour-Ure, 1968, pp. 176-185).

Media Impact on Government

It might be said, however, that government secrecy is itself a kind of
tribute to the vigilance of the news media, a recognition of the watchdog
function of the fourth estate. Certainly, the theory of the fourth estate
emphasized the oppositional role of the media, not only in investigation
of government activities, but in every area of the political arena. The
press, wrote *The Times* in 1854, lives by disclosure. It speaks when the
statesman is silent; it tells the truth when he dissembles. It is "a power,
a branch of government, with inalienable weight in lawmaking." The
press was a means of creating discontent among the people, and thus of
removing the defects of vicious government, wrote James Mill. It provided a quicker, more certain, means of securing redress of individual
grievances than did the courts of justice, wrote Henry Reeve, editor of
the *Edinburgh Review*, in 1855. W. T. Stead, one of the founders of the
"new journalism" of the 1880s, advanced these arguments and spoke of
"government by journalism" (Boyce et al., 1978, chap. 1). The refusal by
government to allow the modern news media, radio and television, to
become "newspapers of the air", with editorials and a recognizable
political bias, did not prevent them from asserting their role as educa-
tors and informers of public opinion, and, latterly, as "honest brokers"
between government and people. Indeed, both the old-fashioned fourth
estate theory of the media, and the new-fangled social responsibility
theory, shared an assumption that the news media did exercise a
profound influence on public opinion and on the practice of government.

But did this belief have any founding in reality, or were journalists,
like kings and queens, suffering from what Leonard Woolf described as
"vocational influence and self-deception" (Stubbs, 1978, p. 320)? Were
they and are they the victims of a delusion about power, playing out
their respective roles quite apart from the true centres of political power
in Britain? Certainly, modern research in many respects seems to con-
firm that media influence on government amounts to very little. Politicians adapted themselves to the media: in the 19th century giving press
interviews; in the 20th century learning to use radio for broadcasts to
the nation; accepting that, whatever the technical difficulties, they must
discover the mysteries of television appearances. And, meanwhile, the
public went on its way regardless, voting on grounds of class, religion,

habit, or whatever, with little attention paid to the media; switching off their TV sets when party political broadcasts were screened; reading their newspapers for entertainment or sport; and deriving their political views from their environment, their families, their work places and only marginally, if at all, from the media—whether it be a fourth estate or a socially responsible organ. Real political power in the 19th century lay with Parliament and then the political parties; real power in the 20th century lay with ministers, bureaucrats, and pressure groups, especially with the trade unions. Any attempts to construct a "controlled experiment," to discover a "cause and effect" relationship between a particular political event, or government decision, and the media, seemed either to yield contradictory results, or to demonstrate that the influence of the media could not be separated from other influences present in the process under examination, or to show that the influence of the media was a negligible factor (Smith, 1973, pp. 119-127).

Nevertheless, politicians have continued to rate the media as profoundly important; hence, indeed, their various attempts to control or influence it, from Lloyd George's purchase of the *Daily Chronicle* in 1918 (Boyce, et al., 1978, pp. 32-33) to Harold Wilson's decision to make Lord Hill of Luton Chairman of the BBC Board of Governors (Smith, 1973, p. 145). Are politicians also, then, suffering from that "vocational influence and self-deception" which bedevils the journalist? Perhaps; but one of the main tasks of the historian and political scientist is to understand and recreate as far as possible the world of which he is an observer, and to see events through the eyes of those who experienced them. Therefore, it can be said quite simply that if politicians rate the media as of political importance, then, in a real sense, it is of such importance. Politicians in the early 20th century feared that Lord Northcliffe spoke for the millions, and they treated him with circumspection, especially when it was believed that he had played a major part in the making of the coalition government in May 1915 and in the accession to power of Lloyd George in December 1916 (Inwood, 1971). Politicians believe that television coverage of the Northern Ireland crisis since 1968 provides a construction of events which shapes, not only British public opinion, but even the nature and unfolding of the crisis itself (Chibnall, 1977, pp. 39-40; Whale, 1977, pp. 60-61, 127-128).

Moreover, government itself constructs its picture of political events partly at least from the news media. Lloyd George, for example, was an avid reader of newspapers, who "committed the error" of reading too many of them (Boyce, 1972, p. 181). The media are carefully combed for issues, potential issues, material which might present a minister with problems, material which might provide him with welcome—or unwelcome—publicity, or perhaps appear in the form of parliamentary questions. The politician, anxiously scanning his mass public for some indications of what they want, or how they might possibly react to some shift in policy, finds that he relies to a large extent on the press. Thus in 1961 it seems that the moment when the Conservative government decided to "stop havering and start negotiating about the Common Market" came when the *Daily Mirror* burst out in support of Europe. With the *Mirror* behind them, the Cabinet thought, public opinion should be malleable enough to enable a line of policy to be followed (Windlesham, 1966, pp. 157-158). Alarm can be created in the ranks of a party when a normally sympathetic newspaper turns against the party leader, as the *Daily Telegraph* and *The Times* did in 1956 when they announced their dissatisfaction with Sir Anthony Eden (Grainger, 1969, pp. 24-25).

Government, therefore, rates the news media as important in constructing a picture of the world of politics that it inhabits; and it is not surprising that government has altered its style to cope with the political impact of the media. The technological complexity, in particular, of radio and television has caused a change in the way in which government communicates with its public. To influence mass opinion is reckoned an expert job; hence political parties have increasingly used men who know something about the art of persuasion. Since 1946 the Labour and Conservative parties have built up specialist publicity departments with full-time staff. They have consulted journalists, economists, public relations men. By 1957 the Conservatives had built up a very efficient publicity organization under the overall supervision of Dr. Charles Hill (former secretary to the British Medical Association), and he was followed in 1962 by William Deedes, M.P., onetime journalist and Lobby correspondent. Both these men had a seat in the Cabinet. In 1962 the Labour party at last overcame its suspicion of such "business" methods and organized its publicity. Its appointed a director of publicity, a deputy director and a broadcasting officer; in 1965 it transferred responsibility for publicity to a coordinating committee under the Chairmanship of Richard Crossman, M.P., a wartime publicity expert. Crossman too was a member of the Cabinet and of Labour's National Executive Council (Windlesham, 1966, pp. 35-80, 242-248).

But was all this a waste of time? Were politicians misguided in taking

the media so seriously? After all, the news media are not simply—
perhaps not even mainly—*news* media. They are entertainment media,
and modern research demonstrates that entertainment is primarily
what the reader and the viewer and the listener want from them. The
editorial—that great Victorian institution, whereby the newspaper
bared its soul to a (hopefully) eagerly waiting nation, was discovered to
fall mainly on deaf ears (Mass Observation, 1949, pp. 48-50). Television
producers were more concerned with high audience ratings than with
fulfilling their classical fourth estate role of educating public opinion
(Burns, 1977, pp. 132-144). Nevertheless, there is that power which
James Mill, in his exposition of the virtues of the fourth estate, emphasized: the power of publicity, based itself on the fact that people—and
especially politicians—are anxious about their public reputations and
can be chided into certain courses of action by exposure in the press
(Mill, 1967, pp. 9-13, 19-21, 25-27).

Bonar Law disgusted the Secretary of the Cabinet, Lord Hankey,
when in 1917 he said that "anyone who was publicly attacked and
unpopular, whether a Minister or a public servant, ought in the public
interest to retire in war time." Whereupon A. J. Balfour "flippantly
commented 'Oh! Vive Lord Northcliffe' " (Roskill, 1970, p. 407). Mill
was concerned to allow a newspaper to print almost anything about
public men, but the modern laws of libel, the Official Secrets Act and so
on, all militate against such merciless exposure. Despite these draw-
backs, it remains true that publicity exercises control over public men,
can shape political crises, can influence the course of political events.
Thus, as Colin Seymour-Ure (1968, pp. 266-276) has shown, it was
press reporting that brought to a head the simmering pot of the liaison
between a Cabinet Minister, Mr. John Profumo, and Miss Christine
Keeler, whose friends included a Russian Naval Attache.

MEDIA AGENDA SETTING

Publicity not only affects public reputations, and, in the modern
jargon, public "images"; it also affects the course of political events, and
often in ways which governments find disagreeable. In May 1915, for
example, the publication in *The Times* of a dispatch from its military
correspondent, Colonel Repington, revealing a shortage of munitions on
the Western Front, aroused public opinion, and, together with an internal Cabinet crisis over the resignation of the First Sea Lord, Admiral Sir
John Fisher, precipitated the crisis which resulted in the formation of a
Liberal and Conservative coalition (Inwood, 1971). In 1962 a report in

the *Daily Mail,* predicting important Cabinet changes in Harold Mac-
Millan's government, helped force MacMillan's hand and turned a
gradual process of Cabinet replacement into an apparently ruthless
piece of political butchery. Seven out of 21 Cabinet ministers lost their
jobs; others remained in the Cabinet but got different jobs; seven new
men were promoted to the Cabinet; and three days later nine other
members of the government, not in the Cabinet, resigned—a total of
some 36 appointments, and all in the space of a few days. "The widespread speculation in the press," confessed MacMillan, "and the unde-
sirability of a period of uncertainty made it necessary to complete a
reconstruction of the government as rapidly as possible." "Mac admits 'I
was pushed'," gloated the *Daily Mail,* whose political correspondent
had broken the story (Seymour-Ure, 1968, pp. 289-300).

As in the case of the 1915 "shells scandal," other factors were present
in the events, internal factors which may indeed have been as important, perhaps more so; but that the press at least acted as a catalyst in
the unfolding of the events cannot be doubted. Media reporting and
speculation in times of economic crisis, in 1931 (Mowat, 1966, pp.
386-387; 1970, p. 155) and in the 1967 devaluation of the pound sterling,
intensified the crisis and made it all the more difficult for government to
handle it (Seymour-Ure, 1974, pp. 33-34). The intensity and timing of
media coverage of a speech by Enoch Powell on immigration in April
1968 to a small audience of Birmingham Conservatives helped create a
crisis of party unity for the Conservatives and obliged the Tory leader,
Edward Heath, to deprive Powell of his post in the shadow Cabinet.
Moreover, from that moment, Powell's speeches were rated by the
media as "newsworthy" items, and a whole debate on immigration—
which until then had been a very muffled one, insofar as it existed at
all—was opened up with an emotional intensity that has survived to
the present day (Seymour-Ure, 1974, chap. 4).

By a process of highlighting certain features of the political scene, the
media can help convert a potential crisis into a live issue. "The Cabinet,"
confessed a former Conservative minister, "increasingly tends to be
most concerned with the agenda that the press and media are setting
out as the crucial issues before the nation at any one time" (Seymour-
Ure, 1974, p. 36). The converse is also true: that the media can keep
items off the agenda. "The power of the press is to suppress," Northcliffe remarked in a characteristic aphorism (Gardiner, 1932, p. 252).
And certainly examples of this "converse power" can be cited. In 1936
the entire British press was aware of most of the facts leading up to the

abdication crisis surrounding King Edward VIII long before a line appeared in the papers. But they kept silence, partly out of a traditional deference to the monarchy, partly because they feared repercussions if an official denial of the rumours brought the wrath of their readers down on their heads. So the vast majority of the British people remained ignorant of these matters until near the end of the affair (Political and Economic Planning, 1938, p. 260).

THE ROLE OF THE MEDIA IN ELECTIONS

Nowhere is this more important to government than at the time when it offers itself to the public for a verdict on its conduct of the nation's affairs—in general elections. The role of the media in general elections is perhaps the most written about, and yet least understood, phenomenon in the political process in Britain. The problem is that, on the one hand, politicians emphasize, indeed exaggerate, the part played by the media in elections, usually in the form of condemnation of the media—and especially the BBC—for showing bias in its treatment of the issues. Antagonism between the Labour leader, Harold Wilson, and the media, had flared up briefly after the 1966 campaign, when Labour complained that the BBC's questioning, probing style clashed with Labour's desire for a "low key" election. In 1970, Labour claimed that the BBC's concentration on Wilson's "walkabouts" (which were dull) showed anti-Labour bias. The Conservatives also managed to object to the 1966 coverage by claiming that the BBC was so biased towards Labour that it showed Mr. Wilson even when he was only puffing his pipe (Butler & King, 1966, p. 146-147; Butler and Pinto-Duschinsky, 1971, p. 207).

While politicians charge the media with a major responsibility for the outcome of an election, academic studies seem to prove that the media plays little or no part in deciding how a voter actually votes. Usually about 80 percent of voters have made up their minds about voting before the election takes place, and some 70-80 percent will vote for the same party as they did last time. Election broadcasts by politicians seem to make little difference. The media reinforces people in their political attitudes; it does not convert them (Blumler and McQuail, 1968; McQuail and Trenaman, 1961), Labour complaints about Fleet Street consisting mainly of conservative newspapers have not prevented them from winning three out of four general elections since 1960.

Here again, however, the desire to find a causal relationship between media and government, or, in this case, the political fate of governments, obscures rather than elucidates the role of the media in British

politics. It is almost a truism, but one that is too often forgotten, that
even if the media influence only a few voters, these few voters could
make the difference about which party is elected to govern the country,
especially in times of political fragmentation and realignment in Britain, when the smaller parties emerge as challengers to the larger, or
when a great political party is in the process of breaking up, as the
Liberals did between 1918 and 1939. But even apart from this most
obvious and direct influence, the media helps shape the character of
general elections in Britain. Politicians and the media vie with each
other about whose election it is, and what kind of election it should be.

Once again the ideology of the media plays a role in the way it treats
political issues. The socially responsible journalist, acting as the eyes
and ears of the modern democracy, takes the campaign to the parties,
especially to the party in power. A whole series of election programmes
evolved since 1945, programmes such as Election Marathon, Election
Forum, Campaign Report, and the theme of these programmes was that
the public had a right to ask, or have asked on its behalf, certain
questions of the politicians, and that it was the duty of the journalist to
ensure that the public received good answers (Goldie, 1977, pp. 263-
281). Moreover, since the media thrives on news, it was natural for it to
try to make elections into news-worthy events; "quiet" elections were
anathema to the journalist. Since at least Northcliffe's day—and possibly before—"people" were more news-worthy than "things," and once
again the media's natural desire to personalize a campaign, to cast it as
the clash of two or more great political figures, has obliged politicians,
whether they like it or not, and whether they are good at it or not, to face
the nation and perform.

The growth of the mass media, moreover, and its centralization in
London, helped break down the long established process in Britain in
which elections were essentially regional affairs, concerned mainly
with regional issues and fought in local centres of power. It is probably
true to say that as late as the 1880s British politics and British elections
were not "general"; yet by the interwar years they were, and not even
the rise of Nationalist parties in Wales and Scotland and the special
political problems of Northern Ireland can exclude from the agenda the
key modern issues of jobs, prices, income policies, and housing. And
politicians, when they comment on these issues—and comment they
must—find that the timing and venue of their utterances is largely
decided by the need to feed the media with information that it wants to

use at a time and place when it can most easily collect and distribute this information to the nation (Seymour-Ure, 1974, chap. 8).

Some aspects of media coverage of the political process, and especially of general elections, has given rise to disquiet about the whole impact of the media on government in modern Britain. Media concentration on personalities, on the "bloody good row" between personalities, on news-worthy items such as strikes (always a bone of contention between the Labour party and the media), even the fact that the media tries to forecast the result of an election, and therefore might influence its outcome, since voters might not bother to turn out to back an apparent loser—all these and other considerations have given rise to the charge that the media trivialises general elections in particular, and British politics in general (Seymour-Ure, 1974, pp. 224-227).

This accusation has been leveled against broadcasting—particularly television—rather than the newspaper press, of which the "quality" variety, at least, gives full, serious, and sustained treatment of political affairs. Broadcasting has become indispensable to the process of political communication, yet broadcasting is primarily an entertainment medium. On 21 October 1968 Richard Crossman accused television of trivialising politics.

> The coverage of politics outside the news bulletins consists chiefly of interviews, arguments and confrontations between the spokesmen of the two parties which play up the gladitorial aspects of politics and gives the impression that it consists of mere conflicts of personalities rather than a conflict of ideas carried by personalities. . . . The fault I suspect lies in the first place with the producer who feels that he must popularise what he regards as a dull, musty subject.

Crossman gave a few examples of this downgrading of serious issues: a housing white paper could be made more palatable by staging a "shouting match between the minister and the studio hecklers"; or the commentator feels that a discussion about Rhodesia would be the ruin of his reputation "unless he can set off a personal row in the round table argument he is managing." Interviews were short and were sandwiched between a "couple of 'really entertaining' items" (Smith, 1974, pp. 194-196).

There was much justification for this complaint. Yet politicians have largely themselves to blame, in that they do generally accept the "show business" nature of television. They rarely insist on reasonable time for interviews, and they frame their contributions in stark items, using catch phrases like the "pound in your pocket" slogan which Harold

Wilson employed on the spur of the moment in 1967 because he wanted a good, short phrase which would get through to the mass audience. The Treasury draft of Wilson's broadcast read "Devaluation does not mean that the value of the pound in the hands of the British consumer, the British housewife at her shopping, is cut correspondingly." Moreover, Wilson sounded optimistic—at the advice of the very Richard Crossman who a year later complained about trivialisation of politics—and this style of broadcast rebounded to his great discredit as the value of the pound was soon seen to be much diminished (Wilson, 1971, pp. 463-464).

Politicians, discussing the possibility of televising Parliament itself, and so throwing open the last bastion of "old style" political debate direct to the mass public, via the television producer, seem torn between a desire to reach a wider audience, and thus make Parliament more central to the nation's concept of politics, and a fear that in so doing Parliament would radically change its nature for the worse. Parliament might become yet another television programme, with the cameras focusing on the most dramatic, not the most important, events, tempting members to play up to the cameras, even altering the rules of the House, since certain procedural points which M.P.s could exploit might no longer be exploited because they would not make sense to the public (Seymour-Ure, 1974, chap. 5; Wilson, 1970, chaps. 4-6). Fearful of the "universal eye," the most that Parliament would allow was a series of sound broadcasts of parliamentary proceedings.

Nevertheless, the fact had to be faced: by the 1970s political parties in Britain found that the idea of a nonpartisan press and a "balanced" broadcasting system had deprived them of the main means of communicating their policies to a mass electorate. In putting their policies before the public, politicians had now to accept that fact that they must make the best terms they could with a media that perceived its role as one of acting as "honest broker" between government, parties, and the public, and which imposed its own pattern on the style of political communication itself.

The Nature of the News Media

This role was mainly a reflection of the changing nature of the news media itself, especially the development of professionalism among journalists and broadcasters, a professionalism which marked them off from the kind of people whose business was governing the country. The early 19th century was a period of government corruption of the press, and government economic controls; but once these practices ceased, around 1850, the journalist found that he could assert his professional role as one of operating in the public interest "to investigate truth and to apply it on fixed principle to the affairs of the world." Moreover, technological developments in the 19th century made the seeking out of truth, especially of truth in the form of facts, objective facts, seem within the grasp of the journalist. Shorthand made possible reporting of facts more quickly; the electric telegraph made fact-gathering more widespread and general; and C. P. Scott could claim that comment was free, but fact was sacred, and that news-gathering was the "primary office" of journalism. Indeed, it was almost a sacred charge, for "at the peril of its soul" journalism must see that "the supply (of news) is not tainted" (Elliott, 1978, chap. 9).

The sort of newspaper for which Scott spoke was politically minded, noncommercial, and almost an extension of the political system itself. Such journalists understood politicians and were understood by politicians. Some journalists, like Scott, began their careers as would-be politicians; some politicians, like T. P. O'Connor, began their careers as journalists. But with the development of the populra, mass-readership newspaper, which might indeed seek political influence, but which was a vast, complex organisation, with highly specialised staff covering various aspects of news, a new form of professionalism emerged. Journalism was regarded as a skill, requiring certain talents, such as speed, accuracy, and the ability to meet deadlines (Elliott, 1978, p. 185).

In the much-governed Britain that was a characteristic of the period after 1945, journalists found it necessary to extend and develop this professional role, as men who stood between a government and society, interpreting complex legislation to a waiting public, explaining what government was doing, but not trying to convince people that it was doing things well (Smith, 1974, pp. 21, 245-249). Political commitment, like the Liberalism of C. P. Scott, or the High Toryism of H. A. Gwynne, was not necessary especially in the age of the commercially minded newspaper, since the main goals of such a newspaper were those of collecting and marketing news which was a commodity just like any other (Tunstall, 1971, p. 53). Political commitments, anyway, for all journalists, might be considered invidious, since the job of the journalist in a modern complex society was to act as a disinterested professional, supplying the public with untainted news, and holding the middle ground between government and the people (Elliott, 1978, pp.

180-181; Chibnall, 1977, chap. 2; Smith, 1974, pp. 249-251, 253-254).

This concept of the nonpartisan, professional journalist was reinforced by the development of broadcasting. After all, broadcasting had from the beginning been charged with the duty of showing impartiality; and added to this was Lord Reith's idea of broadcasting as a public service, with broadcasters members of an independent estate of the realm. But Reith was determined to avoid political controversy by allowing political discussion and analysis to occupy a very small part of the BBC time; this, in fact, was a way of ensuring that the BBC's independence remained unsullied by government interference.

Reith was primarily concerned with culture—plays, music, discussions, talks—and it was here that the BBC exercised its greatest influence over national life in Britain between 1926 and the 1950s. Sir William Haley, Director General, retorted crushingly in 1946 to a suggestion that suitable illustrations could accompany the regular news bulletins. "There is all the difference between a news bulletin and a news reel. The first is a vital public service charged with responsibilities of all kinds. The second, in essence, is entertainment" (Goldie, 1977, pp. 40-41).

In the 1960s, however, the BBC found that it was increasingly drawn into, or at least attracted by, political broadcasting. In 1957 the BBC launched "Tonight," a magazine programme that dealt with current affairs. Its popularity soon assured it of many imitators; and the BBC News programme itself became popular viewing, especially when news announcement was accompanied by moving pictures of a dramatic and controversial kind. These developments were assisted by technological advances, as important in their own way as the printing advances of the 19th century, which made it possible for a compact camera team to film, develop, edit, and produce with commentary a finished product within a single day—later, within a few hours (Smith, 1973, pp. 78-79, 82; Goldie, 1977, pp. 212-219).

In this brave new world of political television, what kind of journalist was best suited to interpret politics to the public? Once again, the ideal journalist was a professional, a man trained in interviewing or broadcasting skills, a familiar figure with whom the audience could identify, in whom, indeed, they trusted. Such professional broadcasters, politically neutral men who sought simply to transmit, or to wring from politicians the "truth," were nonpartisan, standing neither for left nor right, for labour nor capital. Thus they acted for the public, questioning government, questioning trade unions, questioning anyone whose job or function seemed to impinge on the public interest. In the best social responsibility tradition, the broadcaster served his public, providing not only the fact, but also "the truth about the fact," by giving the perspective essential to an understanding of a given situation. He was no longer an advocate of causes, but a professional communicator, a custodian of the public interest (Kumar, 1978, chap. 9; Smith, 1973, pp. 135-136).

Thus, whether the journalist was a straight reporter, gathering news for his editor to market to the reader, or a communicator, who saw his job as one of providing background and analysis about the news, he was marked off from the politician, who was himself more of a "professional," spending more time in the House of Commons, trying to master complex economic skills to enable him to make policy for a modern industrial society. No longer could a broadcaster say, as did Reith in the general strike of 1926, "assuming that the BBC is for the people and the government is for the people, it follows that the BBC must be for the government in this crisis too" (Burns, 1977, pp. 16-17). The government was now considered almost as one sectional interest among many.

Conclusion

It might be argued, however, that although in one sense the relations between government and the news media in Britain have developed to the disadvantage of the former in the last half-century, in other important respects they have contributed to the job of making Britain easier to govern. Firstly, they have come more and more to represent consensual values in Britain, blocking out conflict, minimixing differences, emphasising collective values, affirming the rules under which the political system operates (Curran, 1978, chap. 2; Hoch, 1974; Murphy, 1976). By playing a role in general elections, for example, it could be said that the media reinforce the concept of elections as legitimate means of political behaviour. This stress on the consensual, "natural" order of things in Britain, it is alleged, springs directly from the commercial position of the newspaper press, which must meet the needs of a mass audience in order to stay in business. The professionalism of the broadcaster, which might seem to throw down the guantlet to government, could be interpreted in another way. Since the corollary of this is a self-imposed neutrality on the part of the broadcaster, since it makes him withdraw from political involvement, it deprives him of any truly radical stance, it prevents him from questioning the whole set of rules on which the game of politics is based. Moreover, the audience comes to believe that a neutral position is possible and desirable in politics; and, once again, penetrating criticisms of British society and politics are rendered difficult, if not impossible, to achieve. Thus, the press and broadcasting, for their very different reasons, find that they are simultaneously the scrutineers of government and the tools of government. They help to contain and isolate potential sources of dissidence in modern British politics; and an interviewer giving a minister a trying time on television seems trivial by comparison.

The second point concerns access to the media in Britain. Here the argument is advanced that the number of people who control the media is relatively small, and this small group of people issue all the tickets in circumstances in which admission is by ticket only (Smith, 1973, p. 138). Since the newspaper press has been concentrated in fewer and fewer hands in the 20th century, it follows that fewer and fewer (and, of course, richer and richer) individuals decide how the press shall be run and for what object (Labour Party, 1974, pp. 20-23). Broadcasting suffers from a similar inbuilt bias, despite its freedom from the pressure of the newspaper world, for it too is controlled by a handful of "privileged groups" whose sympathy for certain organizations, such as trade unions, is, to say the least, limited (Glasgow University Media Group, 1976, chap. 6; Smith 1974, pp. 197-201). Broadcasting might aim, as Richard Attenborough, a one-time Director of BBC television programmes, asserted, at playing the role of

a theatre in the middle of a town, and the broadcasters . . . are part of the theatre staff. And it's the job of that staff to find from society, from the town in which they are placed, a whole selection of voices—the most prophetic, the most significant, the most amusing, the most dramatic, the most typical—and to enable those voices to be heard in that theatre (Kumar, 1978, p. 246).

But the expression of these "voices" would still be controlled by trained and trusted individuals.

These criticisms were put forward mainly, though not exclusively, by the Left in Britain; but they represented an important strand of thinking the social responsibility theory of the press. The press was controlled by one socio-economic class, and access to it was difficult for anyone outside that class. Therefore, the free and open market of ideas was endangered. Nevertheless, three Royal Commissions on the Press since 1945 and a spate of reports by committees on broadcasting have made remarkably little impression on the structure of the newsmedia in

Britain, or on its relations with the government. That they have failed to answer the requirements of the critics is because they run counter to the classic theory of the news media, which holds that government control must be absent or at any rate reduced.

The credibility of the press and broadcasting as instruments of political communication depends on their very freedom from any kind of heavy-handed or obvious government control. The failure of party political newspapers in Britain since the early 19th century, and Stanley Baldwin's realisation that a government controlled BBC in 1926 would be a useless instrument in his hands, are only two indications of the way in which government needs a free news media, however much critics might query precisely what is meant by "free."

Moreover, some of the criticisms of the news media on the grounds that they are involved in suppressing dissent and emphasising the homogenity of British politics leave major questions unanswered. It may well be that the idea that there is in Britain some significant source of political dissent left uncatered for by the media is as mythical as Lord Northcliffe's claim that his "tons of words" made "millions think." It may well be true that the public gets the press it wants, and if, for example, a local newspaper stresses community feeling and fails to report conflict in its town, it is because most of its readers do not want their town to be given an unfavourable and economically damaging public image (Cox and Morgan, 1973; Jackson, 1971). To make the BBC an "oppositional" force in society, it has been pointed out, would be to "push the organization in a suicidal direction, outside the confines historically and pragmatically laid down for it" (Kumar, 1978, p. 248).

In any case, television in Britain is increasingly admitting new groups of people, like trade unionists, whose isolation from the medium was largely of their own choice (Smith, 1973, pp. 138-139). Nevertheless observers of the contemporary British scene, while still accepting the classic theory of the news media as a watchdog of the public interest, are, like Sherlock Holmes, concerned to discover not only why the watchdog barks, but—more important—why it does not.

References

Blumler, J. & McQuail, D. *Television in Politics: Its Uses and Influence.* London: Faber, 1968.

Boyce, D. G. *Englishmen and Irish Troubles: British Public Opinion and the Making of Irish Policy, 1818-1822.* London: Cape, 1972.

Boyce, D. G., Curran, J., & Wingate, P. *Newspaper History: From the 17th Century to the Present Day.* London: Constable, 1978.

Briggs, A. *The History of Broadcasting in the United Kingdom.* Vol. 1. *The Birth of Broadcasting.* London: Oxford University Press, 1961. Vol. 2. *The Golden Age of Wireless.* London: Oxford University Press, 1965. Vol. 3. *The War of Words.* London: Oxford University Press, 1970.

Burns, T. *The BBC: Public Institution and Private World.* London: MacMillan, 1977.

Butler, D. & King, A. *The British General Election of 1966.* London: MacMillan, 1966.

Butler, D. & Pinto-Duschinsky, M. *The British General Election of 1970.* London: MacMillan, 1971.

Chibnall, S. *Law and Order News: An Analysis of Crime Reporting in the British Press.* London: Tavistock, 1977.

Cox, H. & Morgan, D. *City Politics and the Press: Journalists and the Governing of Merseyside.* Cambridge: Cambridge University Press, 1973.

Curran, J., Gurevitch, M., & Woollacott, J. (Eds.), *Mass Communications and Society.* London: Edward Arnold/Open University Press, 1977.

Curran, J. "The Press as an Agency of Social Control: An Historical Perspective." In D. G. Boyce, J. Curran, & P. Wingate (Eds.), *Newspaper History.* London: Constable, 1978.

Elliott, P. "Professional Ideology and Organisational Change: The Journalist Since 1800." In D. G. Boyce, J. Curran, & P. Wingate (Eds.), *Newspaper History.* London: Constable, 1978.

Evans, H. "The Half-Free Press." *Granada Guildhall Lectures.* London: Hart-David/MacGibbon, 1974.

Gardiner, A. G. "Two Journalists: C. P. Scott and Lord Northcliffe—A Contrast." *Nineteenth Century and After,* 1932, 111, 247-256.

Gerbner, G. (Ed.), *Mass Media Policies in Changing Cultures.* New York: J. Wiley & Sons, 1977.

Glasgow University Media Group. *Bad News.* London: Routledge & Kegan Paul, 1976.

Goldie, G. W. *Facing the Nation: Television and Politics, 1936-1976.* London: Bodley Head, 1977.

Grainger, J. H. *Character and Style in English Politics.* Cambridge: Cambridge University Press, 1969.

Hirsch, F. & Gordon, D. *Newspaper Money: Fleet Street and the Search for the Affluent Reader.* London: Hutchinson, 1975.

Hoch, P. *The Newspaper Game: The Political Sociology of the Press.* London: Calder & Goyars, 1974.

Inwood, S. *The Press in the First World War, 1914-1916.* Unpublished doctoral dissertation, University of Oxford, 1971.

Jackson, I. *The Provincial Press and the Community*. Manchester: Manchester University Press, 1971.

Kumar, K. "Holding the Middle Ground: The BBC, the Public and the Professional Broadcaster." In D. G. Boyce, J. Curran, & P. Wingate (Eds.), *Newspaper History*. London: Constable, 1978.

Labour Party. *The People and the Media*. London: Labour Party, 1974.

Levy, H. P. *The Press Council: History, Procedure and Cases*. London: MacMillan, 1967.

McQuail, D. & Trenaman, J. *Television and the Political Image: A Study of the Impact of Television on the 1959 Election*. London: Methuen, 1961.

Margach, J. *The Abuse of Power: The War Between Downing Street and the Media, from Lloyd George to Callaghan*. London: W. H. Allen, 1978.

Mass Observation. *The Press and Its Readers*. London: Art & Technics, 1949.

Mill, J. *Essays on Government, Jurisprudence, Liberty of the Press and Law of Nations*. New York: Kelly, 1967 (Originally published, 1816-1823).

Mowat, C. L. *Britain Between the Wars, 1918-1940*. London: Methuen, 1966.

Mowat, C. L. *Great Britain Since 1914: The Sources of History*. London: Hodder & Stoughton, 1970.

Murphy, D. *The Silent Watchdog: The Press in Local Politics*. London: Constable, 1976.

Murray, G. *The Press and the Public: The Story of the British Press Council*. Carbondale & Edwardsville: Southern Illinois University Press, 1972.

Ogilvy-Webb, M. *The Government Explains: A Study of the Information Services*. London: Royal Institute of Public Administration, 1965.

Peterson, T. "The Social Responsibility Theory of the Press." In F. S. Siebert, T. Peterson, & W. Schramm (Eds.), *Four Theories of the Press*. New York: Books for Libraries Press, 1973 (Originally published, 1956).

"Political and Economic Planning," *Report on the British Press*. London: Author, 1938.

Roskill, S. *Hankey: Man of Secrets*. London: Collins, 1970.

Royal Commission on the Press. *Report* (Cmd. 7700). London: Her Majesty's Stationery Office, 1949.

Seymour-Ure, C. *The Press, Politics and the Public*. London: Methuen, 1968.

Seymour-Ure, C. *The Political Impact of Mass Media*. London: Constable, 1974.

Smith, A. *The Shadow in the Cave: A Study of the Relationship Between the Broadcaster, the Audience and the State*. London: Allen & Unwin, 1973.

Smith, A. (Ed.), *British Broadcasting*. Newton Abbott: David & Charles, 1974 (a).

Smith, A. (Ed.), *The British Press Since the War*. Newton Abbott: David & Charles, 1974 (b).

Stubbs, J. "Appearances and Reality: A Case Study of The Observer and J. L. Garvin, 1914-1942." In D. G. Boyce, J. Curran, & P. Wingate (Eds.), *Newspaper History*. London: Constable, 1978.

Tracey, M. "Yesterday's Men: A Case Study in Political Communication." In J. Curran, M. Gurevitch, & J. Woollacott (Eds.), *Mass Communications and Society*. London: Edward Arnold/Open University Press, 1977.

Tunstall, J. *Journalists at Work*. London: Constable, 1971.

Whale, J. *The Politics of the Media*. London: Fontana/Collins, 1977.

Williams, F. *Dangerous Estate: The Anatomy of Newspapers.* London: Longman, 1957.
Wilson, C. (Ed.), *Parliaments, Peoples and Mass Media.* London: Cassell, 1970.
Wilson, H. *The Labour Government: A Personal Record.* London: Weidenfeld & Nicolson, 1971.
Windlesham, L. *Communication and Political Power.* London: Cape, 1966.

VI.
Government, Media, and Politics: Australia

John S. Western and Allan Brown

The relationship between government and the news media in Australia needs to be seen within the context of the political environment of
the country throughout the postwar period. For all but three of the years
between 1949 and 1979, Australia has had a conservative federal
government in the form of a coalition between the Liberal party and the
National Country party (formerly Country party). The Labor party was
elected in 1972 on a moderate-reformist platform, but following the
political crisis of 1975 which culminated in the dismissal of the
government by the Governor-General, the coalition was returned to
office at the election in that year, and again in 1977.

Nevertheless, the reforms and attempted reforms of the Labor years
have had a continuing effect on many areas of government administration, not the least of these being that relating to the media. In particular,
the period since 1975 has seen an unprecedented level of federal
government inquiry and legislation relating to radio and television
broadcasting in Australia. This activity had become necessary because
of the highly unsatisfactory nature of broadcast regulation, and the
need to respond to the initiatives taken by the Labor government in this
area. However, the press, lying outside the constitutional powers of the
Federal Parliament, has been practically unaffected by recent government decisions concerning the media.

This essay examines past and current developments in the structure,
regulation, and operation of newspapers, radio, and television in Australia. The first section provides an outline of the ownership and control
of the media, and gives an account of recent studies concerning journalists, editors, and news content. Then follows an analysis of government
regulation of both the printed and the broadcasting media. The third
and final section describes the process of gathering and disseminating
news on the activities of government departments, Parliament, and the
political parties.

The Nature of the Media

In describing the structure of the Australian media it is necessary to make a distinction between "metropolitan" and "regional" newspaper and broadcasting outlets. For the purposes of this essay, the "metropolitan" cities are defined as the six Australian state capitals—Sydney, Melbourne, Brisbane, Adelaide, Perth, and Hobart. The first five of these constitute, in order, the largest population centres in Australia, but Canberra (the federal capital), Newcastle, and Wollongong are each of a greater size than Hobart. The definition of Canberra, Newcastle, and Wollongong as "regional" is to provide consistency with the definition given in the Commonwealth of Australia Broadcasting and Television Act for radio and television stations. All nonmetropolitan cities and towns are termed "regional."

NEWSPAPERS

The publication of newspapers has traditionally been a highly localised enterprise, and in Australia this tendency is exacerbated by the vast distances between centres of population. Consequently, as can be seen in Table 1, all but about 3 percent of the total circulation of Australian newspapers is accounted for by those papers whose circulation is largely confined to individual towns and cities. The highly urbanised nature of Australian society is reflected by the fact that 81 percent of papers are published in the six state capital cities; while the combined nonmetropolitan centres of population are responsible for only around 16 percent of total newspaper circulation.

Sydney has the highest number of daily newspapers with two competing titles in each of its weekday morning and evening markets; Melbourne supports two morning dailies and one evening daily; one paper is available each weekday morning and evening in Brisbane, Adelaide, and Perth; while Hobart publishes a morning daily only. Of these, only the *Sydney Morning Herald* (which accounts for about 45 percent of the combined circulation of the Sydney morning dailies) and the *Age* (which has around 27 percent of the Melbourne morning market) are considered to be "quality" papers. There is a total of 13 Sunday papers published in the state capitals: three in each of Sydney, Melbourne, and Perth; two in Brisbane; and one in both Adelaide and Hobart. (In addition to those papers whose aggregate circulations are set out in Table 1, there are over 100 suburban newspapers published in

TABLE 1

Structure of Newspaper Publication in Australia

Types of Newspapers	Numbers	Average Weekly Circulation (millions)		Percentage of Circulation	
Metropolitan dailies	14	23.6		70.0	
Metropolitan Sundays	13	3.7		11.0	
Total metropolitan		27	27.3		81.0
Regional dailies	39	3.4		10.1	
Regional nondailies	312	1.9		5.6	
Total regional		351	5.3		15.7
National dailies	2	1.0		3.0	
National weeklies	2	0.1		0.3	
Total national		4	1.1		3.3
Grand total		382	33.7		100.0

Based on the average weekly circulation for the half-year ended 30 September 1976

Australia, which are distributed, most of them free of charge, throughout the residential areas of each of the six metropolitan cities.)

In the regional areas, Newcastle is the only city with both a morning and an evening daily newspaper. Thirty-seven other towns support daily papers, most of which are published in the mornings. As well, there are over 300 smaller towns which support a local paper published less frequently than five days a week.

Considering its vast size and relatively small population, Australia has a high proportion of the nationally circulating papers. Its two national dailies are: the *Australian*, originally a quality, but now a popular, broadsheet which is published simultaneously in Sydney, Melbourne, Brisbane, and Perth; and the *Australian Financial Review*, a specialist tabloid for the business community which is published in Sydney, Monday to Friday. The two national weeklies are the *National Times*, an upmarket tabloid published in Sydney; and the *National Review*, a left-wing, counter-culture tabloid which is published in Melbourne.

As in many other Western countries, the level of newspaper circulation in Australia has declined steadily in the postwar period. In 1950, there were 60 metropolitan and regional daily papers sold in Australia for every 100 people over the age of 15 years. However, by 1975 the comparable figure had fallen to 48.

RADIO

Data on the number of radio and television stations operating in Australia as of 30 June 1978 are set out in Table 2. It groups stations according to sectors and gives separate totals for both metropolitan and regional stations.

TABLE 2

Structure of Broadcasting in Australia

Sector	Radio		Television	
	Metropolitan	Regional	Metropolitan	Regional
Government—ABC	16	83	6	79
—SBS	2	-	-	-
Commercial	30	98	15	35
Public	16	8	-	-
	64	189	21	114

Based on the number of stations as of 30 June 1978

When radio broadcasting was first introduced to this country in 1923, the intention was that it be operated entirely by private business interests. However, Australia's relatively small population severely limited the number of commercial stations which could be supported, especially in the rural regions, and the new medium developed at a very slow pace during its first decade.

The example of the United Kingdom in setting up the British Broadcasting Corporation in 1926, as well as domestic political presure from rural electorates, persuaded the government to establish, in 1932, the Australian Broadcasting Commission. The Commission was required to provide a national radio broadcasting service to as great a proportion of the population as its funds would allow. The ABC has always been prohibited from selling advertising air time on its stations and, during its early years, was entirely financed by revenue received from radio listeners in the form of licence fees. In 1949; it was decided that the commission should be funded from annual appropriations of the federal Parliament, although licence fees continued to be paid by the owners of radio (and later television) receivers, the proceeds going into consolidated revenue. The government abolished listener and viewer licence fees altogether in 1974.

The ABC operates two AM radio stations—Radio One and Radio Two—in each of the metropolitan capital cities as well as in Canberra and Newcastle. The programs of Radio One largely consist of light music, news, and sports; while Radio Two transmits mainly classical music, but also present news, discussions, drama, and programs for school and preschool children. One other ABC AM station, 2JJ Sydney, broadcasts mainly rock music, with a strong emphasis on Australian compositions and performances. In addition to its AM stations, the ABC has an FM network which broadcasts the one (predominantly classical music) program simultaneously to Sydney, Melbourne, Adelaide, and Canberra.

A third ABC AM network, Radio Three, serves the nonmetropolitan areas of Australia. A selection of programs from the capital city's Radio One and Radio Two stations constitutes most of the material for each state's Radio Three stations, although some provincial centres have their own studios for the generation of program supplements of local interest (mainly news). There are also six ABC shortwave stations transmitting to inland Australia from coastal urban centres. (In addition to its radio and television networks, the operations of the ABC include: a Show Band; a symphony orchestra in each state capital city; an overseas radio service, Radio Australia, transmitting to various countries in South-East Asia and the Pacific; and the publication of books and other material on a wide variety of subjects.)

The government sector of broadcasting in Australia can also be considered to include the activities of the Special Broadcasting Service. Established in 1977 and fully funded by the federal government, the SBS provides multilingual broadcasting programs for the country's various ethnic minority groups. By mid-1979 the broadcasting outlets of the SBS were confined to one AM radio station in each of Sydney and Melbourne. However, it is intended to extend the ethnic radio service to other cities and, eventually, to establish a permanent SBS television service.

Commercial radio in Australia has been developed in accordance with the concept of localism whereby stations are licenced to provide transmissions to separate centres of population, with local licensees having autonomy in management and programming matters. The number of commercial radio broadcasters in the metropolitan cities varies roughly in relation to population: in June 1978, Melbourne had eight stations; Sydney, seven; Brisbane, five; Adelaide and Perth, four each; and Hobart had two. There were only four cities outside the metropolitan areas which had more than one station—Canberra, Newcastle, Wollongong, and Launceston: they had two each. In each of the other 90 regional centres there was only one station licenced.

By mid-1979 commercial radio in Australia was still confined to the AM mode of transmission. FM radio commenced operation in Australia in 1975 but, initially, its use was restricted to the government and public broadcasting sectors. However, in July 1979, the first stage in the development of commercial FM was announced when applications were made for two stations in both Sydney and Melbourne, and one each in Brisbane, Adelaide, and Perth. The second stage is to include the establishment of commercial FM stations in a number of regional areas.

Whereas the central production and networking of programs was a significant feature of commercial radio in Australia until the advent of television in 1956, the practice now has almost been discontinued. There still exists a number of commercial radio networks, but their operations mainly involve the sale of advertising on behalf of their associated stations.

During the 1972-75 Labor administration a number of educational and community organisations expressed a desire to operate noncommercial radio stations. In its final months of office, the government hurriedly offered and issued three AM and five FM licences to 12 of these groups thereby establishing the third, "public" sector of radio in Australia. The public sector has now consolidated its position in the country's broadcasting system. The present government has sanctioned the renewal of licences for the 12 original stations, and another 12 were issued in 1978.

Public broadcasting radio licences are issued in three categories: Category E, for *educational* bodies providing programs of continuing and adult education; Category C to *community* groups catering for particular geographically identified audiences; and licences serving the broadcasting requirements of audiences having *special* interests are granted under Category S. Public sector radio stations can be operated only by nonprofit organisations and, under the terms of their licences, they cannot transmit advertising material. Public broadcasters derive revenue from various sources, including listeners' subscriptions, pro-

gram sponsorships, grants, and donations. Government financial support is restricted to indirect funding (e.g., through semigovernment
authorities). State governments, statutory bodies other than educational institutions, and political parties cannot hold public broadcasting licences; and no group can hold more than one such licence.

By mid-1979, there have been 4 Category E and 12 Category S public
radio licences issued for stations in the metropolitan areas—Sydney,
Melbourne, Brisbane, and Adelaide each had 3, and both Perth and
Hobart had 2; and 8 Category C stations had been licenced in the
regional districts. Of the 24 public radio stations, 20 are FM and 4 are
AM. (There are no public sector television stations.)

TELEVISION

From its introduction in Australia in 1956, television has been developed within the framework of a dual system similar to that for radio.
There is a government sector, under the control of the ABC and orga-
nised on a national basis; and a commercial sector consisting of localised, independently operated stations. By June 1978, three years after
the commencement of colour transmission, there was a total of 85 ABC
and 50 commercial television stations.

The government sector consists of one ABC channel in each of the six
metropolitan cities and in 79 regional broadcasting areas throughout
the country. The ABC television service broadcasts general programs
as well as those for special interest audiences not specifically catered
for by the commercial stations. The ABC produces about 60 percent of
its own programs, and purchases the remainder from overseas, mainly
from Britain and the United States.

Fifteen commercial stations are situated in the metropolitan cities:
three in each of Sydney, Melbourne, Brisbane, and Adelaide; two in
Perth; and one in Hobart. Outside the state capitals there is a total of 35
single-channel television markets.

There exists an extensive networking system within Australian
commercial television centered on the metropolitan channels of Sydney, Melbourne, Brisbane, and Adelaide. Three network organisations
are each comprised of one station from each of these four cities. The
principal function of the metropolitan networks is to commission the
production of, and purchase the rights to, programs produced in Australia (mainly in Sydney and Melbourne). Australian programs are
made available for broadcast to each of the network stations; and, in
addition, rights are sold by the networks to the Perth, Hobart, and

regional television channels. Around 40 percent of programs shown on commercial television in Australia are produced locally, with the other 60 percent purchased almost entirely from the United States and Britain. There is also a system of regional television networking in Australia which is similar to that for commercial radio, being primarily designed to facilitate the sale of advertising on behalf of small groups of television stations.

OWNERSHIP AND CONTROL OF THE COMMERCIAL MEDIA

One of the outstanding and disturbing features of the commercial media in Australia is the highly concentrated nature of their control. While the number of individual titles of metropolitan daily newspapers in Australia has remained fairly constant throughout the postwar period, the number of independent owners of these papers has declined dramatically. In 1946, for instance, there were 12 different groups publishing metropolitan dailies throughout the country. But by 1971 the number had fallen to four. In that year, an international comparative study by Nixon and Hahn (1971) found Australia to have the second most concentrated metropolitan daily press ownership (after Ireland) among the 15 countries of the Western World for which it compared data. In 1971, all metropolitan dailies were published by Herald and Weekly Times, John Fairfax Limited, News Limited, and Consolidated Press Holdings. Then, in the following year, the number of metropolitan daily press proprietors was reduced further, to three, with the sale of the Sydney newspaper interests of Consolidated Press to Rupert Murdoch's News Limited. The collective publications of the remaining three newspaper conglomerates now also account for over 90 percent of all metropolitan Sunday papers, and over 50 percent of the country's regional daily newspapers.

The federal broadcasting legislation contains provisions which are designed to restrict concentration of ownership and control within commercial broadcasting. A limit is imposed upon the number of radio and television stations in which a "prescribed interest" may be held by individual persons or companies. The Broadcasting and Television Act defines a prescribed interest in a commercial radio licence as an equity or voting interest in excess of 15 percent in the licensee company. No person or company is permitted to hold a prescribed interest in the radio licences of more than:

1. one metropolitan station in any one state;
2. four metropolitan stations in Australia;

3. four stations (metropolitan and/or regional) in any one state; or
4. eight stations (metropolitan and/or regional) in Australia.

The ownership and control provisions for commercial television are more restrictive than for radio, in that a prescribed interest in a television station is defined as the holding of equity or voting rights in excess of 5 percent in a licensee company. Further, the act provides that prescribed interests in commercial television licences may not be held by a person or company in more than:

1. one metropolitan station in any state; or
2. two stations (metropolitan and/or regional) in Australia.

Nevertheless, certain company groups hold "excess" interests in television (but not in radio) licences. This situation has arisen because the original ownership and control provisions for television, written into the act upon the inception of the new medium in 1956, were circumvented by those groups' use of various legal schemes (involving shares with reduced voting rights, companies limited by guarantee, and other means). When the relevant sections were finally reenacted in 1965, it was the government's stated intention that companies with prescribed interests in an excessive number of television stations be required to dispose of sufficient of their holdings to bring them in line with the amended legislation. However, following strong representations from the companies affected, the government decided that their excess interests could be maintained.

The most contentious feature of the ownership and control section of the broadcasting legislation, however, is that it contains no provisions prohibiting or limiting cross-media ownership. That is, the holders of radio licences are not prescribed from also acquiring television licences (and vice versa); and there is no restriction upon the granting of either radio or television licences to newspaper publishers.

Because of the failure of the act to restrict cross-media ownership, and as a result of the licensing decisions made during the early years of both radio and television, included among the major holders of commercial radio and television licences in Australia are the country's largest newspaper publishers—viz., Herald and Weekly Times, John Fairfax, and News Limited. Collectively, these three groups, at 30 June 1978, held prescribed interests in the licences for: 10 of the 30 metropolitan, and 9 of the 98 regional commercial radio stations; and for 7 of the 15 metropolitan, and 2 of the 35 regional television channels. In addition, the Consolidated Press group (which has considerable magazine and regional press interests) held the licences for two metropolitan and three regional radio stations; and for two metropolitan television channels. It is probable, therefore, that Australia has the highest level of ownership concentration for commercial media among all western developed countries.

MEDIA PERSONNEL

Both in Australia and overseas, information about the people who work in and manage the media organizations is sparse. In the United States, Schramm (1967) has noted: "We have as yet no adequate picture of the media personnel, their training, their jobs, their feeling about their jobs, their financial and other rewards, their codes of responsibility." Since 1967 a number of studies have been reported, but the picture is still fragmentary.

In Australia, Sommerlad (1950), Sparrow (1960), Holden (1961), Inglis (1962), Mayer (1964), and Horne (1966) have each commented on some occupational and other characteristics of journalists. Hudson (1963) however, appears to have made the first systematic investigation of journalists. In a study involving 14 metropolitan newspapers in Australia, he collected data on the status of journalists, their recruitment, education, the conditions under which they worked, and factors associated with their movement from the occupation.

From his investigation we learn that the largest single group of journalists is in the 30 to 34 year age group and that journalism is a male preserve, there being no more than around 10 percent of women employed in the field. Hudson also reveals that no more than 5 percent of 500 journalists surveyed in Brisbane, Adelaide, and Perth had university qualifications. In addition, while in the period 1950 to 1960 there were 285 enrollments in Diploma of Journalism courses at the universities in Melbourne and Brisbane, only 25 students graduated—a dropout rate of 91 percent. The situation has improved somewhat in the last decade, but there is still considerable suspicion within the profession about "brash young university-trained journalists."

Journalists appear not to be joiners. Hudson (1965) remarks that it is probably important for journalists to be in touch with the basic thoughts and attitudes current in society; paradoxically, however, "an occupational hazard of journalism is that it tends to breed in its practitioners a removal from their communities . . . an almost ascetic type of detachment has even been put forward as an occupational necessity of journalism." Hudson (1964) quotes the warning of one Brisbane editor to his cadets: "You are starting out on a career which will give you great satisfaction, but only if you are prepared to give your job all you have in the way of talent, energy, and imagination, to detach from friends, from social habits . . . that is part of the price."

Some preliminary results from a more recent study which Western has been undertaking round out this picture somewhat. The study focused on senior staff of the rank of news editor, feature editor, and above, working in press, radio, and television settings. Both capital and provincial cities in all Australian states were included. Data were collected by means of a mailed questionnaire sent to selected individuals in the different settings. Questionnaires were returned by 155 individuals, a response rate of around 45 percent. The effective sample comprised 70 employed by different newspapers, 61 employed by radio and 24 employed by television. The television group, particularly, was disappointingly small.

Hudson's finding that journalism is a male preserve was reinforced. Only three of the respondents were women; one from newspapers and two from radio. A significant number of those on newspapers came from a journalistic background: 24 percent of them reported a father in journalism or a related area. Such a background was far less common among those working in radio and television although nearly half of them reported growing up in professional and managerial homes. Only four from the whole group had tertiary qualifications. Secondary schooling was all the education that two-thirds of the newspaper and radio managers had had. Those in television were a little more likely to have had some tertiary education.

Findings relating to participation in community affairs are equivocal. The majority of those working in radio and television report no membership in voluntary associations, but around two-thirds of those on newspapers do belong to one or more associations. But minimum political involvement is suggested by the fact that over half of those from newspapers and television and around 40 percent of those working in radio claim not to be consistent supporters of a particular political party. They vote at election time for the "best" candidate. Certainly other studies of comparable socio-economic groups would show a much higher proportion committed to one or the other party.

The majority had worked in the media industry all their lives. Of the press managers, 56 percent had always worked on newspapers; but there was some mobility. Twenty percent reported having worked on one paper only, 40 percent had worked on two to four papers, and the remainder had worked on more than four. Those in radio were a little more variable. A third had worked in radio continuously, a further 13 percent had gone from school to something different but had soon made the break to radio and had not left since that time. Among the television managers, 60 percent had worked only in the industry. Fifty percent had had only one job and 37 percent had had between two and four. Not unexpectedly, movement from radio and press to television was greater than movement in the opposite direction. Clearly, from this sample, it would appear that the careers of media managers are not particularly variable. They move into the industry relatively early in life and the majority of them stay there.

Questions relating to the functions of the media are of perennial concern. In order to determine the views of the sample on this issue, they were asked to indicate how important they felt each of five functions to be. The functions are listed in Table 3, together with the proportion of each group saying "very important."

TABLE 3

Importance of General Functions of the Media as Assessed by
Media Managers

Functions	Percentage indicating functions as "very important"		
	Press (n=70)	Radio (n=61)	Television (n=24)
Providing news about important events	97	89	88
Providing informed comment about important events	64	34	29
Providing entertainment	10	84	96
Providing service features	14	36	25
Acting as a guardian of public rights	69	18	13

As can be seen there is clear agreement concerning the provision of news. Obviously, informed comment is seen more as a function of the press; it is perhaps surprising that it rates so lowly with the television sample. Entertainment, of course, is television's role par excellence, and it is interesting to see the managers and the general public so in accord. Again, the traditional role of the press as a guardian of public rights, perhaps honoured more in the breach in Australia, is in no danger of being usurped by the electronic media.

To investigate this matter further, and to obtain a clearer view of how the executives saw the political functions of the media, a series of questions focussing more specifically on political matters were posed. They are presented in Table 4, together with the proportion of each group indicating that the matter dealt with in the question was "very important."

TABLE 4

Importance of Political Functions of the Media as Assessed by
Media Managers

Functions	Percentage indicating functions as "very important"		
	Press (n=70)	Radio (n=61)	Television (n=24)
To act as a watchdog against encroachments by the bureaucracy	81	39	51
To point out where and when the weight of expert opinion challenges political decisions	74	25	46
To raise important political questions	73	44	71
To mobilize public opinion where necessary	59	34	21
To criticise government on behalf of the people	57	16	21
To point out where and when there are significant differences between experts on political issues	50	36	46
To provide a forum for critics of the government	40	15	25

Clearly, the traditional role of the press as a "watchdog of democracy" (Williams, 1969) is reflected in the responses provided by the press executives. This view is shared to some extent by television executives, but quite clearly those from radio do not see an important political role for their medium.

As has been pointed out earlier in this section, the degree of concentration of ownership of the Australian mass media is exceptionally high. But does concentration of ownership mean a reduction in diversity, or are individual editors able to run their papers as they see fit, free from direction of the parent company?

Several questions in the study of media managers sought information on this issue. First we asked: "If you belong to a mixed media group with associates in other cities, does your group have policies about the treatment of news about specific topics?" And then we asked: "Do occasions arise when all members of your group work together?" Around a third of the media managers with associates in other cities stated that there were policies about the treatment of news which all members of the group followed. The remaining two-thirds said that this was not the case and editors were free to determine how they would make use of any news story. Very few newspaper and radio managers saw occasions when all members of their group worked together. Among those involved in television, however, it was more common: half of those with associations in other cities could name occasions when it had occurred.

TABLE 5

Experiences of Newspaper Personnel With Different
Management Created Situations

Experiences	Percentage indicating situation experienced at least occasionally	Percentage indicating situation never experienced
Instructions being given to you about the emphasis of a story	66	34
Instructions being given to you to treat a story counter to your own interpretation of the facts	20	80
Stories being suppressed or buried because they ran counter to editorial policy	44	51
Stories being suppressed or buried because they conflicted with management interests	41	54
Have you ever written stories which ran counter to editorial policy which were printed?	68	23
Have you ever written stories which conflicted with management interests?	70	21

These findings are obviously far from definitive. The sample is small and the questions cover only part of the issue. Nevertheless, there does seem to be some support for the view that concentration of ownership does not necessarily mean dictation from the head office.

To pursue the issue further, we listed a series of hypothetical situations and then asked: "Have you personally had any experience vis-à-vis newspaper proprietors (not necessarily your present proprietor/ Board of Directors) of any of the following?" The question was given only to newspaper personnel. The situations are listed in Table 5, together with the proportion indicating some experience of the situation and those indicating none. (The percentages do not always add to 100 as on some issues a proportion of the sample indicated uncertainty.)

As with most other aspects of reality the situation is one of some complexity. From the results it is clear that pressures are exerted. Stories are buried because they run counter to editorial policy or because they conflict with management interests: and instructions are given about the emphasis to be given in a story and about the "right" sort of interpretation to place on a set of facts. But at the same time, stories are written which run counter to editorial policy and which are in conflict with management interests. Clearly, control is exerted; but at the same time there is opportunity for resistance.

A related issue has to do with pressure from advertisers. Obviously this is a different dimension of the problem; the concern about concentration of ownership typically is in terms of the reduction of diversity that may follow from it. Reduction of diversity means fewer points of view, fewer interpretations of news and less complete news coverage, all of which act to the detriment of citizens who are attempting to inform themselves about the affairs of the day. The dangers here are hegemonic in a sense. Pressures on diversity from advertising on the other hand, are likely to be more narrowly specific, and concerned primarily with the advertisers' desire to protect their products from unfavourable publicity.

To gain some insight into this issue we put the following question to all three groups: "Because of the large part which advertising plays in the economics of a newspaper/radio station/TV station, advertisers are in a position to exert and may exert influence an editorial policy. How frequently would you consider that editors are subjected to pressure from advertisers?" We asked that they respond in terms of the three factors listed in Table 6.

The data are quite striking. Pressures from advertisers are clearly

TABLE 6

Experiences of Media Personnel With Different Advertiser
Created Situations

Experiences	Percentage indicating situation experienced at least occasionally			Percentage indicating situation never experienced		
	Press	Radio	Tele-vision	Press	Radio	Tele-vision
Pressure from advertisers to:						
•adopt a certain editorial line	65	51	67	33	48	33
•publish a particular item helpful to some interest of the advertisers	97	85	96	3	15	4
•refrain from publishing a particular item harmful to some interest of the advertiser	75	79	89	21	21	11

part of the day-to-day life of the members of the sample. Around
two-thirds of those in newspapers and television report at least occasional pressures from advertisers to adopt a certain editorial line: the
figure drops down to around half for radio personnel. Virtually all the
press and television respondents report at least occasional pressures to
publish or put on air items helpful to some interest of the advertiser,
while 85 percent of those working in radio report the same. Again, there
are pressures to refrain from using items which might be harmful to the
advertiser's interests. It might also be noted that, while for simplicity of
presentation only two categories of data have been given, the category
"situation experienced at least occasionally" includes respondents saying "occasionally," "sometimes," and "often." Those "often" experiencing
pressure amount to around 20 percent of the sample.

The data we have examined clearly suggest that pressures from
advertisers are greater than pressures from owners or boards of management. Space does not permit more than highlighting the issue here.
Further examination of these and important related questions would

necessitate a more detailed analysis of the data than we can provide at the present time.

NEWS CONTENT

The primary source of revenue for each of the major commercial media in Australia is advertising. This fact of course affects the nature of material appearing in the press, and in radio and television programming. In a recent study concerned with foreign and domestic news in a selection of metropolitan dailies (the *Age* from Melbourne, the *Sydney Morning Herald* from Sydney, and the *Courier Mail* from Brisbane) over a 60 year period in Australia (Hughes and Western, 1973, 1974), questions relating to the nature of press content were addressed. Techniques of content analysis were employed, the basic unit of measurement being the square inch. Each paper examined was divided into total editorial space and total advertising space: the two combined equalled total area of print. Editorial space comprised news items which were measured as news space, editorial comment, letters to the editor, features, and what for want of a better term we called "undefined space"—a category used sparingly and mainly arising in recent years through the use of photographs unconnected to either a news item or a feature article.

TABLE 7

Editorial Space as Percentage of Total Area of Print

Year	Age	Sydney Morning Herald	Courier Mail
1907	43%	45%	55%
1917	33	32	39
1927	45	35	50
1937	54	50	56
1947	44	42	45
1957	34	39	37
1967	39	36	31

From a peak in 1937, the proportion of each newspaper given to editorial space has declined to about one-third of total space; and conversely, the proportion of advertising space has risen (Table 7). This trend relates to both the newspapers' increasing dependence on advertising revenue and probably also the increasing affluence of a society able and willing to respond to advertisements.

TABLE 8

News Space as Percentage of Editorial Space

Year	Age	Sydney Morning Herald	Courier Mail
1907	84%	75%	72%
1917	80	75	74
1927	80	71	62
1937	71	59	58
1947	70	55	60
1957	67	63	62
1967	60	59	63

While the *Age* has continued to reduce its news space in relation to general editorial space, the *Sydney Morning Herald* and the *Courier Mail* have levelled off (Table 8). In 1967 all three newspapers showed remarkably similar distributions of their editorial space between news items and other material.

TABLE 9

Overseas News Items as Percentage of Total News Space
Occupied by Items With Identified Geographical Sources

Year	Age	Sydney Morning Herald	Courier Mail
1907	17%	18%	20%
1917	24	35	23
1927	11	15	16
1937	23	27	21
1947	26	30	21
1957	22	20	23
1967	26	32	19

Breaking down news items with overseas news and domestic news provides an index of Australia's readiness to look inwards or outwards. The data are presented in Table 9. What emerges most strikingly is how little change there has been over time. True, there are sharp differences between the proportion of space devoted to overseas news in times of peace (1907 and 1927) as compared with times of war (1917) or war's aftermath, and preparation for war; but there is no regular progression. If, as we believe, newspapers are responsive to the public, then on first sight it might appear that the nature of the public's demand has changed little in the 60 year period we are examining. Specifically, this means that in the normal course of events the demand for news about international affairs is not very different from what it was in the first decade of the century. One further point is worthy of note. While it is apparent that all three papers follow broadly parallel patterns, both the *Age* and the *Sydney Morning Herald* seem to have been marginally more responsive to Australia's external environment than has been the *Courier Mail*, perhaps a reflection of differences between Melbourne and Sydney on the one hand and Brisbane on the other.

TABLE 10

Percentage Apportionment of Overseas News According to Geographical Sources

Year	United Kingdom	Europe	North America	Asia	Multiple Countries
			Age		
1907	52%	9%	8%	2%	7%
1917	28	31	15	1	10
1927	35	15	12	6	4
1937	40	18	9	9	19
1947	29	14	17	11	17
1957	30	9	23	7	15
1967	20	7	15	32	9
		Sydney Morning Herald			
1907	40%	6%	7%	1%	27%
1917	12	33	3	0	47
1927	23	8	9	8	36
1937	30	20	14	11	13
1947	25	18	24	16	5
1957	27	12	38	4	0
1967	21	13	20	25	8
			Courier Mail		
1907	36%	4%	8%	5%	35%
1917	33	38	9	1	6
1927	35	12	12	10	15
1937	33	25	8	11	13
1947	27	6	21	13	18
1957	21	9	26	8	18
1967	18	14	23	27	9

It is possible to move from the broad picture described in Table 9 to a more specific consideration of the geographic sources of overseas news. Four areas were decreed to be of particular interest in the Australian context: the United Kingdom, Europe, North America and Asia. Data relating to these areas and a fifth, "Multiple Countries" which focusses on interactions between countries, are presented in Table 10.

It is clear that the change in emphasis over the years has been considerable. The decline of the United Kingdom and the rise of Asia was hypothesised in broad outline, but some of the details are surprising: for example, the sharp decline in Asian news in 1957 and some of the interpaper variations in United Kingdom news. The rise of North American news after World War II was also anticipated, but its peak in 1957 was followed by a slight decline due to an unanticipated shift of attention to Asia. The rise to prominence of Asia has been quite dramatic. In the years immediately after World War II, Asian news constituted no more than about 15 percent of all overseas news. A decade later the figure had dropped to around 5 percent overall. But, by 1967, between a quarter and a third of all overseas news derived from Asia, and that continent had come to be the main source of Australia's international news. Table 10 also documents the degree of Australian involvement in World War I, as reflected in the primacy given to European news in 1917 in each of the three newspapers. It is quite clear that while Australians may not be becoming more cosmopolitan in their outlook in the sense that they are demanding more overseas news, there is a decided shift in the focus of attention away from the United Kingdom and Europe towards Asia and North America. Horizons may not be expanding, but at least they are changing.

Total space is one dimension of content analysis. Another dimension focuses on particularly strategic and substantial items of information— lead articles, editorials, features, and the like. Although we cannot say with assurance that these were given any special attention by readers when they were published, we can at least assume that the editors concerned regarded them as having considerable significance.

In the analysis, five particular classes of items were identified in the papers being examined: the major news story and second news story, the main and second editorial, and the major feature article. Space does not permit a complete discussion of all the data obtained, but certain of the major trends can be highlighted. Table 11 details the percentage of major news stories, main editorials, and feature articles which are concerned with overseas issues.

TABLE 11

Percentage of Major Articles, Main Editorials,
and Feature Articles Based on Overseas Issues

Year	Major News Story (n=72)	Main Editorial (n=72)	Feature Article (n=72)
1907	42%	27%	23%
1917	83	49	31
1927	36	37	40
1937	60	38	45
1947	26	17	57
1957	30	47	40
1967	31	38	60

It is clear that the trend is very similar for both major news stories and editorials, with both appearing to respond to the international situation. When there is international tension, this gets attention: when the international scene is quiet, attention shifts to domestic affairs. In both cases there is relatively little difference in allocations at the beginning and end of the period. This is not to say that there have been no changes over the 60 year period for, as was suggested before, there are quite significant differences within the "overseas" categories. In the period since World War II, there has been greater variability for editorials, which might cast some light on the greater discretion newspapers have over their strictly editorial columns. Emphasis on the hard facts of political life is unlikely to allow as much variation as editorial argument. On the other hand, there is the prescient observation of Barnard C. Cohen (1963): "These space allocations are not made inflexibly, nor are they made and remade daily, or even frequently. They are matters of fundamental policy in a newspaper, and are subject to considerable inertia; once made they tend to persist until changes in top personnel or in the fortunes of the paper suggest new ones."

Feature articles present a quite different trend. We would not have been surprised to have found their pattern resembling that of the editorials, for both allow greater freedom of choice in focus. But it is clear that this is not the case: features, with only the single downturn in 1957, show an increasing concern with affairs outside Australia.

What impact these changes have had on the newspaper-reading public is, of course, quite a different question. We know that editorials and feature articles are read by only a very small proportion of readers, while the headlines and perhaps a paragraph or two of the main news story on page one was read by many more. So it would not be correct to conclude that the material most likely to reach the great mass of the reading public has, over the years, come to have much more of a cosmopolitan flavour. Other media studies tell us that what people are most interested in reading about is themselves; and lacking that, about their local neighbourhood. But given that important qualification, the data produced by this study tell a somewhat more hopeful story, as they suggest some degree of sensitivity to the contemporary situation. For example, there is the increased attention paid to Asia, albeit quite late in the day. There is the decline in concentration on British affairs, much earlier, we suspect, than many would have believed. And finally, there is the place of North America in the press, from a position of marginal significance at the beginning of the century to one that is surpassed only by Asia on the overseas scene today.

Government Impact on the Media

This section examines the major federal and state government laws, regulations and agreements as they affect both the print and broadcasting media. The six state and two territory governments in Australia possess the power to legislate in matters specifically affecting the printed media, and the federal government in those concerning broadcasting. Nevertheless, certain responsibilities of the states also relate to broadcasting stations; and, conversely, a number of federal provisions impinge upon the activities of the press.

THE PRESS

In 1964, Professor Henry Mayer, in his book *The Press in Australia*, observed that: "the 'press barons' are a striking symbol of laissez-faire capitalism, in a period when big business and, more recently, big labour [are] coming under increasing legal restraints." This statement remains relevant insofar as it refers to the relatively minor degree of government regulation of the business activities of the newspaper industry. However, there are certain state and federal provisions which have the effect of imposing excessive restrictions upon the editorial output of the press in Australia.

Defamation. Australia's defamation laws have long been the subject of criticism because of their alleged archaism and complexity. There are four main areas of concern. Firstly, Australia has a different set of defamation laws for each state and territory. Consequently, it is unlikely that editors of newspapers (and broadcast transmissions) crossing state and territory boundaries will be familiar with all of their provisions. Secondly, a person who claims grievance as a result of an alleged libel is able to prevent further reporting of accurate information on the issue simply by the device of taking out a "stop writ," which causes the matter to be held *sub judice* pending legal action. While this achieves the intended effect of restricting public debate on the subject matter covered by the stop writ, the complaint is seldom proceeded within the courts: one study found that of 831 defamation actions began between 1972 and 1976 only 21, or 2.5 percent, actually went to court. Thirdly, defamation cases which are pursued often take a long time, sometimes years, to come before the courts. (And during this period the principle of *sub judice* remains in force.) Fourthly, the only recompense available to successful plaintiffs is money damages: there is no legal provision for the courts to order the defendant to publish or broadcast a retraction. The combined effect of these defects in the country's defamation laws and judicial procedures is to unduly inhibit the Australian media in their reporting of news.

In 1976, the Australian Law Reform Commission carried out a study of the defamation issue and, in the following year, drafted a model Defamation Bill designed to overcome the problems set out above. Briefly, the Commission formed the opinion that all states and territories of Australia ought to adopt uniform defamation legislation and that the "stop writ" procedure should be abolished. It further recommended that: complaints should come before a court within four months of the alleged defamation, and the action brought to trial within another two months if a defence is raised; in those cases decided in favour of the plaintiff, the court should order the defendant to make a public correction; and the court ought also have the prerogative to award the plaintiff general damages for loss of reputation. These solutions proposed by the Law Reform Commission have generally been well received by interested parties, but their implementation is not yet immanent.

D notices. A system of D (for Defence) notices has operated in Australia since 1952. Under this system, modelled very closely on its British counterpart, the press and the broadcasting stations voluntarily agree to avoid reporting certain topics concerning which a D notice has been issued in the name of national security. This procedure is a voluntary modification of compulsory censorship which operated in Australia during both world wars.

Decisions as to information to be covered by D notices are made by a Defence, Press, and Broadcasting Committee established by agreement between the federal government and the press and broadcasting proprietors (but not editors). The committee has a majority of media representatives and a minority of government appointees selected from the public service. Requests for D notices originate within government departments and are referred to the committee. Approved notices are issued to all editors and managers on a confidential basis, whereupon the media are expected to refrain from reporting any information relating to the notices while they remain in force.

Information concerning the number of D notices issued and the subjects to which they relate is not made public. Nevertheless, it seems that the reporting of the following topics, at least, is currently subject to such restriction: technical information regarding defence force weapons, weapon systems, and equipment; the ciphering and monitoring activities of the defence forces; the activities of the Australian Secret Intelligence Service; and the whereabouts of two former staff members of the Russian embassy in Australia who defected to Australia in 1954. The Australian Journalists' Association opposes the voluntary censorship embodied in the D notice system, arguing that regulation preventing the spread of security information to foreign countries is adequately provided in Australia's official secrets legislation. In addition to the defamation laws and the D notice system, the press is also subject to federal government trade practices procedures and to some degree of self-regulation through the activities of the Australian Press Council.

Mergers. In spite of the high level of ownership concentration of the press in Australia there exists no specific legislation concerning mergers of newspaper companies. However, such mergers are subject to the general provisions of the federal Trade Practices Act. From its introduction by the Labor government in 1974, until 1977, the act prohibited mergers (in all industries) "likely to have the effect of substantially lessening competition in a market for goods and services." During that time seven applications for the merger of newspaper and magazine companies were made to the Trade Practices Commission: three of these were granted outright; one was granted subject to conditions; and the other three were denied by the commission. However, in 1977 the act was weakened to apply only to mergers which would give corporations positions "to control or dominate a market for goods and services." No application for the authorisation of a merger between

newspaper or magazine companies has come before the commission
since the Trade Practices legislation was so modified.

Press Council. The establishment of a "watchdog" over the editorial
content of newspapers was urged for many years by the Australian
Journalist Association. Eventually, in July 1976, following severe public criticism of the role they played in the political upheaval of the
previous year, the country's newspaper proprietors joined with the AJA
in the formation of the Australian Press Council. The council consists
of 13 members, 6 of whom are nominated by the metropolitan and
regional press organisations (with the notable exception of the Fairfax
group which refuses to participate), and 3 elected by the AJA. In
addition, there is an independent chairman who selects 3 members to
represent the public. The operations of the council are financed by its
member bodies.

The Australian Press Council is based upon the British model, and its
main task is to consider complaints from the public against member
publications concerning misreporting, alleged distortion, offensive or
misleading headlines, invasion of privacy, or alleged damage to reputation. However, the council is vested with no power to discipline papers
it finds to have breached its journalistic standards; it simply relies upon
them to publish the decisions of the hearings which it conducts.

In summary, it can be said that the press in Australia has long been
successful in resisting government intervention into its structure and
ownership, but has been forced to adopt a mild form of self-regulation
in an attempt to curb the more immoderate aspects of its behaviour.
And, although both state and federal governments in Australia impose
excessive restrictions over the editorial output of the printed media,
they do not seriously threaten the freedom of the press as the concept is
traditionally interpreted.

BROADCASTING

The overall responsibility for broadcasting in Australia has, since the
federation of the six states in 1901, resided with the national government. In 1942, the legislation governing broadcasting was consolidated
into a single act, the Australian Broadcasting Act. This was amended in
1956 to accommodate the licensing and regulation of television, and its
title was altered to the Broadcasting and Television Act.

The role of government with respect to the different sectors of broadcasting is now considered. However, as public radio stations in Australia are subject to the same regulatory provisions and authorities as

commercial broadcasters, these two sectors are discussed jointly. (The operations of radio and television stations are, as already mentioned, also subject to the defamation laws of the six states and two territories and to the federal government's D notice system.)

THE GOVERNMENT SECTOR

Although nominally an autonomous statutory authority, the Australian Broadcasting Commission has certain restrictions imposed upon it by the act. In particular: the ownership of its transmitters is vested in a separate statutory authority, Telecom Australia; the ABC must obtain the approval of the government for major items of expenditure, of both a capital and operational nature; and, the Public Service Board, rather than the commission itself, exercises the main authority in matters concerning the salaries and conditions of ABC staff. However, in practice, the most significant influence exerted by the government lies in the appointment of commission members and in its financial appropriations.

The board of the commission consists of 11 part-time members each of whom, including the chairman, is appointed by the government of the day. The act provides that the commissioners represent each of the six states of Australia and that at least two be women. The terms of commission appointments are for three years and are renewable. During Labor's period in office one of the commissioners was elected by the staff of the ABC, but when his term expired in 1978 the present government abolished the position of staff commissioner and itself appointed his successor. While the day-to-day management of the ABC is the responsibility of the permanent staff headed by the general manager, the commissioner's liaise with the government decide overall policy matters and plan the development of ABC services.

Dissimilar philosophies of successive governments regarding the extent of ABC financing, and of public spending generally, are reflected in fluctuations in the size of the commission's budget over recent years. The level of funding for the ABC was raised during the period of the Labor government, allowing the commission to expand its production of programs and to formulate plans to extend its AM and FM radio networks into rural areas. In contrast, the current administration has cut the ABC appropriation in real terms, causing the commission to modify its production schedule and to cancel plans for the extension of its services. The total ABC appropriation for the 1979-80 financial year was 189 million dollars Australian.

Of more serious implication for the autonomy of the ABC was a government decision in July 1977 to invoke a seldom-used provision of the act allowing the Treasury Minister (note, not the minister responsible for broadcasting) to stipulate how the funds of the commission are to be expended. The government's purpose was to force the ABC to close down an ethnic-access radio station in Melbourne which was established during the term of the Labor administration. This was carried out under protest from the commission. Another issue involving tension between the ABC and the government concerning autonomy is that of staffing. In 1974 the Labor government introduced the practice of determining the staff ceiling for the ABC. The commission accepted the government's decision in that year, and in subsequent years, as a contribution to government policy aimed at reducing public sector growth. However, between November 1975 (when ABC staff employment was at its highest level) and June 1978, the number of employees was reduced from around 7,500 to below 6,500. The commission has since suggested that it is prepared to resist pressure by the government to further reduce the number of its staff, and in its 1978 annual report felt obliged to point out that, under the Broadcasting and Television Act, it considers that "the number of staff employed by the ABC is a matter for determination by the commission, having regard to its statutory obligations and the funds appropriated to it. "

The Special Broadcasting Service is a separate statutory authority whose six-member administrative committee is nominated by the government. All appointments are on a part-time basis and are for a period of five years. The SBS is under the joint authority of the Postal and Telecommunications Department and the Department of Immigration and Ethnic Affairs. The 1979-80 budget allocation for the ethnic broadcasting stations was six million dollars Australian.

COMMERCIAL AND PUBLIC SECTORS

Before examining the current regulatory provisions and procedures affecting commercial and public broadcasting in Australia, it is necessary to mention the various departments and authorities which have been involved in the administration of broadcasting in the postwar period. Until 1948, commercial radio was regulated directly by the government, through the Postmaster General's Department. In that year, the Australian Broadcasting Control Board was established. It took over most of the department's functions in relation to radio and had the regulation of television added to its charge when the new medium was introduced in 1956. It also assumed responsibility for public radio broadcasting when that sector was established in 1975.

The control board's regulation of broadcasting covered a period of 28 years, from 1948 to 1976. During that time there was no major change in its philosophy or procedures. Indeed, from the introduction of television until the 1970s, very few decisions of government significantly affected either commercial or noncommercial broadcasting.

Upon coming to power, the Labor government retained the Postmaster General's Department, but allocated its broadcasting functions to the new Department of the Media. When the Liberal and National Country parties were returned to government in 1975, the Department of the Media was abolished. Its activities were incorporated into the extant Postal and Telecommunications Department whose responsibilities are, broadly, the same as those of the old Postmaster General's Department.

The government then directed that an Inquiry into the broadcasting system be carried out by the Department, the report of which was presented to the government in September 1976. Notwithstanding the subtitle "A Report on the Structure of the Australian Broadcasting System and Associated Matters," the "Green Report" did not seriously question the existing structure of radio and television in Australia. Instead, the Inquiry concerned itself mainly with that part of its terms of reference requiring it to examine "the machinery and procedures for the control, planning, licensing, regulation, funding, and administration of the [broadcasting] system."

Nevertheless, one of the main recommendations of the Green Report—to abolish the control board and to replace it with a new regulatory authority—was immediately adopted: the Australian Broadcasting Tribunal assumed responsibility for the regulation of the commercial and public sectors of broadcasting from January 1977. The enabling legislation provided for five members to be appointed to the Tribunal by the government, and for such appointments to be for periods up to five years. The tribunal maintained the same permanent staff, premises, and most of the functions of the control board. But its establishment had the effect of removing from the field of broadcast regulation the Labor appointees to the board, whose five-year terms had a considerable period to run.

The major powers and functions of the Broadcasting Tribunal, bestowed upon it by the 1976 amendments to the act, are:

1. to grant, renew, suspend, and revoke commercial and public broadcasting licences;
2. to grant approvals and give directions in relation to the ownership and control of licences;
3. to determine the standards to be observed by licensees in respect to the transmission of programs; and
4. to determine the conditions subject to which advertisements may be broadcast.

Licensing. The most important area of responsibility for the broadcasting regulatory authority, at least insofar as it affects the ownership and control of nongovernment broadcasting, relates to its powers over the licensing of radio and television stations. The past and present licensing policies with respect to commercial and public broadcasting in Australia have had the effect of severely restricting the number of radio stations operating throughout the country. From the incorporation of the Broadcasting Control Board in 1948, to its abolition in 1976, the population of Australia grew by over 80 percent (from 7.6 to 13.9 million), while that of the six state capital cities more than doubled (from 3.9 to 8.6 million). During the same 28 year period the number of commercial radio stations in operation increased by only 18 percent (from 102 to 120), while, in the metropolitan areas, only one new commercial broadcaster was licensed (in Adelaide, in March 1976). Nevertheless, from 1948 to 1966, nearly 2000 applications for new commercial radio licences throughout Australia were rejected by the control board. The two major factors restricting the number of radio stations in Australia throughout the postwar period have been the perpetuation of the myth of shortage of spectrum space for AM radio broadcasting, and the prolonged delay in introducing FM radio.

According to Cole (1966), the nonavailability of frequencies was the sole reason advanced by the control board in refusing applications for new commercial radio licences, and for rejecting continual attempts by the ABC to establish a third metropolitan radio network and a second network in country areas. Cole's article exposed the fallacy of the board's explanation for restricting the number of radio outlets. However, his argument was not accepted by government until nearly eight years later. In 1974, the Minister for the Media confirmed that, by narrowing separations between channels and by making greater use of shared frequencies, the number of radio stations operating within the existing allocation for AM could be doubled at relatively short notice, and at reasonably low cost.

A few months after the minister's announcement, the chairman of the control board seemed to add credence to claims that the myth of spectrum shortage had, for over 25 years, been fostered by both the board and the government. In answer to a question from a senate standing committee as to whether the board had been aware that the radio spectrum could accommodate twice as many stations, he answered: "Yes. The technical people [employed by the board] had certainly always known it." He added, "I do not think that the board or successive governments saw any great need for a great proliferation of the commercial [radio] services."

It was mentioned in the previous section that FM radio did not commence operation in Australia until 1975 when the public broadcasting stations began their transmissions. (The ABC established its four-station FM network in 1976.) The introduction of FM followed many years of indecision on the part of the government and of floundering by the Broadcasting Control Board.

Briefly, the history of FM in Australia, to 1975, is as follows. In 1948, the Labor government announced that FM broadcasting, using the VHF (very high frequency) portion of the spectrum, would be introduced "as soon as practicable." But the Labor party lost office at the 1949 election, and the new Liberal-Country government did nothing to encourage FM, claiming that all resources available to broadcasting were required for the introduction and development of television. Eventually, in 1970, in response to pressure from a number of aspiring broadcasters, the government instructed the control board to conduct an inquiry into the FM issue. The board took two years to prepare its report, which advised in favour of FM broadcasting. However, the VHF frequencies which had originally been reserved for FM had, in 1961, been allocated to television. Consequently, the board recommended that UHF (ultra high frequency) be used for the new mode of broadcasting, a waveband adopted nowhere else in the world for FM transmission. There followed another three years, during which an independent (non-control board) reinvestigation of the question found, inter alia, that "VHF/FM is invariably less expensive and provides greater benefit than UHF/FM." In 1975, the (Labor) government finally resolved to clear the spectrum of the obstructing television stations (by reallocating them to alternative frequencies) to allow FM to be introduced in the VHF waveband.

As well as impeding the establishment of new radio stations, the licensing policies and procedures adopted in Australia in the postwar period have had the effect of vesting de facto property rights in the broadcast licences of existing radio and television stations. During the period of the control board's regulation of commercial radio and television, upon receipt of advice from the board that a station should be established, the minister decided whether to call for applications for a new licence. If the minister approved the proposal, applications would be made to, and considered by, the control board, which recommended to the minister its choice for the awarding of the licence. The minister then had the power to accept the nominee of the board, or to issue the licence to another applicant. (He almost invariably accepted the applicant chosen by the board.) Licences were granted for an initial period of five years and thereafter became due for renewal each year.

On the recommendation of the board, the minister could revoke a station's licence at any time, or refuse its renewal, on a number of grounds including noncompliance with the board's regulatory requirements. However, in practice, once commercial radio and television licences were granted, they were held in perpetuity. Revocation and refusal to renew were considered, by the board and the government, to be excessively severe penalties for even frequent and continual infringement of the broadcasting regulations. Whenever they were breached, the usual response of the board was merely to register its disapproval with the offending stations, while instances of gross violations were reported to the minister and published in the board's annual report to Parliament. No further disciplinary action was ever taken by the board or the government.

Throughout the 28-year existence of the board, therefore, no radio or television licence was ever revoked or refused renewal. In fact, the most recent occasion on which a station lost its licence was in 1941 when the Postmaster General, under the wartime powers conferred on him, not by the broadcasting legislation but by the national security regulations, revoked the licences of four radio stations associated with the Jehovah's Witnesses Church. (This followed an action of the federal government in declaring the Witnesses and certain affiliated bodies "unlawful organisations.") The act also has provided for the suspension of broadcasting licences for up to seven days. However, this power has only once been exercised: in 1975, the Hobart television station was ordered off the air for two hours on a Saturday night for repeatedly exceeding the board's maximum limitation on advertising content.

Since the return to office of the present government and its replacement of the control board with the Australian Broadcasting Tribunal, the licensing procedures for stations have undergone considerable modification. The government, through the minister, still decides the number of new licences to be issued and their specifications relating to location, frequencies, power of signal, etc. Licences continue to be granted for an initial period of five years, but the determination of the tribunal as to which of the contending applicants is to be awarded a new licence is no longer subject to the veto of the minister.

However, it is in the relicensing of the stations that the most apparent change has taken place. This follows the recommendation of the tribunal in its 1977 "Self-Regulation Report" relating to the "public account-ability" of stations. As a licence becomes due for renewal, the public is invited to prepare submissions, relating to that station's programming and general performance during the term of the expiring licence, and to present them at an open renewal hearing. After considering the evidence submitted on behalf of both the public and the licensee, the tribunal determines either to renew the licence for a period varying from one to three years, or, alternatively, to not renew it. A decision by the broadcasting tribunal to not renew a licence, or to renew it for a period of less than three years, cannot be overturned by the minister, but is subject to appeal, by the licensee company, to the Administrative Appeals Tribunal. As well, the broadcasting tribunal has power, under the act, to revoke a radio or television licence following a public inquiry. A licensee can also take a decision to revoke its licence to the Administrative Appeals Tribunal (but it is not subject to ministerial veto).

In the 18 months to mid-1979 licence renewal hearings had been conducted for: the metropolitan commercial radio stations in Brisbane, Perth, and Hobart; the regional radio stations in two states; and the Sydney, Adelaide, and Hobart television channels. In each case the broadcasting tribunal renewed the respective licence for the maximum period of three years. The new regime of "public accountability" under the administration of the broadcasting tribunal is, therefore, yet to provide any indication that it represents a greater threat to the permanency of commercial broadcasting licences than did the licensing policies which applied during the period of the control board.

The regulation of programming and advertising. In addition to the functions of issuing and renewing licences, the broadcasting regulatory authorities have, since 1948, had certain responsibilities in relation to stations' programming and advertising material. However, there have been serious difficulties surrounding this area of broadcast regulation, especially with regard to commercial television.

The problems stemmed from the lack of any clear definition of the powers of the control board from the time it was established. The board formulated regulations concerning the maximum number of minutes of advertising stations were permitted to broadcast in each hour and the minimum proportion of transmission time which they were required to devote to Australian produced programs; and it developed a set of standards relating to matters of taste in programming and advertising. But, concomitantly, the board maintained that it possessed no power to enforce these regulations and standards.

The unsatisfactory nature of this situation was made apparent as early as 1963, when an all-party Senate Select Committee (the "Vincent Committee") carried out an inquiry relating to Australian content on commercial television. In 1960 all television stations had been directed to attain a level of Australian content of not less than 40 percent of total transmission time within three years. However, the Vincent Committee found that, by 1963, only 3 out of the 24 channels then operating in the country had complied with this direction, and that no disciplinary action had been taken against the other stations. In evidence to the committee, the chairman of the control board described its relationship with the commercial broadcasters as proceeding "on the basis of consultation and sweet reasonableness." The committee replied in its report that the board should have long since abandoned its policy of "sweet reasonableness" and taken much firmer action with the stations in relation to its regulation of their operations The report stated: "It comes as a surprise to the committee that the board has neither threatened nor taken disciplinary action against any commercial licensee." Unfortunately, the Vincent Report was only briefly debated in Parliament, and no legislation was ever enacted regarding its recommendation to clarify the powers of the broadcasting control board. (In 1974, the Labor government presented draft legislation to the Parliament which was designed to, among other things, clarify the powers of the board. The bill was passed by the lower house, but was rejected by the Senate where the non-Labor parties held majority control.)

The incapacity of the control board to adequately carry out its regulatory responsibilities continued into the 1970s as was demonstrated by an incident in 1972. One of the standards of the board required television stations to transmit "minority" programs of an educational or religious nature on Sunday mornings. Nevertheless, a Melbourne station began to broadcast, on Sunday mornings, replays of the previous day's football matches which was, of course, a clear breach of the board's standard. The minister intervened in the matter and issued a statement foreshadowing an amendment to the act to clarify the board's power in this area, which he hoped the government would be able to consider "within the next ten days." Of course, no such amendment was ever enacted, and other channels throughout the country soon adopted the practice of broadcasting sports replays and other mass appeal programs on Sunday mornings. They continue to the present time.

Until it was abolished, the control board lamented the lack of legal authority to enforce the various requirements and restrictions that it had promulgated throughout its 28 years of broadcast regulation. In a paper relating to Australian content on commercial television, which it released in December 1976, the board stated: "The threat of legal challenges from stations led the board to consult its own advisers who confirmed quite unequivocally that no powers of direction or requirement existed in this area [i.e. Australian content]. It has therefore been necessary for the board to proceed in small steps in accordance with its view of what stations would be able to achieve."

Since 1976, the regulation of programs and advertising has mainly been debated within the context of a proposal of the Green Report for commercial and public broadcasting stations to have greater responsibility for their own regulation. The broadcasting tribunal, during its first months of operation, conducted an Inquiry into the proposal, and the resulting Self-Regulation Report (1977) recommended that broadcasters be given "a measure of self-regulation in some areas." In particular, it suggested that programming and advertising standards should be developed by broadcasters, approved by the tribunal, and enforced by the various station representative bodies. However, in what it referred to as the three "most contentious and difficult areas of broadcasting"— viz., children's programs, Australian content, and advertising—the tribunal believed that it should continue to establish and regulate requirements for stations' performance. Two years after the publication of the report these recommendations had not been implemented, and the tribunal's powers in relation to commercial and public broadcasters had not been clarified.

Politics and the Media

The discussion to date has been concerned with the nature of the mass media in Australia and the impact that government controls and regulations have had on their activities. We come now to an examination both of the media's impact on government and the manner in which they are used by government. An immediate distinction needs to be made between information systems which relate to the Parliament and the government in power at any particular point in time, and information systems which the public service or bureaucracy employ for the dissemination of material to the Parliament and to the public at large. In the discussion which follows, this distinction will be kept in mind.

GOVERNMENT INFORMATION SYSTEMS

A significant proportion of the energy expended by Australian state and federal politicians is directed towards securing what they judge to be a favourable and adequate media coverage. In this endeavour, they typically employ three main methods: press conferences, press statements, and leaks. All three methods are employed because of the tight control they allow. That is to say, employing these methods, the politician dictates the timing, structure, and the substance of any information released, and subsequently allows journalists only limited opportunities to assess and interpret the divulged material. Nevertheless, the success of these techniques can vary according to whether state or national politics are involved; whether news from other sources is light or heavy at a particular time; and whether particular relationships have been established between politicians and journalists, or the management of the information source for which they work.

Rosenbloom (1978) in *Politics and the Media* suggests that the present Australian Prime Minister, Malcolm Fraser, shows signs of enjoying a special relationship with the News Limited group of newspapers. He grants the group exclusive stories, adopts policies of which they approve, and in return is favoured with friendly news presentation and editorial support. However, Rosenbloom also points out that the most carefully planned information release can disappear without any public sighting if more important news develops simultaneously.

The distinction between state and national politics is also important. State governments in the Australian context are very large fish in relatively small ponds. They possess extensive local power and high local authority. Large organizations, including the media, typically ally themselves with such power centres. This may not always ensure the party in power a favourable press, but it invariably ensures it a vehicle for the dissemination of information. As Peter Blazey shows in his 1972 biography of Henry Bolte, a long-serving premier of the state of Victoria in the 1950s and 1960s, the premier used the media very cleverly and with very considerable effect. He used press conferences to create news, to float ideas, to receive feed-back, and to reinforce his authority. The members of the press who attended Bolte's regular conferences effectively became accomplices in the maintenance of his political power.

The situation is more difficult at the national level. There are more diverse interests involved, power is spread more diffusely, and political pressures are greater. An instructive contrast can be drawn between the information systems developed and utilized by Gough Whitlam, who in 1972 became the first Labor Prime Minister in 23 years, and that currently employed by Malcolm Frazer, who succeeded Whitlam in 1975 with the return of a conservative national government.

Whitlam was committed to a policy of information release which came to be known as "open government." As part of this policy, Rosenbloom (1978) recounts, Whitlam held regular and frequent press conferences: however, as time passed, these became less regular, less frequent, and less informative. This was principally because they provided the journalists in attendance with too much freedom. Conferences became a venue for the expression of opposition and dissent, and for the scrutiny of potentially embarrassing government activity. Both the questions and the responses guaranteed a media coverage of areas which the government would have preferred to face in private. Eventually the political costs of this situation became too great to bear.

As a second arm of his "open government," Whitlam allowed each of his 26 cabinet ministers to appoint press secretaries. Their job was to draft or rewrite press statements, speeches, and articles, to give advice on the media's likely response to policy proposals, to supply information to the media, and to persuade the media of the merits of particular ministers. Press secretaries' jobs became important and powerful. They could control media access to ministers, and they could contribute to policy making by the manner in which they drafted press releases. They could also elicit favourable coverage for their ministers by establishing good personal relationships with the Canberra Press Gallery (comprised of those political journalists resident in the national capital whose job it is to transmit the business of government to the public).

The system, however, soon floundered. The multitude of press secretaries, most of them trying to promote their own minister, created a media log-jam. The media found it virtually impossible to digest the political information with which they were bombarded from numerous quarters. In addition, ministers competed with each other for media coverage and, inevitably, important initiatives were sometimes buried beneath a range of trivia. Eventually, press secretaries were brought under control of the Prime Minister's office, and their number significantly reduced. These two lessons—the dangers inherent in frequent and regular press conferences, and the uncoordinated activities of a multitude of press secretaries—were not lost on Malcolm Fraser when he succeeded Whitlam as Australian Prime Minister.

Since his election, Fraser has proved to be far more selective than a number of his predecessors in the release of information. He gives press conferences rarely, and has prevented all but a few of his senior ministers from hiring press secretaries. He conducts selective background briefings with journalists, keeps in close contact with the major media proprietors, and exercises clearly greater control over the supply and release of information than have previous Prime Ministers. Rosenbloom (1978) argues that this has led Fraser to largely bypass formal channels of information release in favour of informal ones; and this has led him to the third strategy of information release—leaks.

What is a leak? There is no satisfactory dictionary definition, but it has been described as a nonattributable, unofficial, and selective disclosure of information (Rosenbloom, 1978). Essentially, it is a means of disclosing information which would otherwise be withheld or supplied in a different form. Leaks take various forms. Usually sources make disclosures via the telephone; they may provide confidential documents or an authoritative explanation, or report on policy. "Information can be leaked in spite or with pride; it can be aimed at promoting a cause or undermining an individual; and it can be the expression of conscientious dissent, or it can be the outcome of manipulative cunning. A leak can cause a planned result, or undreamed-of chaos; it can destroy its target, or rebound on its source; and it can help the source's enemies, or harm his friends." Leaks typically do not stay within party political boundaries. Backbench members of the Parliament may leak against each other or against their ministers. Ministers may leak against each other or against the Prime Minister. Leaks are clearly weapons in the struggle for power, during which all combatants perceive the media as a crucial resource.

During the period of the Labor government, leaks occurred from most of the organs of government: from the bureaucracy, the backbench of the government, the ministry, and the Labor Caucus. All supplied a steady stream of unauthorised information to the Canberra Press Gallery. The situation has changed somewhat with the return of the conservative government under Malcolm Fraser, but leaks still provide a significant source of information to the public.

It will be clear from the above account that the parliamentary information systems we have briefly described are, to a large extent, informal and importantly dependent on the style and philosophy of the government in power. There is little in the way of institutionalised channels of communication and much depends on the nature of the relationship that is established between the government and the Canberra Press Gallery. The situation as far as state and federal government bureaucracies are concerned is more complex. There is, perhaps, a somewhat greater degree of institutionalisation of information channels, and there is considerable discussion at the present time concerning the public's "right to know."

A recent (1976) Royal Commission on Australian government administration generally emphasised the need for wider public access to information in the possession of government agencies. The issue is not a simple one, however, for governments and their officials frequently insist that they must restrict public access to information they hold, for a number of reasons: on the grounds of national security, to protect the privacy of individuals, to respect confidence placed in them, and to permit and facilitate effective working of the administrative machine.

The proponents of open access, on the other hand, have emphasised that governments operate essentially for and on behalf of citizens, and that they function better when minimum restrictions are imposed on access to the information they hold, and that openness promotes an aware and participatory democracy. The commissioners concluded that "while there is no simple solution to the problems of determining what can properly be withheld, the general sentiment and expectations of the community have been changing consistently in the direction of requiring more openness and access to information gathered and held in the administration."

Nevertheless, it remains difficult to determine just where the right of access of information should stop. Interdepartmental committees set up to develop proposals for freedom of information legislation, consistent with the Westminister style system, have frequently argued for a large number of exemptions from disclosure and also for the reservation to cabinet ministers of the final responsibility for disclosure of certain categories of information.

An alternative approach argues that government departments should be obliged to maintain and publish lists, indices, etc., of the material they hold, and to provide information on request (subject to specified exemption); and that decisions to refuse access should be subject to review by the Administrative Appeals Tribunal.

The three major sources of information within the Australian bureaucracy are the Bureau of Statistics (a federal statutory authority), the National Library (a similar authority), and the Australian Archives. Libraries in Australia are currently experiencing rapid development, both in integration and in the use of more sophisticated techniques. The National Library has been responsible for linking libraries in an Information Service, focusing on the National Library. The Australian Archives is charged with providing access for those within and outside the administration to papers no longer in current use in government departments. Because of the content of the papers, access to this is less readily obtainable than to papers held by the National Library and by other libraries.

In reviewing the activities of the Bureau of Statistics, the National Library, and the Australian Archives, the Royal Commission has concluded that Australia lacks a coherent policy and strategy for the information function generally. They suggested that consideration be given to establishing a Commonwealth Information Advisory Council, with an independent chairman, and which should include representatives from community users of the information held by the Commonwealth government. Other members of the council would be the Australian Government Statistician, the Director-General of the National Library, the Director-General of Archives, a member of the Public Service Board, and representatives of government departments. The primary purpose of the council would be to advise the Commonwealth government on the development of a comprehensive information policy, to review significant technological developments, and to provide a forum for consultation between specialist agencies.

At a more micro level, many government departments and authorities have already established units to provide information for community use. A survey conducted by the Royal Commission revealed that 28 government departments had specially designated information sections, and a further 5 were planning to establish such sections. These sections which employ some 800 people, and whose direct costs appear to be over 50 million dollars Australian per year, are concerned with the publication of material for distribution, while the content of the material is determined by the department or agency. However, the commission concluded that much of this activity appeared to lack a clear objective or programme, and only 13 of the departments reporting the presence of an information section had sponsored or undertaken systematic assessment of the effects of the programmes they ran.

The commission concluded that it doubted the value of much of this department sponsored work. Its relevance to the information needs of the public and its cost effectiveness could be seriously questioned. If it were to be continued, the commissioners saw a clear need for its control by information specialists (rather than predominantly by journalists, as at the present time). The commission also examined departmental relationships with the media. They were of the view that departments should keep their relations with the media separate from publications and publicity.

In general, it would appear that while the importance of a well-developed government information system is recognised, very little has been done to implement such a system on a formal basis within the administrative structure of the federal government. The situation as far as Australian state governments are concerned is even less developed; and the information that is available on the activities of such state-based systems is meagre indeed.

MEDIA IMPACT ON GOVERNMENT

An uneasy truce exists between most levels of government in Australia and the mass media. Politicians of all political persuasions on numerous occasions have complained about bias in media reporting of their parties' activities. In the first of a series of articles in the Melbourne *Age* following the defeat of the Labor Government in 1975, the then Mr. Billy Snedden (who had been the leader of the Liberal/National party opposition and who was to become the Speaker of the House in the new Parliament) had the following to say: "I have no doubt that the media can divert, subvert, or obstruct the individual's judgment of daily politics. An impossible proposal can be presented as an inspired initiative. A reformation of thinking can be stupid or brave, depending on how the media see it."

The following day, David Coombes, the national secretary of the Australian Labor party, claimed that "last year the Australian press allowed itself to be used to destroy in mid-term, a legitimately elected Labor government. The press abandoned its integrity to set the Labor government up for destruction." And later on in the article he says: "what was unprecedented was the way the press used its news columns to campaign against the Labor government. Normal ethical standards were set aside as rumor was reported as fact. Facts were deliberately distorted and argument was suppressed."

Commenting on the same period, in the third of the series of articles, Professor W. McMahon Ball, Emeritus Professor of Political Science at the University of Melbourne, made the following point: "The defeat of the Whitlam government was due, not only to direct experience of economic hardship, but to the picture the media has given of the government's performance over three years." But he then goes on to say that in his judgment, most political news reports, in most of the Australian newspapers and for most of the time, are fair and accurate.

Both at the level of informed and uninformed opinion, there is a widely held view in the community that the media have significant impact on government. In a recent seminar arranged by the Royal Institute of Public Administration (Nicolson and Stokes, 1974), questions of the role of the mass media in the 70s and their impact on public administration were addressed. Again, the views expressed were variable. Media representatives, not unexpectedly, argued that a balanced account of government affairs was typically presented. Alternatively, representatives of government, specifically at the local level, argued that it was frequently difficult to get their message across to the public in the terms they would like to see it expressed.

In the course of the recent Royal Commission on Australian Government Administration, Geoffrey Allen, a political scientist from Melbourne University, was asked to prepare a study on press attitudes toward the public service. In addition, the Commission's Adviser on Community Relations, Max Bourke, wrote to leading newspaper editors seeking their views on government-press relations (1976).

The interchange between Bourke and the late editor of the Melbourne *Age*, Graham Perkin, the most highly regarded newspaper editor in Australia at that time, is worth reporting in some detail. Bourke wrote to Perkin in the following terms:

> As you are aware, quite a deal of money and effort is expended by government departments in producing information for the press. Most departments or authorities have press officers and produce voluminous press releases. Many of these have been described as "apologia" and of little value or benefit to the press.
>
> But the real issue, for which I am seeking your assistance, is this.
>
> The cost/benefit of providing services to the Press can only be measured if the press plays a significant social role in relation to the administration, in other words, if it really does function as the "fourth estate." To my knowledge only one newspaper, and no electronic media at all, has a roundsman actively covering the "administration" as distinct from the

"government" (a fine but important distinction I feel).

Certainly much information is fed unofficially to Canberra journalists by bureaucrats, and certainly much of that information is used.

But from the point of view (my own) of a journalist turned bureaucrat I feel not only is a great deal missed, but equally a great deal is actively "covered up." I admit that Canberra is a "closed society" where, according to foreign correspondents, it is much more difficult to get straight answers than Japan, Canada, or the United States.

However, unless an active coverage of the government administration is undertaken, it is unlikely that this will improve. . . .

My basic question then is: "If the assumptions above are correct, what can be done about it?"

Perkin replied:

Let me begin by disagreeing with two of the propositions you make. It is true that one paper only (*The Canberra Times*) regularly assigns a reporter to what one might call "covering the public service." Yet several other papers (*The Age, The Financial Review*) do make serious efforts to report the administration which is, as you suggest, a different thing from reporting government. And I would *not* argue that the economics of the industry stand in the path of employing specialist journalists for that task, or any other. If one felt the effort would be rewarding, in terms of news, or useful in terms of community service, then there would be no hesitation in appointing someone to the job.

The real problem is that our experiments with such a specialist assignment have been frustrating and pointless—largely because the public service, no less than governments, has become so public-relations oriented. . . .

You observe, and I agree, that there are numerous informal and productive contracts between public servants and the press which work to everyone's advantage. Yet successive governments, with the active help of administrators, have produced a quite terrifying public relations apparatus that seems to me largely counter-productive. I would not argue that the press is blameless in this. The press has acquiesced; it has let the process take place without complaint; it has done an inadequate job in walking around the formalised P.R. machine and exposing the problems the machine exists to hide.

I would not like to over-emphasise these points. I am not sure, for example, that I agree with your assertion that Canberra is "a closed society" even by comparison with Tokyo, Washington, or Ottawa. It could certainly, with advantage, be more open than it is, but I do not really think it is more difficult to get a straight answer in Canberra than in other capitals. Circumstances vary from department to department. There are, for example, several departments which are exceedingly frank and open. . . . I do not think it accidental that these departments . . . enjoy higher public regard than some others.

You ask: what can be done about it? That is the hard bit. Several things occur to me:

1. It would be enormously productive, from the community's point of view, if the higher echelons of the public service were more frequently—even privately—exposed to the higher echelons of the press. There might have to be some selectivity, for I would no more plead equal virtue for all the press than you would plead the same for public servants. But it is simply pointless to attack the press for ignorance, for lack of understanding, for lack of balance, if the only contact a permanent head and his principal assistants have with the press is through a P.R. man and a reporter. Foreign Affairs sends all our principal ambassadors, who are on home leave, in to my editorial conference for a background briefing on high policy. . . . Yet what happened to the other departments? In nine years as Editor . . . I can recall only one or two other senior public servants taking the trouble to spread a little intelligence. . . .

2. It would be productive if someone cut a swathe through the P.R. apparatus of the departments. Most of them are a joke, both professionally and spiritually. Some, of course, are not a joke. In the main, they exist to protect the performance of the inefficient from the attentions of the indolent—and they do not perform that task too well either. . . . If the Australian public service would cross its heart and decide that the volume of "Press releases" is to be cut by half, then we might all get more information.

3. It would be productive if something could be done about accessibility of senior administrators. They are seriously, even gravely, inaccessible now. . . .

4. Which leaves the press itself. If there was the slightest sign that administrators were interested in exposing administrations to the public gaze, I believe there would be a response. Although I can speak only for myself, I would certainly respond. I am sure there would be abuses, tensions, and difficulties, but if we could keep communications open at high levels, I believe the process would be beneficial in the long run.

5. I hope I have written nothing which would give you the slightest inkling of an impending truce between the public service and the press. That would be a disaster. I regard it as one of the press' greatest responsibilities to keep public administration under constant test and examination. The simple fact of your letter suggests you accept that proposition. This comforts me.

The complexities of the interrelationship are well brought out in this exchange. Allen's enquiry was a little more broadly based, being perhaps what was the first systematic examination of the relationship between the media and government instrumentalities. Allen suggests in the introduction to his paper, the following: "As a broad generalisation it can be said that there is a state of mutual hostility and distrust existing between working journalists and public servants, although relations between the Australian Public Service and the press are better than those of the services of most state governments" (1976).

Allen interviewed both journalists and public servants and got from both a variable view on the relationship between the public service and the media. He reports that most journalists he interviewed felt that, apart from a few notable individual exceptions, public servants regarded media approaches as bothersome intrusions on their work preoccupations and, consequently, responded with unreasonable caution and suspicion. From the other side, he reports complaints from public servants that, although a great deal of information that the public ought to know is provided to journalists, it never gets into the media. Additionally, public servants complain that journalists frequently do not "stick to the facts"; rather they offer interpretations which are frequently seen as misleading. Again, it is claimed that newspapers in particular, and also television, tend to over-simplify and sensationalise.

The most common complaint he found, however, was the public service view that journalists were unable to understand issues in depth and report them back accurately. Allen judges these complaints as well placed and sees a basic reason for them lying in the lack of training, experience, and maturity of journalists reporting on political and governmental affairs. Australian journalism, he argues, lacks a professional orientation; for it is only recently that there has been a shift from a craft to a professional career basis for journalists, and only recently have university qualifications become a virtual prerequisite for Canberra reporters.

Both state and federal governments have recently become aware of the need to improve information flows between government and the community; and they are increasingly looking to the press to fulfill an important public function in this regard. A great deal of money is being spent on the build-up of media sections of departments and on an escalation in the volume of reports and documented materials. But there is still the view, quite commonly expressed by journalists in Canberra, particularly, which suggests that "the public service is not serious about developing relations with the media." It is still conservative and straightjacketed by the Crimes Act, the Public Service Act, and regulations.

Since Federation, secrecy restrictions have applied to the state and federal public services; and these, perhaps more than anything else, have conditioned the manner in which government officials respond to the media. The explicit restrictions on employees of the Australian public service have come via two main statutes—one is Section 70 of the Crimes Act, which reads as follows:

> A person who being a Commonwealth officer, publishes or communicates, except to some person to whom he is authorised to publish or communicate it, any fact or document which comes to his knowledge, or into his possession by virtue of his office, and which it is his duty not to disclose, shall be guilty of an offence.

The other specific source of restriction comprises two public service regulations:

> An officer shall not (a) use for any purpose other than for the discharge of his official duties, information gained by or conveyed to him through his connection with the service, or (b) publicly comment upon any administrative action or upon the administration of any department, provided that nothing in this paragraph shall prevent an officer resident in any territory within the Commonwealth, from publicly commenting upon civic affairs relating to that territory.
>
> Except in the course of official duties, no information concerning public business, or any matter of which an officer or employee has knowledge officially, shall be given, directly or indirectly, nor shall the contents of official papers be disclosed by an officer or an employee without the express authority of the chief officer.

In the past, the above section of the statute and these public service regulations have been interpreted strictly. There is, however, as we have suggested in this section, some gradual move away from the secrecy which has characterised public service communication with the public since the time of Federation. Nevertheless, the provisions just described still influence and colour the manner in which the media and the public service relate. The uneasy truce that we spoke of at the beginning of this section is likely to remain a characteristic of the Australian situation for some time to come.

Conclusion

Serious study of the media has been a relatively neglected area of work in Australia until quite recently. Writing in 1971, Western and Hughes could say "Australian sociology and political science have been tardy in studying the role of the mass media in Australian society and politics (and) there exists no substantial research tradition comparable with that found in the United States or even Britain." However, since that was written and particularly since the political upheaval of 1975 (Note 1), interest in the structure and regulation of the country's media outlets has greatly increased: no doubt the widespread criticism of the role played by the media in the events precipitating the crisis in government in 1975 has contributed to the broader attention now afforded media affairs in Australia.

As witness to this fact in the past three years there has been published a history of television in Australia (Hall, 1976), a textbook on the structure and social impact of the media (Barr, 1977), two privately commissioned works on government regulation of the newspaper and broadcasting industries (Wiltshire and Stokes, 1976, 1977), a study of the major media organizations in Australia (McQueen, 1977), and an account of the relationship between government and the media since 1972 (Rosenbloom, 1978). In addition, further studies are underway (Edgar, in press; Western and Hughes, forthcoming) which examine the relationship between the media and government and the picture of government activities that the media provides.

There is, of course, much still to be done. Not a great deal is known about the characteristics of the members of the Canberra Press Gallery, the group of journalists responsible for getting news of government affairs to the public; little is known also about their professional philosophies and values. Likewise, there has to date been only one small study of media executives. Some detailed work on the nature of news content has been undertaken and more is underway, but in this area again more work needs to be done. Given the concentration of the mass media in the Australian situation, this question is clearly of critical importance. The case has been well put by the London *Economist:* "the right to inform the public of the facts of the day and to express opinions about them is one of the safeguards of freedom: and a society in which this right becomes increasingly circumscribed for economic reasons forfeits one of the distinctions that set it apart from societies where the same right is curtailed by political power." The Royal Commission on Australian Government Administration provided some preliminary data on government information systems and the impact of the media on government, but in this area too a great deal more work is clearly necessary before a proper appreciation of media government relationships can be obtained.

Communication is one of the fundamental characteristics of any social system, and a media system of public communication is one of the factors distinguishing a "traditional" from a so-called "developed" society. In media systems the main flow of public information comes from professional communications selected according to skill criteria whose job it is to transmit messages of largely descriptive content through impersonal media to relatively undifferentiated mass audiences. The power of this media to inform, influence, and persuade is undisputed. What continually needs to be redetermined is the nature and patterning of information that the media provides, and the impact this has on the audience to which it is directed.

It is clear that governments are both the transmitters and recipients of information and so may influence and be influenced. We have discussed in broad outline some of the parameters of this interactive process, but, for Australia, a great many of the details still need to be provided.

GOVERNMENT AND THE NEWS MEDIA

Reference Notes

1. In late 1972 the first Labor government in Australia of 23 years was elected with a majority in the lower house of Parliament. However, the Liberal-National Country opposition retained control of the upper house, the Senate. Towards the end of 1975 the Senate would not allow passage of the budget, and the government, refusing to resign, was dismissed by the unelected Head of State, the Governor-General. In the subsequent election the Liberal-National Country parties formed a new coalition government with majorities in both houses of Parliament.

References

Allen, G. & Bourke, M. "The Press and the Public Service." In *Royal Commission on Australian Government Administration Report* Appendix (Vol. 2). Canberra; Australian Government Publishing Service, 1976.

Australian Broadcasting Control Board. *Australian Content in Television.* Melbourne: 1976.

Australian Broadcasting Tribunal. *Self-Regulation for Broadcasters? A Report of the Public Inquiry into the Concept of Self-Regulation for Australian Broadcasters.* Canberra: Australian Government Publishing Service, 1977.

Barr, T. *Reflections of Reality: The Media in Australia.* Adelaide: Rigby, 1977.

Blazey, P. B. *Bolte: a Political Biography.* Brisbane: Jacaranda Press, 1972.

Cohen, B. C. *The Press and Foreign Policy.* Princeton: Princeton University Press, 1963.

Cole, B. G. "What's Really Preventing the Expansion of Broadcasting Services?" *The Australian Quarterly,* 1966, *38* (3), 72-87.

Edgar, P. *The Politics of the Press.* Melbourne: Macmillan, in press.

Hall, S. *Supertoy: Twenty Years of Australian Television.* Melbourne: Sun Books, 1976.

Holden, W. A. *Australia Goes to Press.* Detroit: Wayne University Press, 1961.

Horne, D. *The Lucky Country.* Sydney: Angus and Robertson, 1966.

Hughes, C. A. and Western, J. S. "The Geographic Source of Foreign News in Australian Newspapers." *Australian Outlook,* 1973, *27,* 86-97.

Hughes, C. A. and Western, J. S. "Geographic Sources of Domestic News." *Politics,* 1974, *9,* 166-172.

Hudson, W. J. Metropolitan Daily Journalism in Australia. Unpublished master's thesis, University of Melbourne, 1963.

Hudson, W. J. "Status of the Metropolitan Daily Journalist in Australia." *Australian Journal of Social Issues,* 1964, *2,* 33-45.

Hudson, W. J. "Occupational Characteristics of Journalism." *Proceedings of the First Summer School of Professional Journalism.* Canberra: Federal Capital Press, 1965.

Inglis, K. S. "The Daily Papers," In P. Coleman (Ed.), *Australian Civilization.* Melbourne: Cheshire, 1962.

Mayer, H. *The Press in Australia.* Melbourne: Lansdowne, 1964.

McQueen, H. *Australia's Media Monopolies.* Camberwell: Widescope, 1977.

Nicolson, I. F. & Stokes, C. H. *Mass Media in the Seventies.* Brisbane: Royal

Institute of Public Administration, 1974.

Nixon, R. B. & Hahn, T. Y. "Concentration of Press Ownership: A Comparison of Thirty-Two Countries." *Journalism Quarterly*, 1971, 48, 5-16.

Postal and Telecommunications Department. *Australian Broadcasting: a Report on the Structure of the Australian Broadcasting System and Associated Matters.* Canberra: Australian Government Publishing Service, 1976.

Report from the Select Committee on the Encouragement of Australian Productions for Television. (Chairman: V. S. Vincent), Parliamentary Paper No. 304, 1963.

Rosenbloom, H. *Politics and the Media.* Melbourne: Scribe, 1978.

Royal Commission on Australian Government Administration Report. Canberra: Australian Government Publishing Service, 1976.

Schramm, W. "Communication and Change." In D. Lerner and W. Schramm (Eds.), *Communication and Change in Developing Countries.* Honolulu: East-West Centre Press, 1967.

Sommerlad, E. D. *Mightier Than the Sword.* Sydney: Angus and Robertson, 1950.

Sparrow, G. *Crusade for Journalism.* Melbourne: Wilke, 1960.

Williams, F. *The Right to Know.* London: Longman, 1969.

Wiltshire, K. W. & Stokes, C. H. "Government Regulation and the Commercial Electronic Media." *Committee for Economic Development of Australia,* (Monograph, M. Series No. 43) Melbourne: March, 1976.

Wiltshire, K. W. & Stokes, C. H. "Government Regulation and the Printed Media Industry." *Committee for Economic Development of Australia.* (Monograph M. Series No. 50) Melbourne: July, 1977.

VII.
Canadian Media and the National Imperative

Anthony Westell and Carman Cumming

Canadians, living in communities stretched thinly along 4,000 miles of border with the United States and divided into English- and French-speaking groups, have always assumed that they needed strong systems of national communications if they were to sustain a claim to identity and nationhood. The creation of systems running east and west to tie the country together, instead of north and south to link Canadian regions with their U.S. neighbors, has required government leadership, protection, and sometimes subsidy. Government has in fact been involved in almost every area of communications, and this gives a distinctive cast to relations between journalists and government. There has always been, and remains today, a tension between the national imperative calling for government leadership in developing communications and the libertarian view that the less government has to do with the media the better.

This traditional tension has been complicated in recent years by a new and less understood debate about the emergence of the media as a separate power in society, in competition with political authorities, and having increasing influence over national directions and values. The essence of this critical view is that the media trivialize politics by reducing serious issues to personality conflicts, allow themselves to be manipulated by politicians able to serve their need for entertainment, and emerge as a destabilizing factor in a society in which the preservation of unity and sovereignty is always precarious (Westell, 1977; Cumming, 1977). This public and private criticism of the power of media runs headlong into the new view which many journalists have of themselves, as the real opposition to government in a parliamentary system which has lost its checks and balances.

Relations between government and media are constantly changing, and it is difficult to understand, let alone describe, the current situation. A longer perspective is needed. But it does appear that while government is becoming more deeply involved in the development and regula-

tion of media institutions, journalists are more independent than they
have ever been.

   Most Canadians see no contradiction in endorsing the ideals of a free
and independent press (ideals drawn partly from American free enterprise and partly from British libertarian thought) while calling for more
government intervention to stem the American cultural invasion.

Historical Developments in Government—News Media Relations

   Lest this pattern be taken simply as a sign of current nationalism, it is
important to show how pervasive it has been in Canada's history. As
American scholar James Carey (1975, p. 27) has noted, in a slightly
different context, cultural penetration that is seen by Americans as
simply a matter of freedom of trade and freedom of information is
viewed quite differently by Canadians. The country's most basic system of national communication, the railways and their accompanying
telegraph wires, was built only with huge public subsidies. The railway
telegraphs made possible the national wire service, and the Canadian
Press was given direct federal aid for several years after it was set up in
1917 (Nichols, 1948; Harkness, 1963, pp. 98-99). When movies, radio,
and television arrived, Americans in each case got into the field earlier
and on a scale so massive that it would have been almost unthinkable
for Canadian private industries to compete without stimulation and/or
protection. U.S. dominance of radio in the 1920s, for instance, was so
acute that a Toronto newspaper poll at one point showed the 17 most
popular stations in the city were all American (Peers, 1969, p. 20). It
was natural for liberals, conservatives, and radicals to unite in support
of a public broadcasting agency, designed to develop a "single system"
for the whole country in which private broadcasting would exist only at
the local edges. Television in the 1950s evolved in a similar pattern. The
private broadcasters were by that time strong enough to make sure they
would have more than a minor role, but they, too, were at once coddled
and curbed by public control. On the one hand they were assured of
partial or total local monopolies, while on the other hand they were
required to live with regulations that included, among other things,
minimum Canadian content standards. In films, under the overpower-
ing influence of Hollywood, Canada's tiny industry was tied even more
closely to government apron strings, first through the National Film
Board and later through the Canadian Film Development Corporation, a

financing agency. In each case, fear of American domination was not the only factor. Canadians were strongly influenced as well by a British view of broadcasting and films that put stress on educational and "high culture" values as opposed to more popular entertainment. But the national imperative predominated.

Canada's newspapers and magazines were never so strongly protected or subsidized, but even they did not entirely escape the paternalistic impulse. For newspapers, there was a long tradition of party ties that meant patronage in the form of government advertising, government appointments, and other favors, as well as easy postal rates and exclusion of foreign ownership. For magazines, barriers were set up to prevent a spillover of Canadian editions of American magazines. While these public policies are easy to show, it is much more difficult to trace and evaluate the nature and degree of government influence.

THE PARTISAN TRADITION

Certainly it is striking, in reviewing development of press-government relations, to note how strong and pervasive the party ties were just a few decades ago, and how long they continued in disguised form after they were no longer respectable. If one looks back to the end of the last century, the extent of party control seems almost humiliating. For instance, Sir John Willison (1919), parliamentary writer and later editor of the Liberal Toronto *Globe* in the 1880s and 1890s, tells of deliberately slanting coverage, of asking permission from party figures to write stories, and of being "reproached and condemned" (p. 125) by the party's disciplinary committee for being too kind to a Conservative. And the *Globe* was not merely a party organ; it also served to disseminate party propaganda through a network of smaller papers. Party control was so close that when Willison, on one occasion, was invited to dinner by a Conservative minister, he found it so amazing as to require authorization from head office. "I telegraphed the *Globe* and was assured that acceptance would not be treated as betrayal of the opposition" (p. 123). In the same era, parliamentary reporter Fred Cook (1934) of the Toronto *Empire,* which was directly controlled by the Conservative party, was at one point cut off from government information until his paper hastily corrected an editorial line displeasing to the cabinet. The party control was backed up, as research by Norman Ward (1976) shows, by hard cash, as well as by a long tradition of publisher involvement in politics.

The most blatant aspects of partisanship began to disappear around the start of this century. Willison himself took a leading part in the change, by moving the *Globe* toward a more neutral stance. But the connections remained intact. Arthur Ford (1950), later editor of the London (Ont.) *Free Press,* recalled that as late as 1911 reporters in the Parliamentary Press Gallery were seated according to party. Liberals were on one side of the Speaker, and Conservatives on the other; when a new government came in, the reporters switched seats along with the politicians. "If there were any independent papers in those days they were assigned to the tail end of the gallery," Ford wrote. "They did not count" (pp. 225-226). Charles Bowman (1966, pp. 4-5), later editor of the Ottawa *Citizen,* recalled that his first column for the paper, in 1913, raised an immediate threat that the paper would be stricken from the government's patronage list.

All memoirs of the time make clear that news itself was treated as a form of patronage. Ford (p. 43) says opposition reporters could get government news only through friendly colleagues on the other team or through "underground" sources. Paul Bilkey (1940), who arrived on the Press Gallery in 1903 and spent about 14 years there as a Conservative reporter before becoming editor of the Montreal *Gazette,* gave a similar picture, but added that there were advantages to being on the outside. While the government reporter was "bound and gagged," the opposition reporter had much more latitude. "By putting two and two together, he could upon occasion beat the Liberal side of the Gallery at its own game, and if he was only nearly right it was good enough" (p. 49).

Most accounts of the time also agree that the First World War brought a sharp change in style. For one thing, wartime unity became an over-riding concern, and for another, Liberal newspapers in English Canada broke with the party's French-Canadian leader, Sir Wilfrid Laurier, when he refused to back conscription. More profoundly, wartime meant death or mergers for many newspapers (Rutherford, 1978, pp. 48-53). The remaining papers were not only economically stronger, but found themselves selling to both Liberal and Conservative readers, and hence began to see practical virtues in a neutral stance.

Behind the scenes, though, two aspects of the partisan tradition remained: the system of rewards for good journalistic behavior and the tradition of using journalists as political aides, mediators, fixers and informants. Grattan O'Leary (1977, pp. 44-45), later editor of the Ottawa *Journal* and still later appointed a Conservative Senator, told of being assigned by the paper in 1921 to accompany Prime Minister Arthur Meighen to London—partly as a journalist and partly as an aide—and of how he suppressed a major story that would have embarrassed the Prime Minister. Charles Bowman (pp. 83-85) recalled one occasion in the late 1920s when he helped to rally Liberal members for a crucial Commons vote, and another instance when he set up an important meeting between Prime Minister W. L. Mackenzie King and a pair of opposition M.P.s who held a pivotal voting position in the Commons. Bowman served as a "public relations member" of the Canadian delegation to the 1926 Imperial Conference and also was a member of the Aird commission on broadcasting a couple of years later (p. 121). Hector Charlesworth (1937), editor of *Saturday Night* magazine when Conservative Prime Minister R. B. Bennett came to office in 1930, told of going to Bennett for advice on an exposé he planned on the insurance industry. Bennett cautioned against the planned approach, "and needless to say his advice was accepted" (pp. 25-26). A few months later, Charlesworth was appointed head of the first public broadcasting agency, the Canadian Radio-Broadcasting Commission, predecessor to the CBC.

These anecdotes can be seriously misleading, though, if they leave simply a picture of a slavish and well-managed press corps. The other side of the partisan tradition was that journalists often fought against party policy, from within, and had a strong voice in shaping party directions. The outstanding journalistic figure of the interwar years, John W. Dafoe, editor of the Manitoba (later Winnipeg) *Free Press*, exerted powerful personal influence on the Liberal party, both through his editorials and through a Liberal thinkers' group in Winnipeg dubbed the Sanhedrin (Cook, 1963). Dafoe's correspondent in Ottawa, Grant Dexter, was both a leading journalist and an ambassador from the West to be reckoned with. Henri Bourassa sat in Parliament for a time as a Liberal member, but his Montreal newspaper, *Le Devoir*, reflected passionately his own point of view and established a model of journalistic independence and integrity. Joseph Atkinson, as publisher of the Toronto *Star*, fought a classic battle to separate his paper from Liberal party control and was in many ways a highly original and independent journalist. Yet it was not inconsistent for Atkinson to write, in 1921, an apology to Mackenzie King for a "less than friendly" article written by the paper's Ottawa correspondent, John A. Stevenson (Harkness, 1963, p. 122). Said Atkinson: "Nothing of an unsympathetic character about you should appear in *The Star* as though it represents the paper's viewpoint, or the opinion of its special representatives." When Mackenzie King tried to have Stevenson fired, Atkinson resisted—but certainly did not make a public issue of it. Nor was it inconsistent for Atkinson in

1929 to advise a new Ottawa correspondent, Wilfrid Eggleston (1968, p. 154), that *The Star* remained "broadly a Liberal paper," and that differences between the paper and the party should be discussed in a way that did not harm the party.

Mackenzie King dominated Canadian politics for much of the era from the end of the First World War until the late 1940s, and it is not surprising that his political hegemony to some degree extended to the press. Journalists of the era recall prime ministerial press conferences that in retrospect seem mild to the point of unctuousness—placid encounters in which the Prime Minister released official news but frowned on any attempt by reporters to raise other issues. Arthur Ford (pp. 176-177) reports that when King visited President Roosevelt in Washington during the Second World War, he refused to meet reporters. The only explanation Canadian officials could give was that "he was actually nervous over meeting a brigade of keen and alert American newspapermen." Ford also makes clear that King was not above reminding reporters subtly that the path of good behavior could lead to the ultimate reward: a lifetime appointment to the Senate. On one occasion King announced such an appointment at a Toronto meeting the reporter in question was attending, without telling him in advance. The action could scarcely help but stir fantasies in the minds of other badly paid journalists.

The generally tractable style of journalists before and during the Second World War does not seem to have been affected significantly by the arrival of radio. Neither the CRBC, formed in 1932, nor the successor CBC, created by Mackenzie King's Liberals in 1936, engaged with any great vitality in news of public affairs programming. The CBC did not even set up its own news service until forced to do so by wartime pressures, relying until then on The Canadian Press (Peers, 1969, p. 344). Radio commentators on public affairs were usually newspaper personalities with connections and obligations arising from their primary careers. And they were evidently chosen with an eye to safety in whatever political climate existed at the time. This, too, was a mixed picture, however. Frank Peers (1969), in his detailed study of the early development of Canadian broadcasting, tells a story of gradual emancipation of public broadcasting from government influence (an emancipation set back in wartime, when the CBC became almost a propaganda arm). And as in newspapers, the emancipation reflected at least in part a rising sense of professionalism among reporters.

The nature of the change, as well as the remaining elements of control, can perhaps best be shown in the views of three leading journalists who looked back from the perspective of the mid-50s to assess how journalism had changed. The three are Eggleston and Stevenson, the former Toronto *Star* reporters introduced earlier, and George Ferguson, who like the other two was respected as an independent-minded journalist despite connections with pro-Liberal papers, as managing editor of the Winnipeg *Free Press* and editor of the Montreal *Star*.

Writing in 1955, Ferguson spoke of a growing sense of responsibility among journalists but conceded the press was still largely reactionary in tone.

> Ownership of the press does rest in the hands of the rich and well-to-do, and the opinions expressed in it, as distinct from the facts it contains are, broadly speaking, right wing in character. Sometimes, indeed, the facts are, too. . . .
>
> In the other big media of communication, radio and television, the broad picture is not dissimilar. Expression of opinion by the extreme left is hardly to be found, but generally speaking most other views find their voices. . . . (pp. 14-15)

Eggleston, in an article the following year, discussed with unusual candor the pressures that created an Establishment press.

> It is difficult to work for many years (and, after all, the present administration has been in power for 21 years) among able and eminent men, sharing confidences and accepting news favours, without developing a real affection for them personally. Moreover, as most of them are competent and eloquent defenders of their own policies, and as their technical advisors include some of the most astute and well-informed authorities on Canadian affairs, it is difficult not to become steeped in the philosophy of the administration in power. . . . The charge that this or that Ottawa man has become a government "stooge" is not unknown. I have been called that myself. . . . (p. 563)

John A. Stevenson, also writing in 1956, drew a picture of increasing independence in the press corps.

> Some years ago, when the Canadian Broadcasting Corporation was loath to allow critics of the government to proclaim their views, some members of the Gallery, fearful of losing profitable fees for broadcasts, were disposed to see merit in all the activities of the government and reserve their strictures for its opponents. But now that the CBC gives reasonably free scope on the air to critics of the government, this form of restraint no longer operates.
>
> There is still in the Gallery a sprinkling of docile lackeys of the ruling government, who are fond of boasting of their close intimacy with Ministers and act as useful agents for disseminating propaganda favorable to the government. But they are a tiny minority.

A NEW MOOD EMERGES

The three assessments combine to give what appears from other sources to be a valid picture of a political press still closely bound to political power sources but moving in the direction of independence. The three men, though, were writing at the end of an era. In 1956 the tranquillity of the long Liberal reign was broken by the Pipeline Debate, a raucous Commons outburst against government arrogance in pushing through plans for a trans-Canada pipeline, and an event that united the press corps with opposition outrage. In 1957 John Diefenbaker's Progressive Conservatives were elected as a minority government, and the following year they gained a massive majority. The press corps, after an early flirtation with the Conservatives, quickly turned against the government. And that in turn raised charges that Diefenbaker, a western "progressive," was being undermined by an eastern Liberal Establishment press (Newman, 1963).

To some extent these charges may have been valid, but there were other factors in the mix. Diefenbaker's own volatile personality was one. More important, television was coming of age, creating journalistic power centres detached from the traditional newspaper structures. In French-Canada, especially, television appeared to be nurturing a new breed of journalistic showmen who had come to stardom without passing through the newspaper process in which a reporter was socialized over a period of years before he attained the status of commentator or columnist. It is worth noting that one of the most popular television commentators in Quebec at the time was René Lévesque, later to become head of the province's separatist government (Desbarats, 1977, p. 68).

The new mood showed in a succession of controversies. At the end of 1958, some 80 producers of Radio-Canada in Montreal started a 10-week strike that was meant at least in part as rebellion against a centralized CBC under the thumb of the federal government. The acting CBC president of the day, Ernest Bushnell, called it "an attempt by a power bloc to gain control of an important medium of communications" (Stursberg, 1971, p. 181). The strike's result was mixed, but appears on balance to have been a victory for broadcasters who drew their power from the medium itself, rather than receiving it from a hierarchy appointed by government. The following year, 33 CBC producers in Toronto resigned because they believed a radio commentary show had been cancelled on government orders. The mass resignations successfully forced reinstatement of the program (Stursberg, pp. 189-216). In the same year, Radio-Canada broadcast an interview with an Algerian rebel leader although the government had cautioned against doing so. The minister who reported to Parliament for the CBC, George Nowlan, later acknowledged that after this incident he had spoken to Bushnell about possible firings in the corporation, to "put some discipline into it" (Stursberg, p. 214).

All of these events seem to signal the end of a time when politicians had some degree of control over news media managers, who in turn had firm control of journalists. Diefenbaker and his successors, Lester B. Pearson and Pierre Trudeau, each experienced a pattern of rough treatment in the media after an early period of support. The seriousness and responsibility of the Mackenzie King years went overboard as Ottawa journalists, in the memorable but somewhat overstated phrase of Larry Zolf (1973), became "the camp followers of political warfare, the gossipy fish-wives of the political marketplace." Yet elements of the partisan style lingered as late as the Diefenbaker and Pearson years, as is shown by memoirs of Peter Dempson (1968), Patrick Nicholson (1968), and Bruce Hutchison (1976).

More broadly, of course, the period at the end of the 1950s and the start of the 1960s was one in which Canadian society was experiencing a number of changes. It was the end of a long period of depression, followed by hot war, followed by cold war—all of which had induced a degree of conformity in journalism as well as other sectors. The so-called "alienation of intelligentsia" elsewhere in the Western World had its reflection in Canada. The 1960s mood of rebellion and protest in the U.S. was picked up by Canadian media, in the form of a more iconoclastic and adversarial tone. As one prominent Canadian journalist, Peter Desbarats, expressed it in a 1977 interview: "We started to look, in the 1960s, a lot of journalists like myself, at our own role as running dogs of the Establishment, and we were kind of horrified" (Note 1). In the late 1960s and 1970s, it became conventional wisdom to say Canadian reporters had adopted an adversarial style generated by Americans in the Vietnam and Watergate issues.

Government's Impact On The News Media

Also in the 1960s, concern about the erosion of national identity by the penetration of U.S. business and the overflow of U.S. culture rose strongly and became a matter for political debate and action. One result was a series of government policies designed to protect Canadian media from what was deemed to be unfair foreign competition. Although there were a few libertarian voices complaining that any government action touching on the news media was dangerous, the consensus in the major political parties, probably reflecting public opinion, was that national survival overrode other considerations.

LEGISLATIVE DEVELOPMENTS

The difficulties of Canadian periodicals competing with fatter and usually glossier imports from the United States had been apparent for years, and various governments had tried halfhearted protectionist policies. But in 1960, the Progressive Conservative government, under Prime Minister Diefenbaker, appointed a Royal Commission on Publications to "inquire into and report upon the recent and present position of and prospects for Canadian magazines and other periodicals with special but not exclusive consideration being given to problems arising from competition with similar publications which are largely or entirely edited outside of Canada, or are largely or entirely foreign in content."

The commission was headed by Grattan O'Leary, by this time one of the country's most distinguished Conservative journalists, and soon to become a Senator. Its 1961 report (Note 2) declared, "Only a truly Canadian printing press, one with the 'feel' of Canada and directly responsible to Canada, can give us the critical analysis, the informed discourse and dialogue which are indispensable in a sovereign society." It found that Canadian periodicals were seriously threatened by U.S. periodicals which, at minimal cost, could add thousands of copies to their normal print run for domestic circulation and dump them in Canada. In some cases, U.S. magazines solicited advertising in Canada for low-cost Canadian editions.

The commission proposed among other measures tax legislation to discourage Canadian corporations from placing advertisements in foreign-owned periodicals aimed at the Canadian market. This would have included *Time* and *Reader's Digest*, both of which edited and printed special editions in Canada. The Conservative government accepted the proposals in principle but was defeated in 1963 before it could pass the legislation. The Liberal government broadly adopted the proposals, and indeed extended them to cover daily newspapers with the idea of discouraging foreign takeovers. However, for domestic political reasons and with a wary eye on relations with the United States, the 1965 legislation did not bar the Canadian editions of *Time* and *Reader's Digest,* which in effect were held to be Canadian publications.

The next major development was the appointment in 1968 by the Senate of a Special Committee on Mass Media. The moving spirit was Senator Keith Davey, who had been involved in radio and public relations before becoming national organizer for the Liberal party. Davey proposed a dispassionate study to determine "the adequacy for Canada of its mass media in these changing times." Again there were some mutterings about political encroachment on the press, but with rising interest in the growth and impact of media on politics and identity the general feeling probably was that a study could be useful. The report in 1970 (Note 3) proved to be stronger in research and description than in proposals for change. It did say, however, that Canadian periodicals were still in deep trouble, primarily because *Time* and *Reader's Digest,* with their protected position in Canada, were scooping up more than 50 percent of advertising in consumer magazines. It proposed that unless the two magazines became effectively Canadian-owned and edited, they should be treated as foreigners.

After years of discussion and delay by hesitant politicians, this proposal was implemented in 1976. Regulations made under the law specified that in order to be considered Canadian, publications would have to be at least 75 percent Canadian-owned and would have to carry not less than 80 percent Canadian content. The prospect of bureaucrats combing through periodicals to determine if their content was acceptable gave rise to much concern about state censorship, but not enough to prevent passage of the bill.

So Canadian law now provides that the expense of advertising to the Canadian market in a periodical or newspaper which is foreign-owned cannot be deducted from income for tax purposes. The effect more or less is to double the cost of advertising in publications which are deemed not to be Canadian. This of course discourages advertisers from giving their business to foreign publications, and therefore deters foreigners who might wish to buy a Canadian publication. Faced with the new law, *Reader's Digest* converted its Canadian edition, although not associated enterprises, to Canadian ownership, while *Time* chose to close down its Canadian edition, although it still prints and solicits advertising in Canada.

The Davey committee had less success with its proposal to discourage concentration of ownership of papers and periodicals by establishing a review board with power to disallow mergers and acquisitions except where they could be shown to be in the public interest. The government took no action, perhaps because by the time the report appeared 77 of Canada's 116 daily papers were already owned by chains or groups. It should also be noted that the committee was unable to show that chain ownership produced inferior papers.

Although the government influences ownership of the press through the tax law, it usually claims to have no interest in controlling content. However, there are exceptions, in addition to the normal laws of libel and obscenity. In an emergency, the government can invoke the War Measures Act which has the effect of suspending civil liberties and giving the executive extensive police powers, including the power of censorship. The act has been invoked only once in peacetime, in October 1970, when the government "apprehended" a terrorist insurrection in Quebec. Although ministers were quick to say they were not invoking powers of censorship, the regulations did make it an offense to "communicate statements on behalf of or as a representative or professed representative of the unlawful association,"—that was, the Le Front de Liberation du Quebec. That made it unlawful to broadcast or print the FLQ communiques which had been hot news, particularly on the Montreal radio stations to which they were usually directed (Saywell, 1971).

Another form of pressure appeared when the federal government decided not to place advertisements in Le Jour, a short-lived daily launched by the separatist Parti Quebecois. Ministers argued that it would be wrong for the national government to give even indirect support to a newspaper launched to promote the breakup of the country.

The Official Secret's Act was intended originally to deal with espionage, but it is so sweeping in its scope that it could be used to prosecute almost anyone releasing without permission, or receiving, information classified by the government as secret. While objectionable in theory, there had been no great practical concern until the government used it against a newspaper for the first time in 1978. The Toronto Sun, a daily tabloid strongly critical of the government, was prosecuted for publishing parts of a confidential document prepared by the security branch of the Royal Canadian Mounted Police to describe Soviet espionage activities in Canada. The police claimed that publication gave the Soviet authorities an insight into counterespionage measures. But as much of the document had already been released in Parliament by an Opposition M.P., who was protected by parliamentary privilege from prosecution, it was hard to see what real damage the *Sun* could have done. The evidence in the case was still unfolding in the courts at the time of this writing, but some critics were already convinced that the government's real motive was to intimidate press critics.

Parliament, as distinct from the executive, claims the right, under the ancient law of privilege, to protect itself from false, unfair, unbalanced, or defamatory accounts of its proceedings. In theory, an offending journalist can be called before Parliament and committed to prison, but it is extremely improbable that any such drastic action would nowadays be taken. However, the House of Commons did object to a 1975 report in the Montreal *Gazette* alleging that secrets of the 1974 budget had been leaked to businessmen before they were made known to Parliament. The House appointed a committee to investigate the allegations and recommend action. After taking evidence from the *Gazette* journalists concerned and from the impugned politicians, the committee produced a report in which it said it was "conscious of the balance that must be struck between the principle that Parliament should be protected from improper obstruction of its functions and the principle of freedom of speech of the citizen to criticize the institution and membership of Parliament." It found the *Gazette* allegations to be unfounded—as in fact the paper more or less admitted in its evidence—and declared that the report "fell short of the standards to be expected of a newspaper." With this rebuke, the incident was closed, but it remains a fact that Parliament reserves the right to punish journalists who offend it (Crowe, 1977).

GOVERNMENT INFORMATION SOURCES

The government seeks to influence the media and the public through its information services, and the rapid expansion of these services in the 1960s and 1970s provoked some concern about manipulation of public opinion. During his first election campaign in 1968, Prime Minister Trudeau talked about providing more information to the public to allow more participation in the decision-making process—in short, "participatory democracy." After the election one of his early actions was to appoint a Task Force on Government Information including a well-known producer of public affairs television programs, a public relations consultant from the private sector, and a senior bureaucrat with experience in information services. The task force subsequently produced a rather trendy report (Note 4) which declared candidly that the federal information services were "a mess," and proposed the creation of a new central agency to be called Information Canada. Although the report recommended "the right of Canadians to full, objective and timely information and the obligation of the state to provide such information about its programs and policies be publicly declared as the foundation of new government policies in this field," there was much concern in Parliament and the press that Information Canada would turn out to be a propaganda ministry. In fact, it had a short and ineffective life: set up in 1970, it died in 1975 the victim of an economy campaign, the hostility of the media, the jealousy of existing departmental information services, and its ineptitude.

In the meantime, the regular information services grew like Topsy—as indeed did most branches of the bureaucracy. A Senate committee estimated in 1974 that the total annual cost of information services had risen to between $150 million and $200 million (Note 5). The task force had estimated there were about 400 information officers in the federal civil service in 1969; by 1976, the Public Service Commission reported there were 1,154 (Note 6). In many cases, the information officers had considerable support staffs, some of whom were doing information work without the title. "The federal government information services directly employ about 2,300 persons, not including freelancers, editors, writers, and film makers who are hired under contract," said a 1976 research paper prepared at Carleton University. Most outsiders, and many of the insiders, thought the services were still, as the task force described them—"a mess." In a feature distributed by Canadian Press in 1975, reporter Michael Lavoie described ". . . the days, even weeks, frequently taken by government information offices to produce a simple press release or speech and the bursts of frantic, 11th hour activity on overtime pay when deadlines draw near."

This is not to say, of course, that the government services, however inefficient, have no impact on the media or on public opinion. Obviously they do, but it is probably mostly in the useful and entirely innocent area of providing to the people facts about established programs. Federal ministers normally have on their private staffs, an aide whose principal job is to deal with the media. In many cases, they are former journalists hired from the Parliamentary Press Gallery. While some ministers keep their press aides under tight control, using them mainly as speech writers and tour organizers, others allow their aides considerable scope to promote their own image and that of the government generally by establishing relations with journalists. In any event, ministerial aides are often important sources of political news and gossip.

THE PRIME MINISTER AND THE PRESS

The Prime Minister is of course the subject of greatest media interest and scrutiny, and in turn, has the greatest resources to influence coverage. Professor Frederick J. Fletcher (1977, p. 91) says: "At one level, he can generally get easy access to editors and publishers to explain his case. Private briefings are common. In time of crisis, he can call upon their patriotism to influence coverage. The most recent example is the care with which the CBC handled the October crisis (the FLQ crisis in Quebec in October, 1970). On a day-to-day basis, reporters are susceptible to influence. The Prime Minister can influence not only news reports but also columns and commentaries through judicious use of personal interviews, background briefings, selective leaks to friendly journalists, and the like. Well known commentators have often been used as unofficial spokesmen for government policies."

Under Trudeau, the media relations branch of the Prime Minister's Office grew in size (there is a communications adviser as well as a spokesman, and a number of assistants primarily concerned with logistics) but was less a source of political information than it was under previous Prime Ministers. Trudeau preferred to be his own spokesman, and despite sporadic attempts to establish social relations with journalists—by inviting them for drinks or a meal—he generally maintained an arm's-length relationship (Note 7).

Under previous Prime Ministers, it was customary for reporters to wait outside the cabinet room to interview the Prime Minister at the end of important meetings, or to buttonhole him after a session in the House of Commons. The growth of membership in the Press Gallery to about 250 members in 1978, many of them broadcast reporters carrying mikes or trailing cameras, made this informal relationship more and more uncomfortable for all concerned. In addition, the adversary attitude adopted by some reporters and the combative instincts of the Prime Minister led to embarrassing and politically damaging exchanges and even to some mutual pushing and shoving in what came to be called "the scrum." The Prime Minister then decreed that instead of the informal exchanges several times a week, he would have a formal weekly press conference. This became a major news event, to the dismay of some parliamentarians who saw it as evidence that the Prime Minister was becoming accountable to the media rather than to the House of Commons in the daily question period.

A conventional criticism of the Trudeau government, in Parliament and in the press, was that it was secretive to the point of paranoia.

Whether true or not, the criticism provoked the government to promise a Freedom of Information Act. At the time of writing, the government has outlined its intentions (Note 8), and these have been examined by a committee of Parliament, but legislation has not been introduced. Critics fear that the bill will fall short of the U.S. model in that it will leave final discretion over the release of disputed information to ministers, who are of course ultimately accountable to Parliament, rather than to the courts.

Prime Minister Trudeau tried for years to entrench in the Canadian constitution a Charter of Rights and Freedoms. The most recent draft (Note 9) includes "freedom of the press and other communications media." This would give the media their first constitutional recognition, but how the "freedom" might be interpreted in the courts, which are usually conservative in their judgments and loath to make policy beyond what was clearly stated by legislators, would remain to be seen. The fact is that there was considerable resistance in Canada to the package of constitutional reforms proposed by Trudeau, and it may be years before the freedom of media is "guaranteed" in this way.

THE BROADCAST MEDIA

The broadcasting media, both publicly and privately owned, have always been under more direct control than the print media. The current Broadcasting Act (1962) declares (Note 10): ". . . the national broadcasting service (i.e., the CBC) should be a balanced service of information, enlightenment, and entertainment for people of different ages, interests, and tastes covering the whole range of programming in fair proportion . . . and (should) contribute to the development of national unity and provide for continuing expression of Canadian identity." The act also says that where conflict arises between the objectives of the national broadcasting service and those of private broadcasters, "it shall be resolved in the public interest but paramount consideration shall be given to the objectives of the national broadcasting service."

It is one thing for government and Parliament to make such laws, and another thing to enforce them. The government appoints the president and the directors of the CBC, but over the years, the corporation has developed a tradition of journalistic independence. This tradition may be breached from time to time—the national news reader recently complained that the Prime Minister's Office was influencing decisions about whether or not to cover Trudeau's activities, although not the content of coverage—but the corporation's news service is certainly among the most comprehensive and balanced available to Canadians.

The federal regulatory body, the Canadian Radio-Television and Telecommunications Commission, has concerned itself more with issues of cultural identity and national unity than with political partisanship. It wrestles with the fact that most Canadians can tune in U.S. networks, either directly from the air or through cable systems. In licensing the CBC and private stations, the agency requires them to broadcast a specified minimum of Canadian-made programs. The regulation is hardly excessive: according to CBC President A. W. Johnson, the average Canadian spends three hours and 20 minutes a day watching television, less than one-third of which is Canadian-produced (Note 11). The CBC's modest ambition is to raise the level of Canadian programming to 50 percent.

The CRTC has run into much criticism by proposing to delete advertising from United States television programs distributed in Canada by cable companies. The objective is to force advertisers to buy time on Canadian stations, instead of relying on the overflow from their advertising in the United States. Although United States stations are licensed to broadcast in the United States, they do in fact sell advertising on the basis of their audience in Canada, and they have objected strongly to the idea that cable companies might take their programs but not their advertisements. The interesting point is that they have found much support for their view in Canada, where there is a widely held opinion that to take United States programs without the accompanying ads would be a form of piracy. This controversy indicates the public resistance to policies designed to regulate content of media in line with national policy and goals.

THE PROVINCIAL GOVERNMENT

This survey has focused on the impact of federal government on the media. Provincial governments also have some influence, but it would take an entire volume to examine in detail the policies and activities of all 10. It must suffice to say that several provinces now have their own television stations, mainly educational but branching also into public affairs programming. While the federal government insists on its constitutional power to regulate all broadcasting, the provinces have been trying to establish, through the courts or by amendment of the constitution, their jurisdiction over cable systems.

We must acknowledge also that this survey has referred mainly to English language media. The traditions of the press are rather different in Quebec, where the national imperative is not so much resistance to the influence of the United States as the survival of French language and culture in a predominantly English-speaking country. Always concerned with survival, the Quebec media have usually been supportive of the Quebec government in its conflicts with the federal government. The rise of the separatist Parti Quebecois over the past 10 years has owed much to the support of the intellectual community, including many journalists. But since the PQ formed the government in 1976, the French language press seems gradually to have adopted a more detached and sceptical attitude. Premier Levesque has been highly critical of what he regards as the hostile coverage of his government by the English language papers in Montreal, but the government appears to be backing away from the idea of promoting a Quebec news agency— French papers now take a French language service from the national agency, Canadian Press—and has been less insistent about its hopes to take over from the federal government jurisdiction over Radio-Canada, the French language television and radio services of the CBC. Interestingly, the new leader of the Liberal party in Quebec, in opposition to former broadcaster Levesque, is Claude Ryan, former editor of Le Devoir—confirming again the close ties between journalism and politics in Quebec.

News Media Impact on Politics

It is easier to describe the legislation and regulations by which government seeks to control media, and the sort of influences which exist behind the scenes, than to assess the real impact upon the tone or content of the media (Scanlon, 1976). For example, the sociological convention that the media are the tools of the political and economic elite, serving to preserve the Establishment ideology, seems to us to be less true than it may have been 20 years ago (Porter, 1965; Clement, 1976). The demands of news-as-entertainment journalism, the breakdown of hierarchy in the newsroom, the growth and affluence of media are among the factors that have made journalists less responsive to traditional controls.

Similarly, it is hard to assess the impact of the media on politics and government. The Globe and Mail, of Toronto, describes itself as Canada's National Newspaper and is well read by decision makers in Ottawa. It is commonly agreed that it helps to set the agenda for the day's Question Period in the House of Commons which, in turn, is often the major political story of the next day.

No doubt, the reports and opinions of the *Globe* and of other papers and broadcasts have their influence on opinions and decision making, but according to one experienced observer, Geoffrey Stevens, associate editor and Ottawa columnist for the *Globe and Mail,* the effect is limited.

> The rule is that the media's influence tends to be marginal once legislation has been introduced in Parliament. The media can draw the attention of the government and of Parliament to flaws in legislation, but once a bill has been introduced by the government, the media are as impotent as the Opposition to force the Cabinet to change major principles and provisions. As with the Opposition, the media are unable to do much more than to cause the government to delay passage of a particular bill or to reconsider some of its details. The greatest influence the media have on the legislative process is at the very beginning, before the process formally begins. Pressure from the media can persuade the government to proceed with legislation on a certain subject and it can help to create a public climate favorable to the legislation. The media's influence, however, does not extend to causing the government to follow a course that it does not want to follow or that it feels the public is not ready for it to follow (Note 12).

Stevens probably underrates the power of the media to create a climate of political and public opinion in which the government and the opposition must operate. Asked about the impact of media on the 1976 convention at which he was chosen leader of the Conservative Opposition, Joe Clark replied: "There's no way you can get away from it. You simply have to accommodate to it. Not only (at) the convention; it's also (in) the House of Commons, and I think we simply have to recognize that that is something we have to live with." An unsuccessful candidate for the party leadership, Heward Grafftey M.P., recalled that when he entered Parliament in 1958, the retiring Prime Minister, Louis S. Laurent, had advised him presciently, "The biggest job of your generation will be to combine democracy with the television medium" (Note 13). When the Commons decided in 1977 to permit radio and television broadcasting of its proceedings, some legislators saw the step as a way to circumvent a hostile press and speak directly to the electorate.

We could quote many other examples of the uneasy feelings politicians now have about media power, but perhaps the most striking criticism was expressed by the CRTC, which was headed at the time by Harry Boyle, a former broadcaster and a novelist, and included among its members such distinguished academics as Northrop Frye. There had been suspicions for some years that journalists in sympathy with the separatist movement in Quebec were using Radio Canada as a propa-

ganda vehicle. After the PQ victory in 1976, the concern among Liberal
M.P.s led Prime Minister Trudeau to request the CRTC to inquire
"whether the English and French television networks of the corporation
generally, and in particular their public affairs, information, and news
programming, are fulfilling the mandate of the Corporation." The commissioners set up some analysis of CBC programming content, held
public hearings, and produced a report (Note 14) in which, in effect,
they blamed television for the crisis in national unity. They said that
balance in news reporting meant providing both the essential information on which opinions can be based and some indication of what a
reasonable perspective or attitude toward it could be, and they went on:

> We have bias whenever anyone attempts to cut off essential information
> or balance from someone else, and so tries to force the listener's opinions
> into line with his or her own interests. Such bias, which runs counter to
> the principles of democratic debate, is a form of journalistic malprac-
> tice. . . . If this definition of bias seems reasonable, the damning statistics
> that emerge from Professor (Arthur) Siegel's study (of TV content), in
> particular, indicate that the electronic news media in Canada, English as
> well as French, are biased to the point of subversiveness. They are biased
> because, so far as they are able, they prevent Canadians from getting
> enough balanced information about Canada to make informed decisions
> regarding the country's future. They are biased by their assumptions
> about what is newsworthy and what their audiences want to hear. These
> assumptions really amount to two. First, only Canadians living along the
> St. Lawrence axis, from Quebec to Hamilton, belong in the news; all
> others are some kind of Canadian fauna living in the "boondocks," to be
> noticed only when they do something picturesque. The second assump-
> tion is that English Canadians could not care less about what happens to
> French Canadians, and vice versa. These assumptions are intolerable.
> They are also extremely stupid.

The commissioners pointedly suggested to the CBC that it should
establish a policy for better expressing regional diversity and contributions to national unity before applying in 1978 for a renewal of its
broadcasting licence. Hearings on the application were about to begin
as this paper was written.

Prime Minister Trudeau was closely questioned in Parliament and at
a press conference about his reaction to the CRTC criticism of the CBC
and, by implication, other national media. In one response he said the
best solution would be for the media to discipline themselves, but if
they did not, discipline would have to be applied. He explained later he
was thinking in terms of voluntary councils established by the media to
hear complaints. In a more philosophical mood, he referred to the
television set as an electronic cannon shooting messages, and asked:

"Now, who is controlling that particular message? Should it be the State? Should it be private enterprise with its billions of dollars? Should it be cooperatives of media people? Should it be the community in some sense?" Not unexpectedly, the media at once saw a threat of state censorship.

However, the Prime Minister had at least some public support for his view that control of the media raises legitimate questions for debate. A study of attitudes at the grass roots of Canadian society (Maxwell, 1975) concluded:

> The social power of the media—TV advertising and news reporting especially—worries many Canadians. Occupying the middle ground between policy-makers and the general public, the media select, report, and interpret "the news," and sometimes also "make news." Given this immense power to inform and interpret, Canadians in many walks of life are asking a greater accountability from the media. People are asking, in effect, "Can't the media be required to be more socially responsible, and still remain free?"

Journalist-academic Patrick MacFadden, of Carleton University, has put the issue provocatively (Note 15) by suggesting that the question of Canada's agenda in the 1980s may not be Freedom of the Press, but Freedom from the Press.

In the 1970s, meanwhile, it seems fair to conclude by saying that while government is viewing the power of media with considerable concern, the media conversely have the uncomfortable feeling that their freedoms are being eroded by government.

Reference Notes

1. Interview with author, February, 1977.
2. Report of the Royal Commission on Publications. Ottawa: Queen's Printer, 1961.
3. The Uncertain Mirror. Vol. 1 of the Report of the Special Senate Committee on Mass Media. Ottawa: Queen's Printer, 1970.
4. To Know and Be Known. Vol. 1 of the Report of the Task Force on Government Information. Ottawa: Queen's Printer, 1969.
5. Report of the Standing Senate Committee on National Finance on Information Canada. Ottawa: Information Canada, 1974.
6. Administrative Staffing Program Information Guide. Ottawa: Public Service Commission, 1976.
7. Winter, J. The Trudeau Government and Information. Unpublished research paper, Carleton University School of Journalism, 1976.
8. Legislation on Public Access to Government Documents. Ottawa: Minister of Supply and Services, 1977.
9. The Constitutional Amendment Bill, 1978: An Explanatory Document. Ottawa: Minister of Supply and Services, 1978.
10. An Act to Implement a Broadcasting Policy for Canada. Ottawa: Queen's Printer, 1968.
11. Statement made in a public speech, 1976.
12. Stevens, G. The Influences and Responsibilities of the Media. Paper presented to the National Conference on the Legislative Process, University of Victoria, B.C., 1978.
13. On the sound track of a documentary film, Medium Cool, made by Carleton University journalism students.
14. Report of the Committee of Inquiry into the National Broadcasting Service. Ottawa: Canadian Radio-Television and Telecommunications Commission, 1977.
15. Statement made in a public speech, 1977.

References

Bilkey, P. Persons, Papers, and Things. Toronto: Ryerson, 1940.
Bowman, C.A. Ottawa Editor. Sidney, B.C.: Gray's Publishing, 1966.
Carey, J. W. "Canadian Communication Theory: Extensions and Interpretations of Harold Innis." In G. J. Robinson and D. F. Theall (Eds.), Studies in Canadian Communications. Montreal: Graduate Programme in Communications, McGill University, 1975.
Charlesworth, H. I'm Telling You. Toronto: Macmillan, 1937.
Clement, W. The Canadian Corporate Elite. Toronto: McClelland and Stewart, 1976.
Cook, F. "Fifty Years Ago and More." Daily Province. Vancouver, August 3, 1934, p. 7.
Cook, R. The Politics of John W. Dafoe and the Free Press. Toronto: University of Toronto Press, 1963.

Crowe, D. "Parliament Versus Press." *Carleton Journalism Review,* Spring 1977, I, 7-11.

Cumming, C. "The Coming Battle Over Media Power." *Carleton Journalism Review,* Spring 1977, I, 19-20.

Dempson, P. *Assignment Ottawa.* Toronto: General Publishing, 1968.

Desbarats, P. *René.* Toronto: McClelland and Stewart, 1977.

Eggleston, W. "Leaves from a Pressman's Log—Parliament and the Press Gallery." *Queen's Quarterly,* 1956-57, *63,* 548-564.

Eggleston, W. *While I Still Remember.* Toronto: Ryerson, 1968.

Ferguson, G. and Underhill, F. H. *Press and Party in Canada.* Toronto: Ryerson, 1955.

Fletcher, F. J. "The Prime Minister as Public Persuader." In T. A. Hockin (Ed.), *Apex of Power* (2nd ed.). Scarborough, Ont.: Prentice Hall of Canada, 1977.

Ford, A. R. *As the World Wags On.* Toronto: Ryerson, 1950.

Harkness, R. J. E. *Atkinson of The Star.* Toronto: University of Toronto Press, 1963.

Hutchison, B. *The Far Side of the Street.* Toronto: Macmillan, 1976.

Maxwell, G. *Attitudes at the Canadian Grassroots.* Ottawa: Social Affairs Office, Canadian Catholic Conference, 1975.

Newman, P. *Renegade in Power.* Toronto: McClelland and Stewart, 1963.

Nichols, M. E. *(CP) The Story of The Canadian Press.* Toronto: Ryerson, 1948.

Nicholson, P. *Vision and Indecision.* Don Mills, Ont.: Longmans Canada, 1968.

O'Leary, G. *Recollections of People, Press, and Politics.* Toronto: Macmillan, 1977.

Peers, F. W. *The Politics of Canadian Broadcasting 1920-1951.* Toronto: University of Toronto Press, 1969.

Porter, J. *The Vertical Mosaic.* Toronto: University of Toronto Press, 1965.

Rutherford, P. *The Making of the Canadian Media.* Toronto: McGraw-Hill Ryerson, 1978.

Saywell, J. *Quebec 70, A Documentary Narrative.* Toronto: University of Toronto Press, 1971.

Scanlon. T. J. "How Government Uses the Media." In G. S. Adam (Ed.), *Journalism, Communication, and the Law.* Scarborough, Ont.: Prentice-Hall of Canada, 1976.

Stevenson, J. A. "How the Press Gallery Works." *Saturday Night,* March 19, 1956.

Stursberg, P. *Mister Broadcasting: The Ernie Bushnell Story.* Toronto: Peter Martin Associates, 1971.

Ward, N. "Patronage and the Press." In K. M. Gibbons and D. C. Rowat (Eds.), *Political Corruption in Canada.* Toronto: McClelland and Stewart, 1976.

Westell, A. *The New Society.* Toronto: McClelland and Stewart, 1977.

Willison, J. *Reminiscences, Political, and Personal.* Toronto: McClelland and Stewart, 1919.

Zolf, L. *The Dance of the Dialectic.* Toronto: James Lewis and Samuel, 1973.

VIII.
The Mass Media in America

Delmer Dunn

In America the mass media can be characterized as ubiquitous, with a large number of media outlets. In 1978 there were 1,753 daily newspapers with an average daily circulation of over 61 million ("Letter from the Publisher," 1978, p. v), 986 television stations which reached nearly 74.5 million homes or 98 percent of the homes in America, 9,732 magazines, and 8,532 radio stations ("Closed Circuit and Summary of Broadcasting," 1978; Statistical Abstract of the U.S., 1977).

This picture of the mass media differs from that of 50 years earlier, before the advent of AM radio. In 1925, for example, there were 2,008 daily newspapers with a daily circulation of 33,739,000 ("Daily Newspapers—Total Number, Circulation, and Cost Trend," 1977). The most dramatic development, of course, has been in television. In 1950 only 3.8 million or 9 percent of the U.S. households had television; by 1956 this figure had reached 71 percent; and by 1968, 95 percent (*Nielsen TV 1969*, 1969, p. 10). In 1977, the television set in the average home was in use 26.5 hours a week or a little more than 6 hours a day ("A Short Course in Broadcasting," 1978; Bernstein, 1978, p. 108).

Newspapers and television thus constitute the primary means by which Americans can remain informed about their government. On the other hand, government regulations bear directly upon the operations of the mass media. Before examining the way in which Americans and governmental officials use the mass media for information and functions, let us first examine the role of government in regulating newspapers and broadcasting stations.

Media Regulation

The media in any country must work within the framework of laws written into statutes, constitutions, or judicial decisions. For purposes of this discussion, we are interested in the law as it relates to the American mass media in three contexts.

We are interested first in the law regarding the dissemination of information, that is, the right of the printed media to print and of the electronic media to broadcast. We need to know the constraints, the rights and prerogatives, and in what areas vagueness exists. A second important area for our consideration centers on the rights of print and electronic journalists to gather information. For news to be transmitted, reporters must have access to basic information about events, decisions, and policies of the social, economic, and governmental sectors. Without such access, freedom of dissemination has little meaning. Finally, we are interested in the legal regulations governing the access of citizens to information, particularly the way in which the rules and regulations governing the media in the country either restrict or encourage competing channels of information available to the citizens of the country.

THE FIRST AMENDMENT

In the United States, the broadcast and print media's most fundamental rights are lodged in the First Amendment of the Constitution. This amendment states, "Congress shall make no law . . . abridging the freedom of speech, or of the press; . . ." The rights of reporters to gather news and/or publishers or broadcasters to disseminate it are grounded basically in this constitutional provision. Although there are many issues surrounding the interpretation of the full meaning as well as the limits of this amendment, it has stood through the years to give American journalists broader freedoms to gather and to disseminate the news than exist in almost any other country.

In most cases the electronic media are also governed by the First Amendment protections of the print media; however, there are two important circumscriptions for the electronic media. One is the "fairness doctrine" in Section 315(a) of the Communications Act of 1934. This doctrine requires that broadcast and television stations provide reasonable opportunity for "airing various points of views held by reasonable elements in the community on various issues which arise" (*Fairness Doctrine,* 1968, pp. 5; 3-51). In effect, this doctrine requires that the electronic media cover all sides of controversial issues as fairly as possible. Unless an individual is attacked personally or a candidate for public office is either endorsed or editorialized against, broadcasters may choose to present these various points of view in any way they wish and the time devoted to one side or the other does not have to be equal. Although the vaguely worded doctrine only requires that a reasonable effort be made to present opposing viewpoints, in practice almost any effort is usually interpreted as being reasonable.

A second restriction of the broadcast media in Section 315(a) of the Communications Act requires stations to sell equal time to candidates for the same office, although not necessarily to candidates for other offices. Since 1959 stations have been exempt from the equal-time rule of Section 315(a) in the cases of bona fide newscasts, news interviews and documentaries, and on-the-spot coverage of news events (Note 1). In 1975 the Federal Communications Commission (FCC) ruled that coverage of candidates' debates and news conferences came under the on-the-spot news coverage exemption of the 1959 amendment (Note 2), and these types of programs are still covered by the fairness doctrine. The equal-time rule does not require that stations sell time in the same programming slots to candidates for the same office; it only requires the station to sell equal amounts of time. Thus, one candidate could buy time on a station during a very popular program as long as the station is willing to sell an equal amount of time on any program to other candidates for the *same* office, and the station would meet the requirements of Section 315(a).

Since the First Amendment of the U.S. Constitution with its broad and sweeping powers of protection was written before the advent of broadcasting, the justification of imposing additional requirements on broadcasters that their colleagues in the print media are not required to follow can be questioned, especially since broadcasting is big business and reaches such large audiences. In America the major television and broadcasting networks, as well as the individual stations, are privately owned companies. Nevertheless, in order to operate, they must use the airwave or the electromagnetic spectrum which surrounds the earth to transmit their signals. The public ownership of this resource constitutes the basic justification for the regulation. The fact that this resource is scarce means that only a limited number of broadcasting stations is possible in any one area. In order to justify their use of this scarce resource, stations are under obligation not to abuse that resource by promoting positions or candidates without giving others the opportunity for access to broadcast and telecast audiences in the area. As technological change occurs, it is possible that part of this justification may be abrogated in the future. However, it appears at the present time that the fairness doctrine will be applied to the broadcast media for several years to come.

Thus far, the First Amendment has served as a more effective barrier to permanent government regulation of newspapers and magazines than of the electronic media. In 1974 the U.S. Supreme Court held in a unanimous decision that a Florida statute requiring newspapers to publish free of charge the replies of candidates for public office to published criticism was unconstitutional (Note 3). The court held that there is inherent constitutional danger in any type of forced access to the press. In December 1977, the Ohio Supreme Court refused to hear an appeal by a candidate whose advertising was refused by the *Cleveland Plain Dealer* ("Newsbriefs," 1977, p. 4).

LEGAL ISSUES AND THE MEDIA

The sweeping privileges and rights of the First Amendment, as is true of other amendments and many statutes, acquire their real meaning in court rulings and interpretations, clarifying statutes or laws passed, and by commonly accepted principles of working arrangements. In the United States no constitutional guarantee is absolutely respected in all cases. Frequently, one right conflicts with another, and a balance must be drawn. Most of the issues associated with the First Amendment and its application to American media hinge on the question of which right supercedes the other and what the proper balance is. In recent years most of the concern has centered on the rights of the press to cover matters related to court trials and national security.

Government all over the world seek either formally or informally to use prior restraint in order to control the information which appears in the media. At times government officials attempt to persuade publishers or reporters to withhold certain information in the government's interest. At other times specific laws and regulations are promulgated in an effort to keep the media from disseminating certain information. Within the past several years, the U.S. Supreme Court has issued several rulings which provide media in the United States greater protection than ever before against prior restraint.

In the case of *Nebraska Press Association* v. *Judge Hugh Stewart* (Note 4), the court unanimously declared unconstitutional a "gag" order imposed by a Nebraska judge which prohibited reporters and the press from providing any pretrial publication of information related to the trial of person accused of mass murder and sexual assault. However, this decision did not cover bans prohibiting court personnel or others officially connected with a trial from disclosing matters related to the trial or prohibit judges from closing court proceedings to the public and press entirely.

Several recent developments, however, have made coverage of court proceedings easier. In certain states it is possible to televise and broadcast court proceedings, and cameras have been allowed in some state courts in Florida, Georgia, and Wisconsin.

One relatively recent development in many state and local governments and more recently at the federal level has been the passage of "sunshine laws." These laws were originally propounded by Common Cause and other citizen groups and strongly supported by most news organizations who saw them as ways those not ordinarily a part of government decision making might be better able to find out what those decisions were and how they were made. Today 50 states, as well as the federal government, have various "sunshine laws" ("State and Local Watch," 1977). (Of these 50 state laws, 37 require advance notice, 32 require written minutes, and 34 provide for sanctions for violations.) Most of these laws have various exemptions, for example, the necessary discussion of personnel matters in a public meeting. In some states they are not enforced vigorously. One impact of these laws has been to provide somewhat better access by reporters to the internal decisions and activities of governments in this country.

A second development has been the Freedom of Information Act which became law in 1967 (Note 5). It provides a procedure by which the media or citizens can obtain unreleased documents from federal agencies. Exemptions provided by this act pertain to trade secrets, medical files, and security. The 1974 Amendments to this act were designed to weaken the power of agencies to determine what could and could not be released (Note 6). Still, news organizations complain that many agencies routinely refuse requests. In August 1977, ten years after the law's passage, there were 600 court challenges of denials of requests (Weaver, 1977, p. 1). Conflicting with the Freedom of Information Act are more stringent federal rules regarding the rights to privacy of government records, particularly those pertaining to specific individuals.

Do reporters have rights to gather information about governmental institutions that ordinary citizens do not have? This is still an unanswered question. Recent decisions have indicated that the Supreme Court looks unfavorably upon the rights of news organizations to interview inmates of federal penitentiaries or other corrections facilities (Note 7).

National security has always presented difficulties for newspapers and broadcasters, operating under the First Amendment. In times of war, reporters have refrained on many occasions from publishing information that might have been beneficial to enemy forces. Often this has been done voluntarily. At times, it has been done at the request of a persuasive public official who convinced news organizations that printing a story would be detrimental to the interest of the United States. Once such instance occurred when the *New York Times* learned of the planned Bay of Pigs invasion of Cuba in the early 1960s. The *Times* was persuaded by the government not to publish its knowledge about the pending assault.

The most dramatic developments, however, have occurred in the wake of the Vietnam War. News organizations have given notice that they will not be compliant in the future as they have in the past. In the celebrated Pentagon Papers case, Daniel Ellsberg, who worked at the RAND Corporation, had access to the classified Pentagon study of the Vietnam War. He copied this secret document and turned the information over to the *New York Times* for publication. The U.S. Justice Department successfully sought an injunction to stop the publication of the papers, and the *Times* complied after three installments. Ellsberg then gave the papers to the *Washington Post*, the *Boston Globe*, and other news agencies.

In the *New York Times* v. *United States* and *United States* v. *the Washington Post Company* (Note 8), the Supreme Court overruled the government's attempt to impose prior restraint on the *New York Times* and refused to punish the *Washington Post* and other agencies which had subsequently published the materials. Most observers believe that the ruling eliminated the feasibility of most prior restraint moves by government agencies. It is likely that the government in the future will seek to persuade news organizations to voluntarily withhold sensitive material, particularly as it relates to security matters.

RESTRICTIONS ON REPORTERS' ACCESS TO NEWS SOURCES

Even if the government is unsuccessful in preventing publication or broadcasting of materials it does not want disseminated, there are other ways it can block the effective dissemination of information about its actions and affairs. In fact, there is a body of opinion which holds that it is not the press' responsibility to maintain secrecy but the government's. Under this principle if reporters learn of a secret and if it is newsworthy in the editorial judgment of the news organization, it should be published. Any punishment associated with the publication would therefore rest upon the party who released the material, presumably in violation of the law (Simons & Califano, 1976, pp. 19-23). One of the problems faced by news organizations covering government at all levels is that, since generally government is so large, engaged in so many activities, and making decisions at so many locations, it is very difficult for them to keep tab of all that is going on. Moreover, the problem is compounded when much of the government's business is conducted in secret.

One of the most sensitive problems of government/press relations is the right of reporters to protect the confidentiality of their sources from government knowledge. Reporters regard protection in this area as essential to their effectiveness in properly covering government since they must rely upon sources for much of their information. They believe that their ability to protect these sources from divulgence is crucial to their continuing reliance upon them for information. Without some legal protection, reporters fear that they may not be able to protect their sources in a way that is necessary in gathering information for their stories.

The precise legal rights of reporters in gathering news have not yet been fully defined. The Supreme Court recognizes that news gathering qualifies for First Amendment protection and states ". . . without some protection for seeking out the news, freedom of the press could be eviscerated" (Note 9).

In order to counter the problem of disclosing sources under a court-ordered subpoena, many reporters and news organizations have advocated the use of "shield" laws which would protect or "shield" them from divulging their sources, even under court order. By 1976, 26 states had passed "shield" laws for individual reporters providing a qualified privilege from testimony when confidential sources are involved (Note 10). Many of these "shield" laws, however, have been subjected to negative rulings by state courts, and it is unclear as to whether or not they will, in fact, provide the kind of protection which reporters seek. Further, even with "shield" laws, reporters and/or news organizations are frequently subjected to subpoenas which must be contested in court. The expenses of contesting subpoenas are too great to be borne by news organizations, particularly smaller ones (Goodale, 1975, p. 709).

The deliberations of the Supreme Court in this area are not yet complete. It is clear from court rulings that reporters must testify about crimes which they witnessed (Note 11). The Court has also held that reporters must appear before grand juries investigating evidence of crimes, although to date it has not set an absolute obligation to testify about confidential sources in such hearings. The question of the legal requirements of reporters to appear and to testify about confidential sources has been decided on a case-by-case basis with some decisions going one way and some the other (Note 12).

One of the most recent developments in this area of law centers on Myron Farber, an investigative reporter for the *New York Times*. Farber's reporting of a dozen mysterious deaths which took place in a New Jersey hospital over a two-year period led to the indictment of a physician on charges that he murdered five of the victims by administering dosages of curare. In the trial, attorneys for the accused attempted to subpoena Farber's private notes in order to prepare their client's defense. The reporter and his news organization refused to honor the subpoena on grounds that divulging sources and other notes would restrict the flow of information and violate the First Amendment protections of the reporters. Farber was cited for contempt of court, fined heavily, and sent to jail. Whether this case will constitute clear grounds for developing further court tests on this important matter remains to be seen. The issue is clouded somewhat by Farber's reportedly selling the rights to a book-length manuscript, which will presumably use much of the material which he now refuses to turn over to the lawyers for the defense. This case juxtaposes the basic rights of the First Amendment (free press) and the Sixth Amendment (fair trial). It also indicates that protection of newsmen may be questioned by nongovernment lawyers as well as by those who represent the government in a given case. In fact, the U.S. Justice Department in the early 1970s issued guidelines restricting the powers of U.S. attorneys to subpoena reporters who refuse to reveal confidential sources or provide testimony regarding court cases. Under these guidelines no U.S. attorney may issue a subpoena to a journalist unless all of the sources of the desired information have been exhausted and the Attorney General's permission has been obtained (Note 13). The effect of the guidelines is to extend reporters' protection against subpoenas by government attorneys.

PROTECTION AGAINST LIBEL

Even when reporters have access to sources and there are no legal impediments blocking the right and ability of news organizations to disseminate information, if figures prominently in the news could successfully sue newspapers for real, perceived, or possible damages from the information which appears, then the full information that might be provided by a free press would be impeded. Developments in the area of libel law as applied to news organizations have in the last 15 years greatly broadened the freedom of news organizations to present information about public figures. Although many of the specific court cases have grown out of newspapers or printed media, in general most observers believe that, with the important qualifications of the fairness doctrine, the electronic media now enjoy similar protections from libel suits.

The major case extending protection from libel suits to news organizations is New York Times v. Sullivan (Note 14). This case held that public figures who believe that they have been falsely maligned by the news media must prove not only negligence but also malice in order to successfully pursue a libel case against news organizations. In such cases they must prove that the information in question was provided with the foreknowledge that it was false or most likely false. Later cases have extended this protection by holding that unintentional errors by news organizations in the haste of publishing cannot constitute grounds for a successful suit by public figures (Note 15). The "unintentional error" protection, however, does not apply to magazines, which presumably have longer deadlines than newspapers (Note 16).

These decisions by the Supreme Court have effectively made it very difficult, if not impossible, for public figures to successfully sue news organizations for information about them appearing in the news. The scope of this protection has been narrowed somewhat in recent decisions. The Court has ruled that persons not playing significant roles in deciding public issues were excluded from the public figures definition used in previous cases. This is true even if the persons involved are well known (Note 17).

Still the court has provided considerable protection for news organizations in printing or broadcasting stories about private individuals. The court has indicated that private individuals must prove negligence (as opposed to malice as outlined in the Sullivan case) to successfully pursue a libel action and that private persons proceeding under this standard could collect only actual damages and not punitive damages in such a judgment (Note 18). Further, plaintiffs would have to show that actual damage had occurred in order to collect.

PRIVACY

In recent years both Congress and the federal courts have increasingly emphasized the right to privacy as pertaining to individuals. As these rights are more clearly developed, it is possible that they will impinge directly upon the ability of news organizations to gather and disseminate information. Prosser's standards of violations of individuals' privacy include (1) truthful disclosure of private facts, (2) physical trespass in the course of gathering news, (3) interference with the right to sell or use one's name or likeness for commercial gain, and (4) placing an individual in a false light in the course of description (Prosser, 1971, pp. 802-818).

The U.S. Supreme Court has yet to rule definitively on whether or not news organizations can disseminate true facts without running afoul of the privacy rights. Thus far, it appears doubtful that they can be held libel for publishing true facts, even of a private nature, as long as they can be demonstrated to be newsworthy. Likewise, no Supreme Court decisions have yet spoken to the problem of physical trespass in obtaining news or potential violations by broadcast electronic media. It has held that the First Amendment does not protect the news media in a broadcast of a performer's act without his or her consent (Note 19).

Media Economic Regulation

In a democracy one of the important media principles is that citizens have access to a variety of media communication channels to ensure some diversity in the information available about government activities. Media competition may enhance the quality of political information available, because reporters from the various news organizations vie with each other for "scoops" (exclusive stories) and for quality of event coverage. Moreover, since the American political system seeks to structure decisions into two alternatives, for example, a Democratic and Republican candidate for a given office, diversity of media ownership and control allows citizens access to information which relates to more than one side of any question.

Two developments relate directly to reducing the diversity of media access in America. One of these is the chain ownership of newspapers in which one company owns several newspapers in a state, a group of states, or throughout the country. For example, in 1930, 43 percent of the daily circulation could be attributed to newspapers which were owned by chains. By 1960 the figure had increased to 46 percent, and by early 1977 to 71 percent (Bagdikian, 1977, p. 17). More newspapers are owned by chains, and the largest chains account for ever greater totals of daily circulation. Newspapers belonging to the 12 largest chains, for example, controlled 16 percent of the daily circulation in 1930, 30 percent in 1960, and 60 percent in 1977. Most independent newspapers in America today have circulations of less than 10,000 (Bagdikian, 1977, p. 17).

The second phenomenon which reduces media diversity in America is that of media monopolies. In this case one parent company owns a major television station as well as a major daily newspaper in a given media market.

Concentration of ownership of television stations is also occurring. Although the FCC limits the total number of stations owned by any one company, this prohibition has not had a marked effect on reducing the number of group-owned stations. In the top one hundred markets, 76 percent of the VHF television stations were the property of group ownership in 1975 (Howard, 1976, pp. 402-403). In 1956, nearly 20 years earlier, just about half of the VHF television stations in these markets were owned by groups (Howard, 1976). Interestingly, in the especially competitive top 10 market areas where millions of Americans live, 95 percent of the VHF stations were owned by groups in 1975 (Howard, 1976, p. 404).

In spite of similar trends in both newspaper and broadcast ownership, there has been a total growth in media outlets since 1922. This has occurred primarily because of the development first of AM radio in the 1920s and later television and FM radio in the 1940s and 1950s. One study of media outlets indicates that the number of daily newspapers declined between 1922 and 1970, while the number of broadcast stations increased dramatically (Sterlin, 1975, pp. 251-252). The total growth in the number of media outlets in this period was 270 percent. This study, however, also found growing concentration of ownership of both broadcasting stations and newspapers over the period (Sterling, 1975, pp. 251-252).

Scholars are divided on their assessment of the impact of media concentration (Sobel and Emery, 1978). Verne E. Edwards, Jr., for example, argues that chain ownership can pool resources in an efficient and effective way, allowing publishers to increase and improve their staffs and to free themselves somewhat from their dependence on individual advertisers (Edwards, 1977, pp. 214-215).

Others are less positive in their findings on the impact of media concentration. William T. Gormley, for example, concludes that common ownership tends to restrict the variety of news available in the affected market and that the impact of this limitation is greater in smaller cities than in larger ones. Cross-owned agencies often share

joint physical plants and staff members, and they formally or informally cooperate in news gathering and reporting (Gormley, 1977, p. 38).
Another study found that editorials in independently owned daily
newspapers became less vigorous after the newspapers had been purchased by chains. Moreover, this same study found that editorial writers of independently owned newspapers were more likely than their
counterparts in chain-owned situations to express their opinions more
vigorously on controversial subjects related to the local area (Thrift,
1977, pp. 327-331).

It is possible that the growing cable television industry will provide a
new technology comparable to that of the development of television and
radio stations earlier and that its use will provide more diversity in
media outlets. The FCC now requires some local programming effort on
the part of cable television franchise holders. In many areas this coverage consists merely of automated scanning devices which provide
instruments measuring various characteristics of the weather. But, in
some locations, local news and other programming are provided. It is
not yet clear what the impact of the growing development of cable
television will be. At least two writers have argued that it, too, will be
captured by networks and will provide less diversity than its potential
would suggest (Brunner and Chen, 1978, pp. 81-84).

The federal government, particularly the FCC and the U.S. Justice
Department, has become more active during the last 10 years in seeking
to implement policies which will slow the trend toward concentration
of ownership in media outlets. Before that time, in 1953 and 1954, the
FCC limited the number of stations which could be held by a given
group to a total of seven, with no more than five of these being VHF
stations (Note 20). At least one writer has argued that this policy,
although restricting the size of individual groups, has also become a
guideline which has encouraged the development of group broadcasting (Howard, 1976).

The concern of the U.S. Justice Department centers on its enforce-
ment of antitrust legislation. One of its successful challenges prevented
the Los Angeles Times Mirror from acquiring the San Bernardino Sun
on grounds of overlapping advertising market areas (Note 21). The
Justice Department has, however, been unsuccessful in developing
guidelines to govern newspapers' mergers or acquisitions by chains.
The authority provided by the Clayton Act is directed toward preventing monopolies in a discrete economic area (either local, regional, or
national). According to at least one author, the level of newspaper

ownership concentration is still far below that in other areas, for example, the steel and the automobile industry (McIntosh, 1977, pp. 48-50).

The FCC has, however, attempted to formulate policy on the joint ownership of newspapers and broadcasting stations in one market area. In 1975 the agency ruled that no future cross-ownerships within the same market area would be allowed unless they could be shown to be in the public interest (Second Report and Order, 1975). In the same order, the commission directed the breakup of 16 existing ownership arrangements in cities where there were no competing outlets. The order was contested by the National Citizens Committee for Broadcasting, headed by the former FCC commissioner, Nicholas Johnson, because it did not believe the ruling went far enough in breaking up existing combinations as well. On the other hand, the National Association of Broadcasters and the American Newspapers Publishers Association appealed the decision because they believed the FCC had exceeded its authority.

The FCC divestiture rule was appealed first to the Court of Appeals, which held that the FCC had the power to instate a divestiture order but also ruled that the divestiture of the 16 combination ownerships in which a single owner owned both the sole newspaper and sole radio or television was arbitrary and capricious. The Court of Appeals ruled, therefore, that all local media combinations should be prohibited.

The Supreme Court, in effect, upheld the FCC's original directive by overturning the portion of the Court of Appeal's rule relating to cross membership combinations which by the time of the ruling, had declined to 13 markets ("Crossowners Win Claim on Crossownership," 1978, p. 27). The limited divestiture, therefore, applies to those combination in which the daily newspaper and the broadcasting or television station are the sole outlets in a given market (Note 22).

The Use of Media in Campaigning

It is an understatement to say that the media are important in campaigns for public office in America. The growing size of the American electorate, the expanding diversity of groups seeking and gaining recognition in the American political arena, the increasing complexity of American lifestyles, and new technology, particularly television, have drastically altered campaigns for public office in America.

This is true for campaigns in all levels of government. When George

Washington was president, he presided over a nation of 4 million people, and each member of the House of Representatives at that time represented 30,000 thousand persons. The U.S. population now stands at over 200 million people and after the 1980 census each congressional district will have well over 500,000 thousand constituents.

Combined with the increased size of the American electorate is the more active competition for the individual voter's time. In an urban society with many demands on time, it is very difficult for campaigners for public office to capture the attention of the American voters, and it is impossible in today's complex American society for a candidate for public office to campaign from village to village or from city to city and hope to reach all potential voters individually.

Candidates have thus turned increasingly to the media, especially radio and television, in an effort to reach the voters. Campaign organizations can still be important in American political life, particularly in some large urban areas, but the top-level strategists in most campaigns, especially at the national and state level in America, are the media specialists rather than the party bosses. Today's campaign is planned as a media event supplemented by political advertising as candidates seek to establish their public identities and to persuade the voters to support their candidacy. A large array of high-cost technology is used to plan and implement the media campaign. Public opinion polls, talented script writers and producers, and computers are employed primarily to ensure the effective use of the media (Nimmo, 1970; Perry, 1968; Agranoff, 1972).

One reflection of this emphasis is the increase in expenditures by presidential (Table 1) and other candidates (Table 2) for radio and television time. For example, between 1956 and 1972 expenditures by all candidates for television time soared by 367 percent, as shown in Table 2. This sizable increase does not account for large candidate expenditures made to prepare material for use on television stations. It was estimated in 1968 that a 30 minute television documentary would cost from $50,000 to $200,000 to produce and a package of 10 spots from $25,000 to $75,000 (Dunn, 1972, p. 42).

There are some general trends in candidates's use of the media. First, increasingly, candidates are using individual stations rather than television or radio networks (Table 3). In 1956, 44 percent of all television expenditures in America were made on networks; by 1972 that figure had dropped to 20 percent. One reason for the declining use of networks is that candidates for office at all levels of government are increasingly

Table 1

Presidential Campaign Expenditures
for Broadcasting, 1956-72

In dollars

	1956	1960	1964	1968	1972
Broadcast expenditures[a]	4,723,147	b	11,081,565	20,376,595	10,810,367[f]
For television	3,669,897	b	8,895,613	14,637,750	8,624,482
Networks	2,865,633[c]	b	3,807,011[d]	7,362,240	4,840,041
Spots	386,051	b	n.a.	3,518,456	n.a.
Programs	2,124,006	b	n.a.	3,843,784	n.a.
Stations	804,264	b	5,088,602	7,275,510	3,784,441
For Radio	1,053,250	b	2,185,952[d, e]	5,738,845	2,184,141
Networks	318,261	b	119,365	662,674	475,162
Stations	734,989	b	2,066,587	5,076,171	1,708,979

Sources: *1956 General Election Campaigns*, Report of the Subcommittee on Privileges and Elections to the Senate Committee on Rules and Administration, 85 Cong. 1 sess. (1957), Exhibit 24, pp. 4, 14 (cited hereafter as Gore Committee Report). Federal Communications Commission (FCC), *Survey of Political Broadcasting*, 1964, Tables 3, 9A, 22A; and *Survey of Political Broadcasting*, 1968, Tables 5, 9, 20. *Federal Election Campaign Act of 1973: Appendix A*. Hearings before the Subcommittee on Communications of the Committee on Commerce. U.S. Senate, 93 Cong. 1 sess., pp. 4-5 (cited hereafter as *Communications Subcommittee Hearings*).

n.a. Not available.

a. Figures for 1956 are for September 1 to election day, for other years for the general election period.

b. Figures not collected separately for the presidential campaign by the FCC in 1960.

c. Total is greater than the sum of costs for spots and programs because it includes production and preemption charges.

d. Figure is for network spending by all candidates, but those below the presidential level spend little on network television.

e. Figures include no FM stations programmed separately from AM Stations.

f. Includes $1,744 in cable television expenditures.

using television. In 1956, for example, presidential candidates were more likely than candidates for other offices to use television. That has now changed. Since few candidates, other than presidential hopefuls, can afford time on networks which cover the entire country, they do not use them for campaigning.

But even presidential candidates are increasingly using individual stations rather than networks, as shown in Table 1, because this allows them more flexibility in their campaign strategy. They can buy time on stations in states where they need to concentrate their efforts and bypass states where they either are well ahead or have no chance of

Table 2

Election Campaign Expenditures
for Broadcasting by All Candidates, 1956-72

In dollars

	1956	1960	1964	1968	1972
Broadcast expenditures[a]	9,907,006	14,195,278	24,603,989	40,403,498	38,126,904[d]
For television	6,685,709	10,052,322	17,496,405	27,087,027	24,566,710
Networks	2,930,514[b]	2,927,235	3,807,011	7,362,240	4,911,383
Spots	386,051	n.a.	n.a.	3,518,456	2,466,259
Programs	2,171,808	n.a.	n.a.	3,843,784	2,445,124
Stations	3,755,195[b]	7,125,087	13,689,394	19,724,787	19,655,327
Spots	1,917,759	n.a.	10,608,579	17,459,730	17,714,823
Programs	1,521,079	n.a.	3,080,815	2,265,057	1,940,504
For Radio	3,221,297	4,142,956	7,107,584[c]	13,316,471	13,510,005
Networks	320,940	78,867	119,365	662,674	489,459
Stations	2,900,357	4,064,089	6,988,219	12,653,797	13,020,546

Sources: Gore Committee Report, Exhibit 24, pp. 1, 4, 14. FCC, *Survey of Political Broadcasting, 1960*, Table 1; *1964*, Tables 1, 9; *1968*, Tables 3, 5, 8. *Communications Subcommittee Hearings*, p. 219, 221, 222, 224, 227.

n.a. Not available.

a. Figures for 1956 and 1960 are for September 1 to general election date, for 1964, 1968, and 1972 for the general election period.

b. Total is greater than the sum of costs for spots and programs because it includes production and preemption charges.

c. Figures include no FM stations programmed separately from AM stations.

d. Includes $50,189 charges for cable television.

winning. Further, by pinpointing geographical areas, it is possible at times to identify particular interests which can be emphasized on a commercial for a given area. Targeting of voters with a message which is especially designed to appeal to them is less possible on a national network.

Table 3

Percentage of Broadcasting Expenditures for Television Network
and Station Time by All Candidates, General Election, 1956-72

	1956	1960	1964	1968	1972
Network	44%	29%	22%	27%	20%
Station	56	71	78	73	80
Total	$6,685,709	$10,052,322	$17,496,405	$27,087,026	$24,566,710

Source: Table 2

But even presidential candidates are increasingly using individual stations rather than networks, as shown in Table 1, because this allows them more flexibility in their campaign strategy. They can buy time on stations in states where they need to concentrate their efforts and bypass states where they either are well ahead or have no chance of winning. Further, by pinpointing geographical areas, it is possible at times to identify particular interests which can be emphasized on a commercial for a given area. Targeting of voters with a message which is especially designed to appeal to them is less possible on a national network.

A second trend has been the increasing utilization by candidates of "spots"—short 15, 30, or 60 second commercials—rather than longer program times (Tables 4 and 5). Candidates prefer the shorter spots because viewers are more likely to listen to them than the longer programs and because they can be placed as commercials on popular television programs. It is usually possible to reach much larger audiences with spots than with the 30 minute program alternative (Dunn, 1972, pp. 35-41).

Table 4

Percentage of Broadcast Expenditures for Network Television Spots and
Program Time by All Candidates, General Election, 1956, 1968, 1972

	1956	1968	1972
Spots	15%	48%	50%
Programs	85	52	50

Source: Table 2

Table 5

Percentage of Broadcasting Expenditures for Television Station Spot and Program Time by All Candidates, General Election, 1956-72

	1956	1960	1964	1968	1972
Spots	56%	n.a.	77%	89%	90%
Programs	44	n.a.	23	11	10

Source: Table 2
n.a. Not available

A third development over the last 20 years has been increasing use of radio by candidates for political office at all levels. In fact, expenditures grew at even faster rates for radio time than for television between the years 1956 and 1972 (545 percent for radio versus 235 percent for television for presidential candidates and 419 percent for radio and 367 percent for television for all candidates as noted in Tables 1 and 2). Radio has become attractive because candidates believe it is increasingly effective in reaching voters, particularly in what is called "drive time." These are the times during the early morning and late afternoon when American commuters by the millions get into their automobiles and drive from their suburban residences to their jobs, often many miles away. With the increasing trend toward suburban living, many Americans now live great distances from their work, and more and more they prefer the convenience of their automobiles to get them to the city. In addition, as cities become more congested, even those who live relatively close to their work may spend an hour a day in their automobiles as they travel between office and work. The automobile radio is almost universal in America, and in metropolitan areas it reaches a relatively captive audience, at least twice on every working day.

A final and important impact on the changing campaign styles of American candidates is the increasing desirability of conducting a campaign so as to maximize their chances of appearing on television news. In order to do this, candidates must do or say something that reporters consider newsworthy. Their campaign strategy must be designed to create events, activities, or statements of sufficient news value to capture the attention of reporters.

Getting the news coverage is important for a candidate. Beginning with the 1972 elections, the federal government and many states placed limitations upon the expenditures which can be incurred by candidates for national, state, and local offices. One result of this is that most candidates can now spend less for media time than formerly, as reflected in the 1972 figures in Tables 1 and 2. Not only is getting in the news free, but it also reaches many voters who would either not be watching or would ignore political commercials. Thus, candidates still travel extensively when campaigning for public office in America, and their primary reason for doing so is to maximize their chances of free news coverage (Whitcover, 1977; White, 1973).

The Media in Government

The use of the media by public office holders continues after the campaign. In fact, the role of the media is no less ubiquitous in making and implementing policy than in campaigning. Elected and appointed public officials at all levels of government utilize the media to transmit and receive information that is relevant for their work.

The complexities of American government, particularly at the state and national level, make it difficult for any individual public official, sometimes even the chief executive, to have an impact on making and implementing policy. News transmitted through the media constitutes one of the weapons in public officials' arsenals for accomplishing their goals. These goals might include creating or destroying a policy coalition, circulating information inside government, or going over the head of one's superiors in order to surface a policy idea (Sigal, 1973, pp. 7-34; 131-133; 143-148; 153-158; 180-181). Naturally, public officials try to generate news coverage in order to build support for their proposals. Since other officials who must acquiesce or agree if the proposals are to be implemented are among the most attentive consumers of news, the media constitute a very efficient way to accomplish this goal. Thus, public officials often use the media for communicating program ideas, issues, and support to other public officials. Media can be directed to generate support among citizens or specific publics for given program ideas or proposals. Both officials who make and those who receive news sometimes gauge interest on a given policy question by whether news of it appears on the evening television programs or by the number of column inches it receives in a newspaper. Thus, the media are important tools in the attempts of officials to win approval of their policy ideas.

Public officials, especially those who are elected, are also interested in all levels of government getting in the news in their local districts. In order to increase voter acceptability of their performance in office, their general desire is to build an image of "doing a good job" by appearing in the news as advocates of popular public policies or defenders of the public. More importantly, the mere feat of appearing in the news builds name identification with the voters. If this is done frequently enough between elections, the necessity of buying paid advertising for exposure during the election is greatly lessened. There are also the added advantages that appearing in the news not only reaches wider audiences but gives the message more authenticity than a paid advertisement. This is, thus, a primary goal of many elected officials and of those appointed officials who want to build citizen support for their administrations.

The techniques public officials use to make news include news conferences, press releases, direct interviews with individual reporters, meetings, tours, and speeches. Most public officials prefer mechanisms of transmission which give them maximum control over the media message. Some prefer television and radio news coverage because there is a chance for direct interviews. Others prefer press releases directed to either the print or electronic media since this mechanism allows them more control over the message than news conferences or direct interviews where hostile or unwanted questions could be asked.

In America a variant of the technique of direct interviews with individual reporters is termed the "background" or "leak." In both cases, the official's desire is to transmit an anonymous message in order to further his goals (Sigal, 1973). If he is going to be successful in enticing reporters to write news without attributing it directly to a source, the government official must have a story which reporters will find very newsworthy. Usually the official is one of the few persons who is informed about the matter in question. The reporter is willing to grant anonymity to the source to get the story. The source is willing to give the story to achieve his or her goal. The use of unattributable sources by reporters is generally deplored, but it is likely that reporters will continue to use such sources because they provide them with information not otherwise available. Often backgrounders and leaks are funneled through one favored reporter who would have as the additional incentive for cooperation getting a "scoop" on his or her opposition.

Public officials also look to the media to bring them information (Sigal, 1973). In fact, media are a major way in which government officials can gather intelligence about their larger political environment. Because decision makers need the cooperation of others and must often accommodate them or anticipate their reactions, they frequently check the media to learn the plans, proposals, and moods of the people with whom they must work to achieve their goals. On most civic matters public officials find out the reactions to and opinions about policies or activities associated with their work through the media. These reactions may come from other government officials, perhaps in other branches or at other levels of the government, as well as from specific individuals or groups outside of the government who have some interest in the matter under question. Often public officials rely on the media to gauge how their constituents view a given situation, then decide how their constituents are reacting, and respond accordingly. Now with their desired goals in mind, they can introduce new information to the news channels to change the message being presented there, if that needs to be done. Thus, the media serve as "instant" public opinion polls which provide public officials reactions to specific events and activities of government.

Another use of the media by public officials is that of monitoring potential problems of society with which government must deal or of checking on the activities of government itself. In the summer of 1978, for example, stories in several Washington newspapers dealt with alleged bribes offered to and kickbacks received by General Service Administration officials in the awarding of building and service contracts for government office space. Much of the information appearing in the news was apparently not previously known by the agency's top administration or by members of Congress. Frequently television documentaries and newspaper series cite critical conditions ranging from hunger to mine safety which bring to the attention of government officials societal problems which are amenable to government actions. Also singling out these problems suggests potential issues to public officials. By focusing on a particular situation, the news organization demonstrates interest in that area. Public officials who desire publicity know that they will find it easier to get coverage on that situation than on ones with less news interest.

Finally, officials use the press for suggestions, ideas, and interpretations. While documentaries or series may suggest issues, news commentators' interpretations of events may be helpful to public officials and editorial writers, news columnists, and commentators and may provide ideas which public officials find useful for action.

The information, reactions, opinions, and other intelligence made available through the media are especially important in the intergovernmental structure of the United States with its multiplicity of governments providing services. Many federal government programs, for example, are implemented by state and local governments, and other policies at the state and local level are regulated or influenced by the activities and rules of the government in Washington. State and local government officials themselves are increasingly attempting to impact policy in Washington because they know that it affects directly their work performance. Although many of these officials rely upon specialized communication from associations or other informed sources, they also depend on the media to keep them abreast of the developments and activities of the federal government which affect their own positions. Thus, just as we have seen that the media is playing a role in intergovernmental communication throughout the multiplicity of branches and agencies of American governments, it also plays a similar role in intragovernmental communication among the multiple levels of American government.

Reporters and News Definitions

The relationship between reporters and public officials has often been called a symbiotic one. Reporters need to uncover news stories in the basic work of producing their stories. On the other hand, as we have seen, public officials have a variety of goals which can be served by getting news coverage. In order to do that, they must meet the basic definition of news and call it to the attention of reporters in time for them to gather it and meet the deadline for a given broadcast or newspaper edition.

One writer has indicated that government news is essentially the product of two types of organizations—the news organization in which the reporter works and the bureaucratic organization in which the government official works. In each of these organizational settings, the actors have work which they must accomplish and goals which they must achieve which impinge directly upon the newsmaking process in America (Sigal, 1973). The goals of the bureaucratic organization are similar to the ones discussed earlier in this chapter. The goals of the news organization, however, are important to reporters because they determine whether or not stories that they like or uncover will, in fact, make the news.

News definitions are not precise. There is a great deal of uncertainty in the minds of reporters and editors as to what is and is not news. News is also defined relatively. On some days the competition for space or time is not great. Items which ordinarily would not have appeared in the news appear on these "slow" news days. On the other hand, cataclysmic events, such as large natural disasters, deaths of political leaders, or crises of war or foreign policy, may crowd out items which on other days would have been considered top news stories.

With this uncertainty, the reporter must work at producing news stories. In most news organizations in America, reporters are expected to turn in stories almost every day. There are several clues to assist the reporter in defining what is news. Frequently because of the uncertainty over news definitions, reporters protect themselves by writing the same material other reporters write. They are sensitive about the movements of their colleagues to make certain that the competition does not write about items that they know nothing about and to validate what they believe is news (Rosten, 1937, pp. 19-77; 97; 113; 221; 225; 261; Dunn, 1969, pp. 25; 29-30; 35-41; 103-104; 164-167; Nimmo, 1964, pp. 118; 128; 148-154; Cohen, 1963, pp. 56; 81-83; 90; 224-230;

Breed, 1955a; Grey, 1966). This mutual validation process is reinforced by the editors to whom reporters report. Reporters who miss stories run the risk of being criticized by editors for not getting them. There are thus great pressures for reporters to keep up with what other reporters are covering.

Another major factor in the reporters' environment is the news organization for which they work (Sigal, 1973; Breed, 1955b; Rosten, 1937; Cohen, 1963; Nimmo, 1970; Sigelman, 1973; Warner, 1971). This includes most importantly the editors or, in the case of television, the producers who are responsible for the ultimate selection of stories which will appear. Since one major goal of reporters is to get their stories printed or broadcast, a reporter is sensitive to the way in which stories are handled by the news organization. If certain stories do not appear at all, are cut drastically, or appear in an undesirable location, the reporter naturally deduces that his editors are not interested in stories on that topic. On the other hand, if they are prominently displayed in print or emphasized in broadcasts, the reporter knows that his editors are interested, and he will be influenced to write more stories on the same or a similar topic.

Ideas for stories develop out of daily conversations among reporters covering the same beat, the agenda of the governmental agency or government they cover, or suggestions given by editors. The easiest stories to write are about meetings, including hearings, and press conferences, or ones based on press releases (Rosten, 1937; Nimmo, 1964; Brandt, 1936, p. 175). The first two items are action events which in themselves may be newsworthy. Press releases present more of a problem since reporters usually view them as self-serving. But they may suggest additional areas of inquiry for a reporter, or they may sufficiently meet the definition of news to constitute the basis of the story in themselves.

Another determiner of the subject for stories for reporters is the sources with whom they work. This is particularly true for stories which do not cover specific meetings or activities. Many dramatic stories originate in this way. The coverage of Watergate by *Washington Post* reporters Carl Bernstein and Bob Woodward illustrates dramatically the utility and necessity of sources to initiate and sustain a story (Bernstein and Woodward, 1974).

Television news reporters behave similarly to newspaper reporters. One recent study, however, has indicated several important differences. In his study of television network news Edward Jay Epstein

(1973) found that network reporters have less freedom in choosing their stories than most newspaper reporters and that networks also tend to assign reporters on a rotating basis so that none become more expert in their areas than their supervisors. He also found that television network news seeks out expected events because of the necessity of having complex equipment available for coverage. It was also necessary to centrally assign this equipment because of the expense of camera crews to accompany reporters (Epstein, 1973, pp. 25-27; 54-59; 135-144). Finally, affiliates' concern with government regulation placed networks in a position of presenting their news coverage so as not to offend them (Epstein, 1973).

In spite of the ambiguity of what news is, there are some guidelines reporters use to determine what is news. Conflict, controversy, and attack are almost always at the top of any definition of news. Acrimony, misunderstandings, and opposition always increase the likelihood that the situation will be come news (Dunn, 1969; Cohen, 1963; Rosten, 1937). Change can also be newsworthy. New courses of action and departures in a different or unexpected direction, particularly on items of great interest to news consumers, are also likely to have news value. Unique events, too, make the news, again because reporters believe that others will find them interesting. The importance of unique events is immaterial; they may include a governor who rides a bicycle backwards, a candidate who runs for office by walking through the state, or a political leader who in an unguarded moment behaves in a bizarre manner. Unique events are, of course, very elusive because once they have occurred their uniqueness wears off fairly quickly. Finally, reporters are also interested in well known top public officials who are sometimes covered incessantly (Grey, 1966a). U.S. presidents, for example, find it almost impossible to take a vacation privately. Governors of states can take a tour of state facilities or call a press conference almost at will and capture the attention of the press. Lesser public officials find this more difficult.

On any given day reporters take these basic news definitions and apply them to what is occurring. They are thus preoccupied with action, and news is usually that day's activities or events (Grey, 1966b; Valleau, 1952, p. 163). Choosing what to cover is a function of what other reporters are covering, anticipations of reactions by editors or producers, considerations of whether the events can be covered before the day's deadline for stories, whether the activity can be written about in a straightforward way which, in part, is determined by how well the reporter understands the activity or action, and whether the reporter is personally interested in the event (Tuchman, 1973).

There are several implications in reporters' news definitions and routines which affect the ways officials make news. Obviously, for officials to make the news they must understand the routine and engage in activities or stage events which will capture reporters' attention by meeting their news definitions.

Since reporters emphasize events and actions in their definitions of news, meetings and press conferences are therefore important ways to attract their notice. The pressures upon reporters lead them to cover these events rather than to study problems or situations not currently covered by meetings, press conferences, or press releases. Because reporters believe that events guarantee stories, they are disinclined toward independent study and investigation because they risk the possibility of not getting stories. Thus, officials provide much of the initiative for stories, particularly officials who choose what meetings to have and who stage them to receive favorable publicity. This is particularly true of the state and local levels of government in America. On the national level, some news organizations are willing, at least on occasions, to devote great resources to undercover stories and are willing to encourage reporters to engage in activity which may not make the news. Still, most news organizations are hesitant to provide this kind of support because of potential law suits by those who are being covered, the possibility of being misled by sources, and nagging uncertainties about the newsworthiness of events—particularly when other organizations do not join in covering the situation (Bernstein and Woodward, 1974).

The Impact of the Media in America

The role of the media as a mechanism through which citizens and officials (or candidates) can exchange information is important in the policy and electoral process in America. All politically relevant activities or news constitute too much information for all of it to be transmitted through the media. Newspapers do not have enough space, and electronic news programs do not have enough time to permit this. The media thus determine to a large extent which symbols will be communicated and which will not be allowed. Decisions about what will become news are determined by a complex set of criteria that emphasizes conflict, change, and uniqueness. Some events and situations that meet the definition of news become news and others do not. To get free

media coverage, an individual's or public official's messages must conform to the media's news definitions.

Of course, if a publicity seeker with a message cannot capture news
attention with it, there are other resources. The primary one is to buy
advertising. But buying what cannot be obtained free is possible only
within limits. The credibility of news is higher than that of advertising.
Those who receive information are much more likely to believe that
advertising is self-serving, biased, and distorted than they would the
news. Moreover, advertising costs money, and those with limited
resources may not be able to mount a paid media campaign. Those who
determine what can and cannot become news through the media thus
possess a valuable political resource with great potential impact on the
policy and election process in America.

CREATING ISSUES

Perhaps the most important potential impact of the media is its
ability to focus attention. It can direct the attention of both citizens and
officials to certain governmental issues or candidates (Dunn, 1969). By
continual emphasis on certain items, the media can create issues.

This power to create issues can have a range of potential impacts.
Generally, the media can alter both citizens' and officials' perceptions
about what is important (Cohen, 1963). In the policy arena the media,
either by generating within itself or by permitting officials, citizens, or
interest groups to transmit information through it, can change the
priorities of what is important and can put items on the agenda for
decision that would not otherwise appear. This is done by providing
information about problems that call for government solution and by
presenting ideas, suggestions, and proposals for public action. Once an
item has become an issue, the potential results are exponentially
expanded as more and more individuals, both citizens and officials,
alter their perception of what is important. Since officials have time for
only a limited number of items, what is placed on the agenda for action
is important because this determines what will obtain government
attention (Cobb & Elder, 1971). Other items are, in fact, excluded. This
is important because when it is implicitly decided not to decide, what
some call nondecisions, the status quo is perpetuated and this, too, is
important in allocating resources and determining values to be served
by governmental policies (Polsby, 1963, 96-97; Bachrach and Baratz,
1962; Bachrach and Baratz, 1963). But once perceiving that the media
think a matter is important, the officials often equate media attention
with public interest in the matter (Dunn, 1969). The officials then

perceive that they must demonstrate that they are doing something constructive in the area, and they may view the situation as an opportunity to catch public attention in order to promote their own images or programs.

Citizens are also affected by what become issues. They may see problems which they did not see previously that demand some government solution. Issues like hunger, pollution, civil rights, and medical care have become a part of the policy agenda in the last 15 years, in large part because of media attention. Once an item reaches public attention, however, citizens are more willing than they were previously to consider government activity in the area as advantageous and may be more inclined to support public officials and agencies proposing to deal with the problem.

As for the electoral arena, the media, by devoting attention to certain candidates, can influence the public in making judgments about who is important enough for serious attention, particularly in the prenominating and primary stages of the election. How does a person become a serious contender for the presidency or a governorship? In part, this is determined by reporters for the media who watch potential candidates and make judgments about whether they constitute appropriate "timber" (Broder, 1969). Once newsmen make that judgment and begin writing, they can, in effect, create the timber they think they have discovered. And in a primary with 15 or 20 candidates, the media, by devoting attention to only a few, actually create impressions which may have an impact upon voters about who are the "serious" candidates with a chance of winning.

By focusing attention upon an issue, the press may also intervene in the normal decision making process in government. Generally in this process officials considering a decision consult most closely with those they believe will be most directly affected by the decision. Normally the consultation is limited to those who have previously demonstrated to these officials that they are the legitimate spokesmen for the affected interests. By intervening, the media make the issue visible, and this alerts additional groups and decision makers to their stakes in the outcome. As the scope of conflict has thus been increased, it is possible that officials will be sensitive to different considerations and that the outcome will be different (Schattschneider, 1960, pp. 1-19).

MEETING THE INFORMATION NEEDS
OF OFFICIALS AND CITIZENS

Another way in which the press makes an impact on the policy and election processes is through its ability to meet the information needs of officials and citizens as they seek to learn about their larger political environment. The public official often seems desperate in his attempt to learn about his environment, and the information available through the media is helpful in this quest. He can learn about the strategy of his opponents in controversies. He can also ascertain the reactions of other officials and nongovernmental groups to his actions and proposals and can learn of the proposals of others.

Implicit in this discussion is that the media also has the ability to provide both citizens and officials with a mechanism through which to exchange information. Since each desires to influence the other in a variety of ways, some exchange of communication must occur. Most of the time such exchanges cannot occur directly in face-to-face encounters. Since such encounters are less and less possible in our society, the media fulfill an increasingly larger exchange role.

CONDITIONS AFFECTING THE IMPACT OF THE MEDIA

In general, the impact which the media can exert on a policy or electoral decision is determined by the extent to which it can monopolize communication channels. At the national level in this country there are three networks, many national magazines, and several newspapers that have important audiences. At the local level, however, there are usually only a few of these, but there are more informal channels of information exchange in such face-to-face encounters as social clubs, telephone calls, and various organization meetings.

Of course the presence or absence of competing media can be determined individually as well as structurally. It is possible that even when several sources are available certain individuals or officials will not sample widely among available sources. When analyzing such individuals—whether they be officials or citizens—it becomes clear that the media will have a greater impact when they serve as the only source of information.

In terms of the national, state, and local policy and electoral arenas, this discussion leads to the conclusion that the media probably have more impact at the local or state level where there were few competing information channels than at the national level where competition abounds. The situation is not that clear, however. It is possible that the informal channels compensate, at least in part, for the lack of formal media competition in most areas at the state and local level of government.

In spite of the potential impact of the media, there are several constraints to their strength. Perhaps the greatest impediment to their impact is the availability of other sources of information, whatever they may be. The media themselves seldom speak with one voice, particularly at the national level of government. There are additional institutional sources which may be important, including interest groups, which act as cue givers to segments of the public on given policy and election questions. As with any other potential agent of influence, the streams of information emanating from the media must interact with preexisting attitudes and values held by those receiving the message. A classic example of this occurred during the 1948 election when supporters of Harry Truman perceived that he agreed with their position on the Taft-Hartley Act (a labor management relations act) and supporters of Thomas Dewey did likewise, regardless of the true positions of the candidates.

Social psychologists generally hold that people frequently interpret information so that it agrees very closely with what they already think. (The "theory of cognitive dissonance" advanced by Leon Festinger [1957], explains why this might be so). The way they do this varies, but individuals tend to selectively perceive—hearing only what they want to hear or failing to hear any part or all of a message that does not conform to their preexisting opinions and beliefs (Berelson, 1954, pp. 215-222). Some scholars also believe in the efficacy of the "two-step" flow of information through various segments of the public. This theory holds that an attentive audience first gets messages from the media and then reinterprets them by word of mouth to individuals with whom they come in contact (Katz, 1957). These individuals thus filter the stream of information transmitted by the media and diffuse its impact.

Reference Notes

1. 47 U.S.C.A. §315(a).

2. *Petition for Aspen Inst.*, 55 F.C.C. 2d 697 (1975); aff'd. *Chisholm* v. *F.C.C.*, 538 F. 2d 349 (D.C. Cir. 1976).

3. *Miami Herald Publishing Company* v. *Tornillo*, 418 U.S. 241 (1974).

4. 427 U.S. 539 (1976).

5. 5 U.S.C.A. §552.

6. 5 U.S.C.A. §552(a) 2.

7. See, for example, *Saxby* v. *The Washington Post* 417 U.S. 843 (1974); *Pell* v. *Procunier*, 417 U.S. 817 (1974); *Houchins* v. *KQED Inc.* 98 S. Ct. 2588 (1978). For discussion of *Saxbe* and *Pell* see Pember, D. *Mass Media Law*. Dubuque, Iowa: William C. Brown & Co., 1977, pp. 443-445.

8. 403 U.S. 713 (1971). For discussion see Pember, D. *Mass Media Law*, Supra note 8, pp. 76-79, and Devol, K. *Mass Media and the Supreme Court*. New York: Hastings House, 1976, pp. 42-54 & 61-68.

9. *Branzburgh* v. *Hayes* 408 U.S. 665, 681 (1972).

10. For a discussion of "shield" laws see Pember, D. *Mass Media Law*, Supra note 8, pp. 303-307.

11. *Branzburg* v. *Hayes* 408 U.S. 665, (1972).

12. See *Cervantes* v. *Time*, 446 F. 2d 631 (1972); *Baker* v. *F. and F. Investment*, 470 F. 2d 778 (1972); *Carey* v. *Hume*, 429 F. 2d 631 (1974); *U.S.* v. *Liddy*, 354 F. Supp. 208 (1973).

13. 28 C.F.R. §50.10.

14. 376 U.S. 254 (1964).

15. See *Associated Press* v. *Walker* 388 U.S. 130 (1967).

16. See *Curtis Publishing Company* v. *Butts* 388 U.S. 130 (1967).

17. *Gertz* v. *Robert Welch Inc.*, 418 U.S. 323 (1974); *Time Inc.* v. *Firestone*, 424 U.S. 448 (1975).

18. *Gertz* v. *Robert Welch Inc.*, 418 U.S. 323 (1974).

19. *Zacchini* v. *Scripps-Howard Broadcasting Co.*, 433 U.S. 562 (1977).

20. "Multiple Ownership of AM, FM, and Television Broadcast Stations," 18 FCC 288 (1953). See *U.S.* v. *Storer Broadcasting*, 351 U.S. 192 (1956), which upheld the regulations.

21. *U.S.* v. *The Times Mirror Co.*, 274 F. supp. 606 (1967) affirmed 390 U.S. 712 (1968) rehearing denied 391 U.S. 971 (1968).

22. *FCC* v. *The National Citizen's Commission for Broadcasting* 98 S. Ct. 2096 (1978).

References

Agranoff, R. *The New Style in Election Campaigns.* Boston: Holbrook Press, 1972.

Bachrach, P. & Baratz, M.S. "Two Faces of Power." *The American Political Science Review,* December 1962, *56*(4), 947-952.

Bachrach, P. & Baratz, M.S., "Decisions and Non-Decisions: An Analytical Framework." *American Political Science Review,* September 1963, *57*(3), 632-642.

Bagdikian, B. H. "Newspaper Mergers, the Final Phase." *Columbia Journalism Review,* March/April 1977, *15*(6), 17.

Berelson, B. R., Lazarsfeld, P. F. & McPhee, W. N. *Voting.* Chicago: The University of Chicago Press, 1954.

Bernstein, C. & Woodward, B. *All the President's Men.* New York: Simon and Schuster, 1974.

Bernstein, P. W. "TV Networks Get Some Bad News From Dunedin." *Fortune,* January 16, 1978, 108.

Brandt, R. P. "The Washington Correspondent." *Journalism Quarterly,* June 1936, *13*(2), 175.

Breed, W. "Newspaper 'Opinion Leaders' and Processes of Standardization." *Journalism Quarterly,* Summer 1955a, *32*(3), 277-284.

Breed, W. "Social Control in the Newsroom: A Functional Analysis." *Social Forces,* May 1955b, *33* (4), 326-335.

Broder, D. "Political Reporters in Presidential Politics." *The Washington Monthly,* February 1969, *1*(1), 20-33.

Brunner, R. B. & Chen, K. "Is Cable the Answer?" *Journal of Communication,* Spring 1978, *28*(2), 81-84.

"Closed Circuit and Summary of Broadcasting." *Broadcasting,* September 4, 1978, 9-52.

Cobb, R. W. & Elder, C. D. "The Politics of Agenda-Building: An Alternative Perspective for Modern Democratic Theory." *Journal of Politics,* November 1971, *33*(4), 892-915.

Cohen, B. C. *The Press and Foreign Policy.* Princeton, N. J.: Princeton University Press, 1963.

"Crossowners Win Claim on Crossownership." *Broadcasting,* June 19, 1978, 27.

"Daily Newspapers—Total Number, Circulation, and Cost Trend." *Encyclomedia,* Newspaper Edition, 1977, *1*(1), 29.

Dunn, D. D. *Financing Presidential Campaigns.* Washington, D. C.: The Brookings Institution, 1972.

Dunn, D. D. *Public Officials and the Press.* Reading, Mass.: Addison-Wesley Publishing Co., 1969.

Edwards, V. E., Jr. "News Media Ownership." *Journalism and a Free Society,* Editorial Research Report, Suzanne de Lesseps, March 11, 1977, *1*(10), 214-215.

Epstein, E. J. *News from Nowhere.* New York: Random House, 1973.

Fairness Doctrine. A Staff Report Prepared for the Senate Committee on Commerce 90 Cong. 2 sess., 1968.

Festinger, L. A Theory of Cognitive Dissonance. Evanston, Ill.: Row, Peterson Co., 1957.

Goodale, J. C. "Branzburg v. Hayes and the Development of a Qualified Privilege for Newsmen." Hastings Law Review, 1975, 26, 709.

Gormley, W. T. "How Cross-Ownership Affects News-Gathering."Columbia Journalism Review, May/June 1977, 15(7), 38.

Grey, D. L. "Decision-Making by a Reporter under Deadline Pressure." Journalism Quarterly, Autumn 1966a, 43(3), 427.

Grey, D. L. "Supreme Court Headlines: Accuracy v. Precision." Columbia Journalism Review, Summer 1966b, 5(2), 26.

Howard, H. H. "The Contemporary Status of Television Group Ownership." Journalism Quarterly, Autumn 1976, 53(3), 402-404.

Katz, E. "The Two-Step Flow of Communication: An Up-To-Date Report on an Hypothesis." Public Opinion Quarterly, Spring 1957, 21(1), 61-78.

"Letter From the Publisher." Editor and Publisher Yearbook 1978. 1978.

McIntosh, T. J. "Why the Government Can't Stop Press Mergers." Columbia Journalism Review, May/June 1977, 15(7), 48-50.

"Newsbriefs." Editor and Publisher, December 31, 1977, 110(53), 4.

Nielsen TV 1969. Chicago: A. C. Nielsen Co., 1969.

Nimmo, D. Newsgathering in Washington. New York: Atherton Press, 1964.

Nimmo, D. The Political Persuaders: The Techniques of Modern Election Campaigns. Englewood Cliffs, N.J.: Prentice-Hall, 1970.

Perry, J. M. The New Politics. New York: Clarkson N. Potter, 1968.

Polsby, N. W. Community Power and Political Theory. New Haven, Conn.: Yale University Press, 1963.

Prosser, William. Law of Torts. St. Paul: West Publishing Co., 1971.

Rosten, L. C. The Washington Correspondents. New York: Harcourt, Brace and Co., 1937.

Schattschneider, E. E. The Semi-Sovereign People. New York: Holt, Rinehard and Winston, 1960.

Second Report and Order. Fed. C. C. Dockett No. 18110, FCC, memo 29942, January 29, 1975, 75-104.

"A Short Course in Broadcasting 1978." Broadcasting Yearbook 1978, A-2.

Sigal, L. V. Reporters and Officials: The Organization in Politics of Newsmaking. Lexington, Mass.: D. C. Heath, 1973.

Sigelman, L. "Reporting the News: An Organizational Analysis." American Journal of Sociology, 1973, 79(1), 132-151.

Simons, H. & Califano, J. The Media and the Law. New York: Praeger Publishers, 1976.

Sobel, J. & Emery, E. "U.S. Dailies' Competition in Relation to Circulation Size: A Newspaper Data Update." Journalism Quarterly, Spring 1978, 55(1), 145-419.

State and Local Watch. Intergovernmental Perspective, Winter 1977 3(1), 9.

Statistical Abstract of the U.S. 1977. U.S. Government Printing Office, 1977, 584.

Sterling, C. H. "Trends in Daily Newspaper and Broadcast Ownership, 1922-1970." Journalism Quarterly, Summer 1975, 52(2), 251-252.

Thrift, R. R., Jr. "How Chain Ownership Effects Editorial Vigor of Newspapers."
    Journalism Quarterly, Summer 1977, 54(2), 327-331.
Tuchman, G. "Making News by Doing Work: Routinizing the Unexpected,"
    American Journal of Sociology, 1973, 79(1), 110-131.
Valleau, J. F. "Oregon Legislative Reporting: The Newsmen and Their Methods."
    Journalism Quarterly, Spring 1952, 29(2), 163.
Warner, M. "Organizational Contort and Control of Policy in the Television
    Newsroom: A Participant Observation Study." *British Journal of Sociology*,
    1971, 22, 283-294.
Weaver, W. "U.S. Information Act: Difficulties Despite Success." *New York
    Times*, August 8, 1977, 1.
Whitcover, J. *Marathon: The Pursuit of the Presidency 1972-1976*. New York:
    Viking Press, 1977.
White, T. H. *The Making of the President 1972*. New York: Atheneum, 1973.

IX.
Government and the News Media: Mexico

Marvin Alisky

Mexico began this century with an inherited dictatorship under Porfirio Díaz dating from 1876, and a political history of governmental control of the press. In November 1910, a struggle against the past began with military battles and evolved into elaborate social reforms embodied in the federal Constitution of 1917. The civil war between rebels seeking social justice and the entrenched forces of age-old landed gentry raged for a decade, to 1920, in which one million Mexicans—out of a population the of only 15 million—lost their lives, civilians as often as soldiers, women as often as men, children as often as adults. Out of so much bloodshed came the ongoing institutionalized social reform called The Revolution, spelled in Mexico with a patriotic capital "R" to distinguish it from the many revolts and coups d'etat which preceded it.

Individual political freedoms seemed central to the slogan "Effective Suffrage, No Re-election" espoused by the intellectual articulator of the Revolution's theory and plans, ill-fated President Francisco Madero, who was murdered in 1913. A more central concern of those peasants who actually fought and won the battles was the slogan "Bread, land, and justice," the credo of peasant general Emiliano Zapata. As Wilkie (1970) has emphasized, the Revolution's program of government-directed integration of Mexican social and economic life since 1917 has continued to be justified by establishment leaders as the principal priority of Mexican public life. The goal of truly representative government, complete with vigorous opposition parties and a completely independent system of mass media could wait until the Revolution could create a viable middle class, an expanding economy, and a discernibly developing nation.

In an open society, such as that found in the United States, the privately-owned news media certainly influence government by influencing official attitudes through emphasis or de-emphasis of governmental policies, programs, and performances, as Rivers, Miller, and Gandy (Chaffee, 1975) point out. In the less open society of Mexico,

privately-owned newspapers, magazines, and radio and television stations also similarly exert such influence, but not to the same extent.
This chapter will examine a few of the entities with which the Mexican
government attempts to guide the flow of news and with which the
media attempt to chronicle public life.

Governmental Mechanisms of Control

Mexico's power elite has not had to fall back on overt censorship.
Built within the Mexican governmental and political structures are the
mechanisms of control, ranging from the regulatory agencies to the
informal techniques categorized by the concept of "news management."

Newspapers and magazines cannot publish unless newsprint (paper)
suitable in texture for offset or direct-type printing remains continuously available at prices feasible for the fiscal solvency of the publications involved. In Mexico, all production of newsprint and its importation and distribution under federal law remains a monopoly of the joint
private-public corporation PIPSA (Productora e Importadora de Papel,
S. A., or Producer and Importer of Paper, Inc.) (Note 1).

Radio and television stations must receive assigned frequencies and
transmitter power to avoid engineering chaos and the cacophony which
would result if two rival stations tried to broadcast too near each other
in the broadcasting spectrum for transmitting clarity. In addition, in
Mexico in the name of public service, the government requires daily and
weekly reports to be aired (Alisky, 1953a, 1953b, 1953c, 1954a), centered in the radio, television, and film office of the Ministry of Internal
Affairs or Government (Secretaria de Gobernacion).

Although not labeled as control mechanisms, the Mexican government's Cabinet ministries and agencies, and the state and municipal
governments dominated by federal policies in a day-to-day practical
sense also help the government manage the flow of news through their
role as sources of information for the media. Not all major news stories
stem from official sources, but a majority of the events and announcements shaping Mexican public life certainly do.

NEWSPRINT CONTROL

Mexico's paper mills are concentrated in the Federal District and in
the states of Oaxaca and Mexico. Most pulp production turns out
cartons, wrapping paper, stationery, and other nonpublishing products, with the amount of newsprint for newspapers and magazines
remaining a small percentage of the mills metric ton total.

As Brandenburg (1964) noted, modern large-scale paper production in Mexico geared to domestic needs began in 1936 with the founding of the Titan Corporation by the Garza Sada financial investors group in Monterrey. In the 1950s, the government's development bank, Nacional Financiera, launched the joint public-private Celulosa Corporation with Kimberly-Clark as a partner in the state of Chihuahua and, in 1958, the newsprint plant, Papel Túxtepec, in the state of Oaxaca.

By 1960, Mexico was producing 30,000 metric tons of newsprint a year, forcing publishers to import 82 percent of the newsprint their newspapers and magazines required from Canada, the United States, Sweden, and Finland. In the 1970s, Mexico, along with the other developing nations, continued to import a majority of its newsprint needs. On June 1, 1976, the Villa de Reyes newsprint mill opened in the state of San Luis Potosí, giving Mexico its first paper plant able to recycle old newspapers in the production of newsprint. In 1978, Mexican newsprint plants achieved an annual production of 110,000 metric tons, or 40 percent of the newsprint needs of Mexican newspapers and magazines. Thus, in an 18 year period, the percentage of imported paper had been reduced from 82 to 60 percent (UN Statistical Yearbook, 1977).

Although the republic of Mexico has 240 daily newspapers, provincial papers have grown slowly, due in part to the fact that seven Mexico City dailies circulate nationally. In 1973, the three largest metropolitan centers of the republic—greater Mexico City, greater Guadalajara, and greater Monterrey—had 59 percent of the total daily newspaper circulation of the republic. The remainder of Mexico, with 80 percent of the total population, bought only 41 percent of the newspapers. Five years later, in late 1978, the imbalance had worsened, with 60 percent of the daily papers selling in the three largest metropolitan areas.

Deciding how much imported and domestically-produced newsprint may be purchased by each newspaper is PIPSA. This corporation, controlling all importation of newsprint and every publicly-owned or privately-owned newsprint plant in the republic, has a board of directors made up of the publishers of the Mexico City major dailies, plus the head of the Association of Newspapers of the States. Serving as substitute board members are the major magazine publishers of Mexico. In addition, the federal government designates three commissioners to coordinate the administration of policies the board enacts. As noted in the newsmagazine *Tiempo* (1960), these *Comisarios* sit with the voting board members and the nonvoting substitutes at annual meetings.

Publications ranging the political spectrum from left to right receive newsprint quotas based on their paid circulations and the number of pages customarily printed for each issue. Most Mexican newspapers and magazines can be classified as either progovernment, neutral, or benignly antiestablishment. Political scientists such as Pablo Gonzalez Casanova (1965), L. Vincent Padgett (1976), Martin C. Needler (1971), and Kenneth F. Johnson (1971) have differed on various aspects of the locus of power in Mexico but agree that at the apex the Revolutionary coalition can be identified. Scholars and observers do not agree as to the scope of that coalition. Who besides the President, his Cabinet ministers, a few key industrialists, labor leaders, and investors are involved? Regardless, analysts of Mexican public life, in classifying newspapers and magazines, should not use as calipers solely the government as a benchmark, but rather the Revolutionary coalition, thereby entwining key governmental entities, the power elite within the dominant Institutional Revolutionary party (PRI or Partido Revolucionario Institucional), and selected management and labor union leaders ranging from industrial to agrarian.

As Ronald Chilcote observed in 1963, working with PIPSA is the government's Publications Classification Commission (CCP or Comision Calificadora de Publicaciones), which enforces unevenly and sporadically a Code of Ethics formula. Any violation of that code could prompt the CCP to have PIPSA halt distribution of newsprint to an accused publication, thereby halting its operations without ever utilizing formal censorship as practiced in various countries of the world ranging from Communist to right wing.

In June 1962, the semimonthly news magazine *Política*, which had a physical format resembling *Time*, Marxist in philosophy and enthusiastically pro-Castro in editorial stance, was suspended for two weeks from receiving PIPSA newsprint deliveries. This action by the CCP prevented the circulation of the issue prepared for the visit of President John F. Kennedy with Mexican President Adolfo López Mateos in Mexico City. That issue had been set in type, with a few copies run off for the benefit of *Política* editors and advisors from the Cuban Embassy, which secretly had been subsidizing the slick-paper magazine. *Política* reported only 5,000 paid subscribers to tax authorities but claimed 257,000 street sales at 3 pesos (U.S. 24 cents) each. In 1968, after the magazine had ceased operations, a government audit revealed that 75 percent of its operating costs had come not from its meager advertising sales, nor subscribers or street sales, but rather from subsidies both foreign and domestic—Communist in nature. It had indeed circulated 262,000 copies of each issue twice a month as claimed, but thousands of those copies had been given away in the name of political propaganda.

The anti-Kennedy issue, which never circulated because the magazine could not get sufficient newsprint from PIPSA, contained personal, abusive attacks on President Kennedy, calling him a war criminal in league with Mexico's oligarchy, planning further exploitation of Mexican farm hands in the United States under the U.S.-Mexican Bracero Treaty, which ended in December 1964.

A *Política* staff member smuggled several copies of the limited run of the suspended issue out of the plant and sold them for large sums to interested Mexican officials of the Foreign Relations Ministry. The author of this chapter was able to read briefly through one of those copies before having to return it to a Mexican administrator.

In the 25 years since the Mexican government has been able to utilize its control over the distribution of newsprint, only a relatively few such suspensions have taken place. And in most of these few cases the suspended publication has been far left rather than far right, though the fascist overtones in one issue of the weekly *Orden*, organ of the far right Sinarquista Movement, in 1969 almost caused a suspension. The issue in question attacked the government's distribution of free textbooks to primary schools because a historical reference to the Catholic Church was severely critical. The principal article in that issue then demanded that public education be phased out in favor of parochial schools. Newsprint delivery at *Orden* was delayed five days before the CCP decided that the ethics code had not been violated, and PIPSA then supplied the paper, allowing *Orden* to publish late.

The demise of *Política* finally came at the end of 1967. Begun in 1960, the magazine soon reached a circulation of 28,000, distributed mostly in the Federal District. But after 1962, with Cuban subsidies, its press runs rapidly increased and its distribution quickly spread to university and prep school campuses all over Mexico. Its editor, Manuel Marcué, echoed the world views of Fidel Castro. Its publisher, Edmundo Jardón, had been chief of the Mexico City bureau of Prensa Latina, the news service which the Cuban government had created to compete with the Associated Press and United Press International in Latin America.

The issue of *Política* dated December 15, 1967, never appeared. After almost eight years of publishing twice a month except for the suspended issue in June 1962, during the Kennedy visit, the magazine had again missed an issue. Late in December, the final edition of *Política* appeared bearing the date December 1-31. On January 3, 1968, the magazine officially announced it had ceased publication permanently.

PIPSA board members had halted any further newsprint shipments to *Política* based on a CCP ruling that the magazine had violated the ethics code of the nation. Although the magazine in late 1967 had gradually increased its hints that it would encourage protestors against the government's hosting of the 1968 Olympics in Mexico City—a protest which did materialize during the July-October 1968 period, culminating in bloody riots—no issue of the magazine during the last quarter of 1967 triggered the adverse CCP ruling. Rather, the issue dated June 1-14, 1967, with the headline "Libertad de prensa en Mexico?" ("Press freedom in Mexico?") had been the edition serving as the basis of the CCP indictment (Note 2).

Throughout the 1970s, the CCP and PIPSA have not dealt primarily with ethics code violations and the withholding of newsprint shipments to publications. Rather, the thrust of the government to guide the editorial straying from unofficial limits has centered on control through stock purchases.

Control through stock purchases. The major example of stock-purchase guidance occurred in 1972 when the government owned and operated Mexican Industrial Credit Society (SOMEX or Sociedad Mexicana de Crédito Industrial) took over the García Valseca (GV) chain of 37 daily newspapers (Alisky, 1960). Colonel Jose García Valseca, an advertising salesman and investor, over a 20 year period, built himself into the largest publisher of provincial dailies in Mexico, with newspapers in 36 provincial cities plus Mexico City. But by 1970, he had spent far beyond his income: and outstanding debts owed to the government's Nacional Financiera, for social security taxes for his employees, and to several private creditors resulted in the chain losing its credit ratings.

Behind the scenes, another motive besides the government's desire to see the republic's major chain of provincial dailies remain solvent lay in political pressures from Chambers of Commerce of every principal city in the Mexican borderlands within 200 to 300 miles of the U.S. border. GV dailies, such as the morning *El Mexicano* and the two evening papers, *El Fronterizo* and *El Continental,* featured large numbers of advertisements from retail stores in U.S. cities of the borderlands. At the 1971 annual conference of Mexico's Chambers of Commerce, the Minister of Industry and Commerce pledged to help find a way to de-emphasize that advertising trend. No government official ever so stated, but the pending insolvency of the GV chain certainly proved convenient for the Luis Echeverría administration to justify its acquisition of these newspapers.

To preserve a facade of independence from direct political pressures, SOMEX stressed that its managerial role is that of trustee for the many creditors of the GV chain, and that some private participation remains via the route of stock purchases by private individuals in limited amounts, when SOMEX began to offer to the public shares in its Cadena García Valseca subsidiary.

The other major move by the Revolutionary coalition of government-political-investment leaders to change a leading newspaper's management involved an incumbent president of Mexico and a few of the dominant party's politicians loyal to him. The newspaper was the leading daily of Mexico, *Excelsior*, rated by scholars and specialists alike as the republic's elite paper (Alisky, 1960; Merrill, 1968; Merrill, Bryan, & Alisky, 1970). As Armando Vargas (1976), *Excelsior's* chief correspondent in Washington until his resignation, noted, Mexico's most influential daily lost some of its editorial independence of the government in a "scenario of intimidation."

Founded in 1917, *Excelsior* became ostensibly a full cooperative in 1932, although not all of its employees fully participated in the corporate organization or even in the selection of the newspaper's management. Perhaps fewer than 100 of its key employees shaped the framework under which a publisher and editors were chosen and retained or changed. Still, *Excelsior* did achieve fame in world newspaperdom as one of the few successful cooperatives among the major dailies of the world. Meeting in general assembly, key workers voted to ratify the slate of editors and staffers preselected by those key administrators themselves. Periodically, changes occurred as a kind of innovation within a system of self-replenishment, not unlike the process operating within the dominant political party of Mexico (the PRI) and in the selection of new federal adminstrations for the government every six years.

Quietly, behind the anti-*Excelsior* moves was the Chief Executive of Mexico himself, President Luís Echeverría. At the riotous general assembly on July 8, 1976, the presiding chairman and every orator he allowed to hold the floor to dominate discussion were identified as part of the political clique (camarilla) of Echeverría. Each had been groomed for the assembly coup by public relations experts in a leftist group of journalists headed by José Pagés and Luís Suárez, publisher and editor of the weekly news magazine *Siempre*. The magazine officially supports the Popular Socialist party (PPS or Parido Popular Socialista), but in practice always has given support and advice to PRI leaders and members behind the leftward thrust of Echeverría.

At that July 8 assembly, Julio Scherer García, executive publisher and editor-in-chief of *Excelsior,* and five top editors were fired. No charges were specified against them. Not one word was raised about competence or professional standards. In fact, the Scherer staff had won various honors from the Inter-American Press Association, the María Moors Cabot awards of the Columbia University Graduate School of Journalism, and similar professional and academic awards.

A week prior to the July 8 meeting, those slated to attend, a cross-section of *Excelsior* employees, had been contacted by spokesmen for the PRI, the Ministry of the Presidency, or from the federal Attorney General's office. At the entrance to the assembly hall, private guards in business suits, but with pistol shoulder holsters discernible, checked those entering and challenged at length several veterans of past *Excelsior* assemblies. Later on, the newspaper's legal counsel, Adolfo Aguilar y Quevado, commented that unparliamentary procedures, ineligible voters, and arbitrary rulings by the presiding officers made the assembly vote to fire the newspaper's management illegal. But no governmental authority or private citizen challenged the action in Mexico's politicized courts.

Prominent newspapers of the world—the *New York Times, Le Monde* of Paris, the *Washington Post, O Estado de São Paulo* of Brazil, the *Arizona Republic* of Phoenix—editorially condemned the action. Some 200 *Excelsior* reporters, writers, editors, and photographers walked off the job in protest. Some never returned, whereas others stayed away only for a few days or weeks.

Excelsior angered Echeverría in 1972 when it reported the fact that he personally encouraged SOMEX to take over the García Valseca newspaper chain. Also in 1972, the daily had been alone among Mexico's media in pointing out that Echeverría forced the expropriation in that year of a prosperous tobacco growers' industry although sales had been at an all time high, there had been no labor unrest or grievances against private management, and no public push for the move. Similarly, in 1975 *Excelsior* revealed that the president's own economic advisors had urged him not to expropriate the motion picture studios. That action became overkill in government guidance of the film industry, for the government already controlled most theaters which exhibit films and the government Cinema Bank already made the loans for the major Mexican film productions.

Echeverría, during his final year in office, campaigned to become Secretary General of the United Nations, a post denied him when the UN reelected the incumbent. Echeverría had to settle, as an ex-President of Mexico, for the post of Mexican Ambassador to UNESCO in Paris. In his unsuccessful bid for the UN Post, Echeverría tried to out-posture leaders of North Vietnam, Angola, Cuba, and East Germany in his criticism of the United States, the western democracies, and nations not part of the Communist or Socialist or Third World blocs. When Echeverría ordered Mexico to support the Arab attack on Israel via the anti-Zionist resolution in the UN, Excelsior followed up on the contraction of tourism among both Jewish and non Jewish habitual visitors to Mexico. The newspaper reports intensified Echeverría's anger with Excelsior's investigatory reporters and caustic editorialists.

Scherer García had served as a political reporter for Excelsior since 1947, being promoted to assistant publisher in 1963, then editor-in-chief, and finally executive publisher in 1968. Until then a prominent politician could purchase a front-page story praising himself for 100,000 pesos (U.S. $8,000), a practice belatedly revealed in the prosecution of corruption by President José López Portillo (Alisky, 1978). Scherer ended that practice abruptly and added topflight writers to his staff, ranging from economist Daniel Cosío Villegas to Ricardo Garibay.

After the firing of Scherer and his key personnel, Excelsior evidenced a lowering of writing style standards and less vigor in its investigatory reporting for a few months. The paper had customarily emphasized, in its budget of news, stories about civil rights violations by both rightist and leftist governments. Excelsior correspondents had personally investigated human rights abuses in Uruguay, Chile, and Bolivia. It ran news service reports of human rights problems in Brazil, the Soviet Union, and Uganda.

For a few months prior to the Scherer ouster, supporters of Echeverría in the television network Televisa began airing stories critical of Excelsior. And key government administrators began challenging Excelsior stories quoting them, questioning the accuracy even when the reporter had tape recordings to back up the quoted statements.

In February 1976, Echeverría and his close associates became major shareholders in the Mexican Editorial Organization (OEM or Organizacion Editorial Mexicana). Immediately OEM purchased the Mexico

City daily, El Universal, which had for decades been owned by the relatives and heirs of the Lanz Duret and Palavicini families, epitomizing conservative nonactivists who were neutral in the rivalries among Revolutionary coalition leaders.

Soon Echeverristas took over the key posts at OEM, with Echeverría's former foreign minister, Emilio O. Rabasa, on Universal's board and Echeverría's former ambassador to the People's Republic of China joining both the OEM board and the Universal board.

OEM then quickly purchased the controlling stock in the SOMEX subsidiary, the García Valseca chain of 37 newspapers, and installed Fausto Zapata as publisher and editor of the GV papers. Zapata had been Under-Secretary of the Presidency in the Echeverría Cabinet (Alisky, 1960; Camp, 1976, p. 338).

OEM papers reported that on June 10, 1976, dozens of slum dwellers invaded a 218-acre property owned by the Excelsior cooperative on the outskirts of Mexico City. The land was slated to become the site of a housing development, and the newspaper had purchased the site as a long-range investment to insure its editorial independence and to finance a new printing plant. The poor land squatters were led by an unlikely affluent organizer, Congressman-elect Humberto Serrano, one of Echeverría's most vigorous supporters in the PRI and an articulate spokesman for the party's left wing. Serrano promised that the squatters would not leave the site until Scherer was expelled from Excelsior. The police made no effort to evict the squatters, who had been transported to the newspaper's land in buses belonging to the governor of the state of Guerrero, another close associate of Echeverría.

The District Attorney of the Federal District refused to accept a formal complaint filed by lawyers for the newspaper. The federal attorney general of Mexico stated, when appealed to, that he would enforce the law against the squatters only after the Excelsior general assembly had been completed on July 8. The newspaper denounced these government actions in an editorial in its July 7 edition. That evening, network television news commentators attacked the newspaper's editorial and protests.

José López Portillo became President of Mexico on December 1, 1976. Luis Echeverría no longer held any power. The makeshift staff he had forced upon Excelsior had by then been muddling through for five months. Several months more were to pass before the daily began to regain some of its journalistic prowess and skills it had acquired during

60 years of labor and dedication to professional standards. By 1978, reportorial professional standards again were in evidence.

BROADCASTING CONTROLS

Licenses for radio and television stations in Mexico were issued to private corporations, or to public entities in many instances, for periods of five years, with renewals invariably automatic. This compares to three year licenses issued in the United States, with license suspensions occurring on rare occasions and even a handful of license revocations during the past half century. In Mexico, since 1934, not one broadcasting license has ever been revoked outright, though a couple of corporate owners have been unofficially pressured into selling to new owners.

In the United States, the Federal Communications Commission (FCC) remains an autonomous board not directly linked to a presidential cabinet post. In Mexico, the Telecommunications Bureau (Dirección General de Telecomunicaciones, or DGT) functions under the Ministry of Communications and Transportation (Secretaría de Comunicaciones y Transportes).

A U.S. president, by law, cannot appoint any more than four of the seven FCC commissioners from the same political party, meaning in practical terms four Republicans and three Democrats or vice versa. The Mexican president functions in a system in which his own party, the PRI, dominates. He is under no restriction to appoint as DGT commissioners anyone from the opposition minority parties (the conservative National Action party, the Popular Socialist party, the Authentic Mexican Revolutionary party, or the Communist party).

In the U.S., an FCC Commissioner serves a seven year term and the terms of the seven commissioners are staggered, so that an incoming president can hope to appoint only one new commissioner from among his own close supporters. By contrast, each incoming president in Mexico selects an entirely new Cabinet and Sub-Cabinet, new boards and commissions, and entirely new top administrators for even semi-autonomous agencies and public corporations.

The Mexican Minister of Communications and Transportation helps a new president of Mexico select the Deputy Minister of Broadcasting (Sub-Secretario de Radiodifusión). The Broadcasting Sub-Ministry (Sub-Secretaría de Radiodifusión), rather than the Broadcasting Bureau (DGT), in practice awards and renews licenses, sets policies, and collects fees. The major policies, however, requiring (1) every licensed station in the nation to air central government-produced programs or news reports, and (2) campaign discussions broadcast before elections, come not from the Sub-Ministry of Broadcasting, but rather from the Ministry of Internal Affairs or Government (Secretaría de Gobernación).

Until early 1977, Gobernación included in its subministries two key bureaus dealing with cinema and with information, the latter concerning itself with political and administrative problems in the radio, television, and theatrical professions. Then came an administrative reorganization, giving Gobernación a Bureau of Radio, Television, and Motion Pictures, headed by Margarita López Portillo, sister of the President of Mexico who had been inaugurated himself as the nation's chief executive only three months before. Aside from the factor of nepotism, her appointment by President López Portillo certainly could be judged on her professional record as a successful writer of film and broadcast scripts, books, essays, and volumes of poetry (Lagos, 1977).

Under the federal Law of Radio and Television, the Minister of Gobernación determines the number of radio and television discussions the registered political parties may have during a campaign and the length each broadcast shall be. For the campaign of 1976, from late March to the beginning of July, there were four recognized registered parties. The minister decided that each party spokesperson representing the presidential candidate and all of the party's congressional candidates could appear on television for 10 minutes every 2 weeks and on radio for 5 minutes each week. A further stipulation required that each program aired must have representatives from all 4 parties. This forced the stations and networks to combine an entire month's allotted time in order to present panel discussions beyond the briefest summary statements.

For the 1979 federal congressional elections, the Federal Electoral Commission on October 24, 1978, promulgated new regulations giving four hours of free radio and television time per month to all political parties. In addition to the dominant Institutional Revolutionary party (PRI) and three minority opposition parties given air time in 1976, for 1979 the recently recognized Communist party of Mexico and the new leftist Workers party also received free air time in 15 minute segments.

The Law of Broadcasting of 1934 had no time formulas or fairness considerations for rival candidates. It simply prohibited all political broadcasts on radio: television being 16 years in the future of Mexico's daily life. Revisions in the law in 1942, 1953, and throughout the 1960s merely brought adjustments to the old law written for radio to accommodate the addition to the broadcasting spectrum of video and frequency modulation services. Not until the 1970s did the Mexican government, itself wedded to its own dominant Institutional Revolutionary party, amend the law to permit the airing of political broadcasts.

GOVERNMENT BROADCASTS

From the beginning of daily radio broadcasting in 1923, Mexico had primarily a system of privately-owned commercial stations, with only a handful of noncommercial educational or cultural stations. When television joined radio as a daily service in 1950, the emphasis did not change much. Only in the 1960s did the number of radio stations, licensed to educational entities and financed substantially by the government, increase to where every one of the 30 states and every one of the 15 largest metropolitan areas had one in its area. In the 1970s, the government began to invest more directly in television and to exert influence through its position as a partner in private-public corporations (Alisky, 1953c, 1954c).

By the late 1940s, realizing that one-third of Mexico's adults were then still illiterate or at least not functionally enough literate to be newspaper readers, the government decided to supplement its few spot announcements and special shows on commercial radio stations with a weekly program designed to saturate the republic's radio stations. Radio had become Mexico's major medium of mass communication. The Ministry of Gobernación hired the republic's leading radio writers, producers, and directors to formulate "The National Hour."

By 1952, the Federal Radio Law required that every radio station in the nation, including the small number of noncommercial outlets and even the three English-language stations near the United States border, must carry "The National Hour" every Sunday from 10 to 11 p.m. A hookup of 100 percent of a nation's broadcasting stations would not have been unusual in countries with a state-operated system of broadcasting. But in Mexico in 1952, of 210 radio stations on the standard wavelength band, 550 to 1600 kilocycles, only two educational and one governmental license existed, the remainder becoming commercial (Alisky, 1953a, 1953b, 1954c).

The format of "The National Hour" consisted of progress reports of various governmental activities and policies, written in newscast or documentary style, sandwiched between popular musical selections featuring the most popular folk singers and the most successful commercial orchestras. Mexico's leading motion picture and stage stars also appeared to boost adult literacy campaigns, drives for innoculations against disease, and similar public service projects.

With the growth of the Sunday night television audience in the 1960s, the impact of "The National Hour" on radio began to lessen. Public relations advisors for the government began to consider more extensive use of the existing commercial television and radio stations. The formula would be daily reports from and about key governmental entities. The broadcasting law was amended in 1960 by the dominant PRI in Congress without any questioning debate by the minority opposition parties so that every broadcast licensee in Mexico, to retain and renew a license, must give 12.5 percent of its daily air time to public service reports from the government.

GOVERNMENT INVESTMENT IN STATIONS

The Mexican government's direct control of selected television service stems from two types of stations, those video outlets owned directly by the government and the educational outlets licensed to educational entities financed by the government.

Rómulo O'Farrill, Sr., publisher of the Mexico City daily newspapers *Novedades* and the English language *News*, in 1950 owned and operated radio station XEX, Latin America's most powerful with 250,000 watts of transmitting power. That same year he opened XHTV, Channel 4, the first fulltime television station not only in Mexico but in all of Latin America.

In 1951, the late Emilio Azcárraga, Sr., owner of Mexico's leading commercial radio station, XEW, and its network of provincial repeater stations and affiliates, launched XEW-TV, Channel 2, as a rival to Channel 4. By then, O'Farrill and Azcárraga had merged the operations and management of their former radio rivals, XEX and XEW. But the television channels would compete for a few years before they too became part of a larger merger.

Also in 1951, Guillermo González Camarena inaugurated Channel 5, Latin America's first television station transmitting in color. Later, Channels 2, 4, and 5 would merge into the Telesistema Management Corporation, maintaining three separate broadcasting schedules from studios located adjacently at the Televicentro.

Mexico's first noncommercial television station was licensed to the National Polytechnic Institute in Mexico City, an engineering and technology university tied to the Ministry of Public Education, Channel 11. By the mid-1960s, five other provincial universities or departments of education also had video stations. Cultural or public television in Mexico, incidentally, encouraged a parallel growth in educational radio. In the mid-1950s, only the National Autonomous University of Mexico and two other outlets were fulltime noncommercial stations. By 1978, the Ministry of Education, using its Mexico City standard-band station as a network anchor, transmitted daily to radio stations operated by the universities of Sonora, Veracruz, Yucatán, Guanajuato, Sinaloa, Michoacán, and Baja California Norte, plus public community radio stations in Chiapas, Nuevo León, Oaxaca, and Aguascalientes. In addition, networks of both commercial and noncommercial frequency modulation stations carry some of the same Radio Education Network programs on a selective basis.

By the early 1970s, the government owned and operated two television stations in Mexico City, Channel 8 and Channel 13. To enhance maximum support for the Revolutionary coalition's politics and programs, the government devised a super holding corporation, Telesistema, with an umbrella management overseeing the friendly competition among commercial Channels 2, 4, and 5, and the government's 8 and 13.

BROADCAST BUDGET EMPHASIS

As political scientists point out, budget analysis often yields the relative importance and scope of various entities in the public life of any nation. Utilizing that premise, a glance at the National Polytechnical Institute's Channel 11 and the government's commercial-style Channel 13 in Mexico City may give some clues as to the relative emphasis the government gives to each type of operation.

For 1978, reported *Tiempo* (1978), Channel 13's budget totaled 480 million pesos (U.S. $21.6 million) for all its operations, whereas Channel 11's budget totaled 42 million pesos (U.S. $1.9 million). That is, the station which the government operates as a commercial-type outlet with emphasis on entertainment had a budget approximately 11 times that of the educational station the government finances through the National Polytechnical Institute.

Unlike the situation in the United States, where the Public Broadcasting System obtains not only government funding but also generous grants from philanthropical foundations and large corporations, in Mexico educational stations subsist on whatever funds are appropriated by the government. Thus Channel 11 cannot hope for extra funds to purchase Italian operas, British dramas, or cultural series from the U.S. or from other Latin American countries. With strong pressures from labor unions to pay its personnel on a par with the employees of the commercial stations, Channel 11 therefore finds a relatively large part of its budget going for payrolls. It must get along with fewer employees and a smaller selection of program types than its commercial rivals.

In productions costs for programs, Channel 13 can spend many times the sums allocated by Channel 11. This contrast also holds for news and information programs. Yet with respect to the purpose of the government to project a positive image of stewardship to citizens, that difference may have little political meaning. The Ministry of Gobernación can arrange to air as elaborate a production on the educational outlet as it can on the commercial-type station. That it seldom chooses to do so can be explained in terms of audience ratings. Channel 13 draws larger audiences for its light comedies, popular musical reviews, and dramas than does Channel 11 with its discussion panels, programs on science, and old movies.

Pablo F. Marentes, general manager of Channel 11, when interviewed by Mexico's leading weekly news magazine, *Tiempo*, stated flatly: "This (educational) station is a channel of the government, not of special interests within the government" (1978, p. 15). In everyday practice, that statement may be meaningless, given a political system in which the Revolutionary coalition power elite formulates basic public policies after filtering out the strongest divisions among rival factions in the government, the dominant political party, and the economic sectors (González Casanova, 1965; Instituto Mexicano de Estudios Politicos, 1970; Needler, 1971; Padgett, 1976; Ross, 1975; Scott, 1964; and Turner, 1968).

PUBLICIZING A GOVERNMENT PROGRAM

Not until April 1972 did any Mexican government official discuss the national need for family planning, even though the decreasing death rate and the high birth rate in the 1960s had brought social and economic problems which political leaders chose to ignore.

Population imbalance and demographic disequilibrium strain tend to strain distribution and communication facilities. So, in addition to population pressures in which young citizens multiply faster than any sources of new jobs, too many Mexicans crowd into select areas, burdening society with urbanization stresses on top of nationwide overpopulation problems. Half of all Mexicans live in 14 percent of the national territory, the central region. Industrial payrolls are bunched in the metropolitan areas of Mexico City, Monterrey, and Guadalajara, even though the government has encouraged some industries to move to outlying states.

The National Population Council, in November 1976, estimated the annual rate of population growth at 3.6 percent. Had the government not launched its program of family planning in 1973, maintaining vigorous propaganda for "responsible parenthood" ("paternidad responsable"), the yearly net increase in population might have soared past 3.8 or 4 percent. Even the escape valve of the United States, where several million illegal aliens have come from Mexico, has not solved that republic's overpopulation dilemma. The papal encyclical against birth control had little impact in predominantly Catholic Mexico, where church and state had suffered a century of mutual antagonism in the political arena. Moreover, machismo, the cult of male virility, has been a chief inhibitor of birth control (Alisky, 1977; Cornelius, 1975; Paz, 1961).

Although social scientists and some government administrators had been warning about the rising unemployment rate fueled by a rapidly increasing potential work force since the early 1960s, the Ministry of Health and Welfare (SSA or Secretaría de Salubridad y Asistencia) and the Social Security System (IMSS or Instituto Mexicano de Seguro Social) each opened the first family planning centers in January 1973. By early 1977, more than 2,000 such centers were operating seven days a week all over the republic, and in 1978, more than 3,800 such centers.

After years of official neglect or even criticism and scorn towards birth control, the government in the 1970s has had to wage campaigns to make Mexicans aware of the need to practice family planning, at two levels. At the popular level, aimed at working class adults without much formal education and at middle class adults without higher education, the National Population Council circulates leaflets, radio and television announcements, advertisements in magazines and on billboards, and various booklets and pamphlets typified by the booklet with a large-lettered title "Better Life for Mexico's Population" ("Mejor Vida para la Poblacion de México"). The 16 page pamphlet of cartoons urges family planning so that children can be fed and can have a chance to find jobs. Numerous family planning centers have reported that women who come in for the first time inquiring about the contraceptive pill, which is distributed free of charge, bring either a leaflet saying "Paternidad Responsable" or an advertisement from a newspaper, or the "Better Life" booklet some friend or neighbor had passed along.

As the nonprofit private Mexican Population Association reported in late 1976, of the childbearing or fertile-age group of Mexican females ranging from 13 to 47 years of age, only 26 percent were utilizing the free centers. Aside from cultural traditions and social pressures against birth control, one inhibiting factor has been widespread functional illiteracy. Although three out of four adults claim rudimentary ability to read, some cannot or do not read newspapers or magazines with true comprehension. In addition, the price of a metropolitan newspaper approximates the price of a stack of tortillas, the cornmeal basic equivalent of bread in the Mexican diet.

Radio obviously offers the greatest mass medium for reaching a majority of Mexicans with a message about family planning, especially when taken into consideration are the factors of inexpensive transistor receivers owned by almost every citizen and the demographic reality that half of Mexico's 65 million people are 15 years of age or under. The very youthfulness of the population portends an even more intense population explosion in the 1980s, given the widespread practice of early mating.

In 1976, for the first time since daily broadcasting came to Mexico in 1923, a dramatic series directly attacked machismo. María Elena Becerril, a young dramatist, wrote 60 episodes of a daily half-hour series or "soap opera" called "Maria the Forgotten One" ("María la Olvidada"). From July to October, each Monday through Friday from 12:30 to 1 p.m., over XEW and the National Network, millions of Mexican women followed the fictional adventures of a factory worker, who is made pregnant by her love, Juan Carlos. María quits her job to have the child and marry Juan, only to find out that he has other children fathered with a girl friend. In dialogue with her physician and with friends, María condemns male chauvinism and vows to take the pill so that she will not bring more children into the world than Juan can support. He reluctantly agrees (Alisky, 1977).

That series provoked widespread praise, denunciations, and other comments, but it helped popularize the idea of birth control among millions of young Mexicans. The Ministry of Gobernación, its sponsor, decided to repeat the taped series on provincial stations in 1977 and 1978.

Aimed not so much at the small town, rural, and city slum dwellers as the radio series, the television series, begun in 1976 and continuing through 1978, "Thanks, Doctor" has been aimed at middle class young adults. The question-and-answer program has been taped after live airing on the government's Channel 13 in Mexico, for syndication in provincial cities. Physicians from Social Security hospitals answer questions on birth control, pregnancy, and contraception telephoned in or mailed in.

The daily morning radio program "Dialogue without Fear" over the XEW network also fields questions about birth control. As of late 1978 apparently the only topic relating to birth control avoided by the pioneering radio and television programs was abortion. When the question came up on talk shows, a spokesman for the Health Ministry usually explained that abortions were still illegal in Mexico. Women were then urged to inquire about the free sterilization program at government centers.

At the second or leadership level, the National Population level, the National Population Council had been waging a campaign paralleling the one at the popular level, to make those in academic, government, and professional life aware of the population problem, and of the need to encourage birth control practices. For civic leaders, the council distributed reports like *The Demographic Revolution,* a 156-page paperback book in pocket size, devoid of the cartoons in the popular-level literature. Instead were included explanations of the Population Law of 1973, from which the Health Ministry and other government entities derived their general policies in this area.

The government, since 1976, has thus been campaigning for more widespread practice of family planning by utilizing its own facilities for printing and distributing literature at the popular and leadership level, advertisements in all the print and electronic media, serialized radio drama, radio and television discussion programs sponsored by the government on both commercial and governmental outlets, plus an increasing number of special announcements circulated via the government's self-allotted time for news on all broadcasting stations. Such announcements may be separate from any surrounding program or part of established news roundups.

A Summary: Government and the Media

We have examined the governmental controls built into the Mexican system of mass communication: newsprint distribution, allocation of licensing facilities for radio and television stations, governmental investment in corporations operating newspapers or broadcasting stations, and a case study of one major governmental campaign in the media to institutionalize a key policy and to encourage widespread participation in its programs.

As Rivers, Miller, and Gandy (Chaffee, 1975) have pointed out, perhaps the most important questions about government impact on media are those which look at the result of impact vis-à-vis news content. Under what conditions do regulatory policies and direct plus unofficial pressures affect the amount and diversity of news and editorial content available to the Mexican public? Neither Mexican or foreign social scientists have provided much detailed information about that news content. An occasional study has indicated in general trends the news content of major Mexican newspapers, but almost nothing about broadcast news stories. In the 1940s and 1950s, most content analyses of the Mexican media concerned only the most basic categories of stories, such as foreign or domestic, politics or sports (Alisky, 1953a, 1953b, 1954a, 1954b, 1955; Erlandson, 1964; Markham, 1961; Merrill, 1962; Underwood, 1965; Velasco Valdez, 1955; Wolfe, 1964).

In the 1960s and 1970s, an added perspective to Mexican media emphasis of various types of stories has been an offshoot of renewed concern by various Mexican leaders with the age-old system of bribery to insure favorable coverage (Gardner, 1967; González Casanova, 1970; Médin, 1972).

Political communication in Mexico divides into two basic categories as to potential audience: the popular and the leadership levels. Given a population not overwhelmingly attuned to newspaper reading but attuned to radio, and given the fragmentary and superficial nature of broadcast news content, one can safely assume a discernible amount of laudatory coverage in the popular media of the Mexican government. At the leadership level, communication may channel itself into impartial emphasis of national resources available to carry out a proclaimed basic policy, such as the information circulated among civic leaders about the need to encourage family planning. Leadership communication may also channel itself into the partisan realm of establishment and antiestablishment media, though the latter must operate in Mexico within the confines of criticism which does not approach overturning the power elite itself, as epitomized by the case study of newsprint distribution to the defunct magazine *Política*.

In this volume about government and the news media, many of the chapters deal with the situations in western democracies: Australia, Canada, France, Great Britain, the Scandinavian nations, and the United States. These nations provide a backdrop of variety in terms of the extent in each in which the public and private sectors of the economy have been mixed.

Chapters on Israel and Italy give us some perspectives on how the cultural milieu of the Middle East or of the Latin tradition, entwined with western political entities, can affect the news media. The chapter on Japan certainly parallels that reportage for Asia's developed areas of mass media. This chapter on Mexico, having to serve as the sole entry from Latin America, has stressed those elements central to government-media relationships which reflect the Mexican experiment. Certainly Mexico does not duplicate Cuba or Chile or Bolivia in its political experiences of this century. Mexico's attempts to institutionalize a social revolution, however, do find counterparts in certain programs which were emphasized in Peru during 1968-1978, in Uruguay during 1907-1969, in Venezuela during 1968-1978, and in Costa Rica during 1948-1978. Further, Mexico's land and population size reflect some of the demographic problems of mass communication found in the other large republics of Latin America, Brazil, and Argentina.

Latin America cannot be adjudged as one unified piece of real estate, located south and east of North America. It ranges in size from the third-of-an-island called Haiti to the half-continent called Brazil, from the participatory democracy of Costa Rica to the rightist dictatorship in Chile and the Communist dictatorship in Cuba. It ranges in literacy from the 92 percent in Uruguay and the 90 percent in Argentina, Chile, and Costa Rica, to the majority of illiterates still found in Guatemala, Honduras, Nicaragua, Haiti, and Ecuador. It varies in mass media development from the sophisticated press and broadcasting centers of Mexico City, Buenos Aires, Rio de Janeiro, São Paulo, Lima, Caracas, and Monterrey, where the overlay of developed national technology pervades both media and public administration.

This chapter does amass some pertinent factors about Mexico, and certainly in the ongoing study of government-media relations in the field of comparative politics, Mexico will recur as one of the key nations considered. With a population by 1979 totaling 66 million, and the processes of industrialization and urbanization operating against the backdrop of population pressures and a governmental tendency to self-replenish its national leaders, certainly our study offers at least one new vantage point for the research in this vital area which surely must follow (Alba, 1967).

Reference Notes

1.   "S.A." stands for "Sociedad Anonima" which in English best translates as "Corporation" or "Incorporated" depending on its use in a sentence.
2.   Members of the PIPSA Board. Personal communication with the author via telephone, January 8, 1968.

References

Alba, V. *The Mexicans: The Making of a Nation.* New York: Frederick A. Praeger, 1967.

Alisky, M. "Mexican Newscasts Link a Nation." *The Quill,* September 1953a, *41,* 12-14.

Alisky, M. "Mexico's National Hour on Radio." *Nieman Reports,* October 1953b, *7,* 17-18.

Alisky, M. "Mexico City's Competitive Radio Market." *Inter-American Economic Affairs,* Winter 1953c, *7,* 19-27.

Alisky, M. "Radio's Role in Mexico." *Journalism Quarterly,* Winter 1954a, *31,* 66-72.

Alisky, M. "Mexico's Rural Radio." *Quarterly of Film, Radio, and Television,* Summer 1954b, *8,* 405-417.

Alisky, M. "Early Mexican Broadcasting." *Hispanic American Historical Review,* November 1954c, *34,* 515-526.

Alisky, M. "Jazz in Mexico City." *Metronome,* April 1955, *71,* 26, 44-45.

Alisky, M. "Growth of Newspapers in Mexico's Provinces." *Journalism Quarterly,* Winter 1960, *37,* 75-82.

Alisky, M. "Mexico's Population Pressures." *Current History,* March 1977, *72,* 106-110, 131-134.

Alisky, M. "Mexicans Jailed for Fraud." *USA Today,* September 1978, *107.*

Brandenburg, F. *The Making of Modern Mexico.* Englewood Cliffs, N.J.: Prentice-Hall, 1964.

Camp, R.A. *Mexican Political Biographies, 1935-1975.* Tucson, Ariz.: University of Arizona Press, 1976.

Chaffee, S., ed. *Political Communication.* Beverly Hills, Calif.: Sage Publications, 1975.

Chilcote, R. H. *The Press in Latin America, Spain, and Portugal.* Stanford, Calif.: Institute of Hispanic American and Luso-Brazilian Studies, 1963.

"Consejo de la PIPSA." *Tiempo,* 1960, *37,* 14-15.

Cornelius, W. A. *Politics and the Migrant Poor in Mexico City.* Stanford, Calif.: Stanford University Press, 1975.

Erlandson, E. H. "The Press of Mexico." *Journalism Quarterly,* Spring, 1964, *41,* 233-234.

"Frente de la Adversidad." *Tiempo,* 1978, *73,* 13-15.

Gardner, M.A. *The Inter-American Press Association.* Austin: University of Texas Press, 1967.

González Casanova, P. *Democracy in Mexico.* London: Oxford University Press, 1965.

Instituto Mexicano de Estudios Políticos. *México: Realidad Política de sus Partidos.* México, D.F.: Instituto Mexicana de Estudios Políticos, 1970.

Johnson, K. F. *Mexican Democracy: A Critical View.* Boston: Allyn and Bacon, 1971.

Lagos, M. de. "Homenaje de cineastas a Margaria López Portillo." *Mujeres,* May 31, 1977, 7, 8-10.

Markham, J. "Foreign News in the United States and the South American Press." *Public Opinion Quarterly,* Summer 1961, 25, 254-256.

Médin, T. *Ideologia y praxis: Política de Lázaro Cárdenas.* México, D.F.: Siglo Veintiuno Editores, 1972.

Merrill, J. C. "The Image of the United States Presented by Ten Mexican Daily Newspapers." Iowa City: Unpublished doctoral dissertation, University of Iowa, 1962.

Merrill, J. C. *The Elite Press: Great Newspapers of the World.* New York: Pitman Publishing Corporation, 1968.

Merrill, J. C., Bryan, C. R., & Alisky, M. *The Foreign Press* (2d ed.). Baton Rouge: Louisiana State University Press, 1970.

Needler, M. C. *Politics and Society in Mexico.* Albuquerque: University of New Mexico Press, 1971.

Padgett, L. V. *The Mexican Political System* (2d ed.). Boston: Houghton Mifflin, 1976.

Paz, O. *The Labyrinth of Solitude.* New York: Grove Press, 1961.

Ross, S. R. (Ed.). *Is the Mexican Revolution Dead?* (2d ed.). Philadelphia: Temple University Press, 1975.

Scott, R. E. *Mexican Government in Transition* (2d ed.). Urbana: University of Illinois, 1964.

Turner, F. C. *The Dynamics of Mexican Nationalism.* Chapel Hill, N.C.: University of North Carolina Press, 1968.

Underwood, B. "A Survey of Contemporary Newspapers of Mexico." Columbia, Mo.: Unpublished doctoral dissertation, University of Missouri, 1965.

United Nations. *United Nations Statistical Yearbook.* New York: United Nations, 1977.

Vargas, A. "The Coup at *Excelsior.*" *Columbia Journalism Review,* September-October 1976, 15, 45-48.

Velasco Valdes, M. *Historía del Periodismo Mexicano.* México, D.F.: Porrua, 1955.

Wilkie, J. W. *The Mexican Revolution: Federal Expenditure and Social Change Since 1910* (2d ed.). Berkeley: University of California Press, 1970.

Wolfe, W. "Images of the United States in the Latin American Press." *Journalism Quarterly,* Winter 1964, 41, 79-86.

Yates, P. L. *El Desarrollo Regional de México.* México, D.F.: Banco de México, 1961.

X.
Government-News Media Relations in Israel

Dina Goren and Rozann Rothman

A tumultuous history, measured in decades rather than centuries, security considerations, and intense political partisanship are major factors shaping the relationships of government and the news media in Israel. Primary has been the historical experience itself and the attendant security concerns. Moreover, there has been the relatively small country and population. In addition, there has been the commitment of the press—first to the achievement of statehood and then to the defense of the state. More immediately, the day-to-day performance of the press has been affected by the legal framework—an amalgam, derived from British mandatory powers, yet influenced by a liberal tradition and cognizant of the requirements of security—which marks the boundaries of the relationship. Finally, even the most stringent of legal restrictions on information dissemination has been offset by the contentiousness of the political process. Israel is a parliamentary democracy; seats in the Knesset (Parliament) are awarded through proportional representation; there are many small parties but no majority party, and the leader of the largest party forms the government. The resulting coalition politics and intense partisanship leave their mark on the dissemination of information to the public.

In the pages that follow, we shall focus upon the interaction of historical, situational, legal, and political factors that necessitate a continous weighing of competing pressures, such as the commitment to the preservation and defense of the state and the conflicting demands of an intensely politicized domestic scene. Specifically we will analyze such factors to explain how, separately and in combination, they have shaped the nature of the news media and determined government's influence on media performance as well as the media's impact on government and the operation of government information systems.

The Background of the Relationship

In the prestate period, politics were characterized by consensus on the necessity of a Jewish state. The press not only shared the commitment, its role was defined by its contributions to the goal. Adherence to the directives of the leaders of the fight for statehood seemed morally sanctioned and did not raise the spectre of role conflict. The restrictive measures imposed by the British government offered ample opportunities for editors and journalists to assert their commitment to press freedom.

The community, although united on the need for statehood, was deeply split over the particular model of Utopia and the means to achieve the objective. Strategy and tactics to use against the British and to counteract Arab hostility were argued and reargued. There were no neutrals, and different political factions adhered with passionate intensity to their respective ideals. The press was organized for partisan activity and engaged in these ideological debates. The pattern which emerged in this period, of press commitment to realization of an ideal against a background of political competition, is the source of some of the idiosyncratic aspects which characterize the contemporary government/media relationship.

Before independence, the leadership of the Jewish community lacked legal sanctions for their directives and relied on voluntary compliance. Improvised methods of obtaining agreement included granting or withholding of access to information concerning political and military matters. After independence, the inability of the country's largest party to win majority status and the necessity of playing coalition politics reinforced the habits formed during the struggle for independence. Resort to a deliberately informal modus operandi provided the flexibility to cope with partisan claims and conflicts of interest and principle. As a result, current laws tend to be less significant determinants of behavior than informal understandings. The consequences are apparent when government/media relations are examined. The severe restrictions of the legal code (Press Ordinance, 1933; Defense Regulations [Emergency], 1945; Penal Revision Law [State Security], 1957; and Section 28 of the Basic Law [Government], 1968) are often circumvented by the claims of personal contacts, the prerequisites of position in the political hierarchy, and the continuing interest of the world press.

Continuing Arab hostility sharpened awareness of the need for internal cohesion and reinforced consciousness of the importance of world opinion. Israelis are avid consumers of reports about Israel in the foreign press and such reports are frequently replayed in the Hebrew press. Local coverage of military and foreign policy issues is constrained by security considerations, but coverage of these subjects in the foreign press expands the opportunities for local coverage.

The constraints imposed by the past have weakened with the emergence of a new generation of Israeli journalists. The younger generation lacked a close involvement with the leadership. Living in an independent state was no longer evidence of a miracle, and it became easier to take a more critical stance on government policy, particularly domestic policy. Security considerations, however, remain significant determinants of publication policies. Israel has become stronger militarily, but its strategic position remains tenuous. The validity of military censorship regulations has never been challenged, but its application in a number of specific cases has been disputed.

The framework in which government/media relations developed will be discussed in detail below. Engagement in the struggle for independence shaped press behavior in the prestate period and consensus on preservation of the state remains the primary determinant of press performance. But there are new pressures for more critical coverage of domestic subjects and more extended coverage of sensitive subjects. Political needs and informal understandings serve to dilute the impact of legal strictures and improvised reconciliations of conflicting pressures produce the compromises that define the present relationship. A study of government/media relations in Israel offers a unique opportunity to explore the juxtaposition of pragmatic needs and conflicting political interests with concerns about national security, against the background of a liberal commitment to press freedom.

The Impact of The Struggle For Independence

The tasks and objectives of the media, its raison d'etre and conceptions of the role of journalists were determined by the history of the Zionist movement and the struggle for independence. From the beginnings of the Zionist movement, there were close ties between its leaders and journalists. In 19th century Europe, Jews, for the most part, were barred from engaging in political careers and a journalistic career served as a substitute for young men with political inclinations. Dr. Theodore Herzl, the founder of political Zionism, began his career as a journalist. While covering the Dreyfus trial as Paris correspondent of the Viennese *Neue Freie Press,* Herzl became convinced that the only solution for the Jewish people was the creation of a Jewish state. Other Zionists came from the ranks of journalists, and reputations earned in journalism often served as springboards to prominence in the movement. Several of the leaders in the drive for statehood, for example, David Ben Gurion, Zalman Shazar, and Moshe Sharett, worked as journalists early in their careers. This mobility and the enduring personal relations which developed had important consequences for the emerging framework of government/media relations.

The Zionist Organization was established in 1897, and was followed by the establishment of a weekly, *Die Welt,* which served for many years as the movement's official organ. The need for an official paper was clear. The movement was new, it was small, it had to publicize its objectives and activities in order to win support for its programs. *Die Welt* would exhort the faithful and provide ammunition to further the Zionist cause in the world.

The Zionist Organization served to concentrate activities for the realization of the Jewish state under one umbrella, but there were intense disagreements over means within the Organization. Distinct factions developed; divergent programs were advocated, and wider support was sought. Each faction created its official newsletter to advocate its respective program. The raison d'etre of these papers was their service to a cause.

The Hebrew press in Palestine started in 1863, when two competing newspapers began publication (Yardeni, 1969). Between 1863 and the outbreak of World War I, many new weeklies and monthlies made their appearance. Most were short lived. Many were published by the younger members of the orthodox religious communities and advocated a religiously based ideology to support resettlement of the land. This ideological commitment to the land became characteristic of all segments of the Hebrew press. Although some of the editors and publishers of these papers came in conflict with the Ottoman authorities, they did not engage in a conscious effort to oppose Turkish rule or advocate its overthrow (Kressel, 1964).

The last of these early papers ceased publication by the end of World War I. It is ironic, but the Intelligence Branch of the British Army in the Middle East was the catalyst for the rebirth of the Hebrew press. As the British Army was conquering Palestine, Intelligence Headquarters in Cairo began publication of a propaganda sheet in three languages addressed to the civilian population in Palestine. Eventually, the

Hebrew sheet was sold to a wealthy new immigrant from Russia, the word "haaretz" was pulled from the paper's lengthy title, and *Haaretz* became Israel's oldest newspaper (Kressel, 1964).

During the 1920s and 1930s, several more newspapers began publication. These papers were affiliated with the various Zionist factions and the number of publications reflected the increasingly political nature of the Jewish community. Both editors and readers came from the newer waves of immigrants; many espoused socialist beliefs and belonged to one of several Zionist Labor factions. Some editors were influenced by the Soviet model of journalism which featured revolutionary correspondents reporting from "field and workshop," and advocated a similar pattern for the Zionist press. A prominent example is Berl Katznelson, who founded *Davar* in 1925 and became its first editor. He organized the paper on the Soviet model of "revolutionary correspondents"—a network of nonprofessional correspondents would report from "field and workshop" (Goren, 1971).

The use of the press to further political objectives was compatible with the traditions of Central and Eastern Europe and the need to so use the press was reinforced by the turmoil of the 1930s. The growing threat of Nazi Germany, open hostility between Jews and Arabs, and vehement opposition to British policy added urgency to the fight for statehood. Editors and journalists placed their services at the disposal of the Zionist leadership. The ad hoc measures that translated willingness into programmed action will be discussed below. Here, the commitment of the press to the struggle for an independent state is stressed because the commitment was the major determinant of press performance in the prestate period. But despite consensus on the need for a state, differences over the means split the community and each of the major factions continued to operate its own newspaper.

Composition of the News Media

The pattern at independence, then, was that most newspapers were affiliated with and subsidized by the factions of the Zionist movement and performed accordingly. However, in the years between 1948 and 1976, there was severe attrition of the partisan press. Eleven partisan papers failed, and at present only four Hebrew papers are so affiliated. Nevertheless, Israelis support a large number of newspapers. There are 26 daily papers—13 Hebrew, 4 Arabic, and to serve the various waves of immigrants, one each in English, French, German, Yiddish, Polish,

Roumanian, Hungarian, Bulgarian, and Russian—for a population of approximately 3½ million people. The foreign language papers account for approximately one-third of the circulation (Moshayov, 1977), but except for the *Jerusalem Post* (the English language daily), they have only marginal journalistic or editorial impact. They share reporters and editorial material and are often several days behind the Hebrew press in their coverage.

Three of the four dominant Hebrew papers, i.e. those with the largest circulations, are privately owned and have no formal affiliation with a political party. *Haaretz*, 50,900 is a morning paper; *Maariv*, 137,000 and *Yedioth Achronot*, which does not publish circulation figures but is assumed to have as many readers as *Maariv*, are evening papers. The fourth major Hebrew daily, *Davar*, 37,000 (Educational Statistics, 1977) is formally the organ of the Israel Labor Federation (Histadrut). When Mapai was the strongest Labor party and dominated the Histadrut, *Davar* tended to follow the party's lead. However, the Histadrut executive committee is presently composed of members of all the parties, and currently *Davar* does not specifically advocate any party program.

The absence of partisan affiliation in the present contrasts sharply with the experience of the past. Attrition of the partisan press has been attributed to the shifting composition of the news audience—from ideologically motivated party members to persons who sought refuge, first, from the Nazis and after independence, from hostile Arab governments. A fragmented, intensely partisan press was supplanted by a press which sought to appeal to a mass audience.

The position of the broadcast media differs from that of the press. Radio and television are a state monopoly, run by the Israel Broadcasting Authority, a public corporation whose status is defined by the Broadcasting Authority Law, 1965. The Authority's policymaking bodies, the general council and executive committee, are in theory apolitical, but in practice, members of the council and committee are partisan appointees chosen by their respective political parties and apportioned according to party representation in Parliament. The Director General of the Authority and the directors of Radio and Television are appointed by decision of the Cabinet and are professionals rather than politicians. Lower echelon appointments are apolitical. The Director General and the Directors of Radio and Television generally conform to government policy, but at times come into conflict with ministers and other government officials. Under the broadcasting law, the Minister of Education and Culture bears parliamentary responsibility for the Broadcasting Authority, but the minister has little influence on the Authority's day to day policies.

Several radio networks cater to different cultural preferences, but all networks carry the same newsprograms. There is only one television network and there is close coordination between the newsrooms of radio and television. Given the monopolistic character of broadcasting, and the existence of only one television network, broadcast news coverage could have significant political impact. Broadcast journalists are subject to considerable pressure from government officials, party leaders and various interest groups, However, they are able, for the most part, to withstand such pressures because they are able to balance one off against the other.

The shift in the orientation of newspapers from support for partisan objectives to cultivation of a mass audience as well as the expansion of broadcast facilities is slowly altering the relation between government officials and journalists. Journalists remain dependent on officials and leaks play an important role in news dissemination, but there are more incentives to take a critical view of the actions of officials.

The incentive to be more critical is buttressed by shifts in the conception of the journalist's role. During the 1920s and 1930s, journalists were influenced by the example of East and Central European journalism. In the 1940s and continuing through the 1950s, the BBC and British journalistic practice was held in high esteem, and provided models for Israeli journalists. In the 1960s and 1970s, Israelis were inspired by American performance. Vietnam, publication of the Pentagon papers and Watergate coverage provided the models for a new generation of journalists. The gradual passing of the generation of journalists who participated in the struggle for independence and had close personal ties with government leaders also contributed to shifts in conception of the journalist's role.

The change in press performance is illustrated by the wider utilization of the techniques of investigative reporting. Originally, use of these techniques focused on the role of government in the economic sphere. A number of "affairs" were researched first by the press, and one eventually led to the resignation of a minister in Mrs. Meir's Cabinet. The Washington correspondent of *Haaretz* published the story of Mrs. Rabin's secret bank account, and the repercussions were more immediate. Rabin resigned as party leader, and his party was defeated at the next election. The cause and effect relation is coincidental, but it suggests that Israeli politicians no longer can afford to ignore the potential of investigative reporting.

Organizational Influences

The final factors to be considered in the discussion of the nature of the media are concentration of facilities and personnel, and the number of journalists and their organization. Israel's media are national; i.e., most newspapers are published in Tel Aviv for nationwide distribution. Both broadcast and print journalists are concentrated in Jerusalem, the seat of government, and Tel Aviv, the publishing center. The small size of the country makes such concentration feasible. Any part of the country can be reached within hours by automobile. Concentration also means that any single reporter assigned to a specific beat can be reached when there is a story. News conferences are attended by representatives of the entire press.

Concentration and the resulting efficiencies of communication are reinforced by journalistic organization. The National Association of Journalists has a membership of over 1,200—650 in the Tel Aviv branch and over 400 in the Jerusalem branch (Moshayov, 1977). The association combines the functions of a trade union with those of a professional association. Journalists are further divided into separate "cells" ("cell" is the literal translation of the Hebrew) according to their specialties; for example, economic, financial, and political reporters and military correspondents belong to different "cells." Each "cell" elects a secretariat to coordinate relations between members and outside organizations, thereby reducing the extent of journalistic competition.

The performance of political reporters is only marginally constrained by organizational stringencies. These reporters receive information through the organizational framework from sources who provide both "on the record" and "off the record" briefings. However, reporters representing the more important papers, (Maariv, Yedioth, Haaretz, and Davar and in some cases the Jerusalem Post) have individual contacts with important political figures. Leaks are a major component of an elaborate exchange system through which these reporters receive politically sensitive information. This is the first step in circulating such information through the mainstream of informed political opinion.

Military correspondents, on the other hand, are subject to more rigorous organizational constraints than their colleagues. All able males serve in Army reserve units until the age of 55. Most journalists, even those who cover nonmilitary subjects, are members of the Army spokesman's unit. In case of war, they become military correspondents, but in peacetime they are not in continuous contact with the Army. The military correspondent must be accredited by the Army spokesman. The process of accreditation is coordinated by the secretariat of the "cell." After accreditation, the military correspondent formally undertakes to comply with certain secrecy regulations, and is assigned to a reserve army unit under the command of the Army spokesman. After assignment, he remains in continuing contact with the Army spokesman (Goren, 1975). Organization, centralization, and the comparative lack of unofficial sources within the military, in addition to the existing military censorship regulations, means that the military correspondent has few opportunities to develop a divergent version of things. Military correspondents also receive a considerable amount of classified background information, which, since it is available to all accredited correspondents, enhances the uniformity of their stories.

However, these limitations do not apply to military analysts. The latter do not need accreditation and are subject to military censorship only to the extent that they discuss concrete military details. Consequently, they have more latitude. The censor, for reasons that will be discussed below, does not interfere with abstract expositions of strategic doctrine or other matters of a conceptual nature. However, there are societal constraints which limit the impact of such articles on the public. Before the Yom Kippur War, there was little public interest in analyses that varied from accepted military doctrine. Nevertheless, several professional military journals, addressed to reserve and regular officers and available to the general public, have published articles debating questions of doctrine. Since the Yom Kippur War, there has been an increase in journalistic articles on strategy. Most of these articles, which appear spasmodically in newspapers and magazines, are the work of free lance writers. Many of the military analysts are high ranking reserve officers, and their views as a rule do not diverge greatly from official military doctrine. However, the cumulative effect of such articles may induce some degree of change in the public's view of the military situation.

The changes depicted above have destablized the balance between government officials and media personnel. Commitment to preservation of the state still defines the boundaries of the government/media relationship, but there is more elasticity in applying the commitment as a criterion of press performance. One measure of a new assertiveness was publication of the controversial book, *The Secret Talks of Henry Kissinger*, by Matti Golan, political correspondent for *Haaretz*. Despite the difficulties of Israel's position in the aftermath of the Yom Kippur War, the fears of diplomatic repercussions, and an attempt to use censorship regulations to stop publication, the book (allegedly a verbatim report of the negotiations between the Israeli Cabinet and Secretary of State Kissinger) appeared in 1975.

The Legal Framework

The laws that regulate government/media relations are an amalgam; one element derives from regulations and statutes originally enacted by the British Mandatory Government; the second comes from judicial protection of freedom of expression, and the third is composed of statutes enacted after independence, which recognize the claims of free expression and balance these claims against other social interests (Lahav, 1978). However, in many instances, the laws that regulate the relationship take second place to habits and procedures which originated in the prestate period and alter the effects of legal restrictions. This section offers a brief historical survey, describes the formation of the Editors' Committee and discusses the role of censorship.

During the 1920s, the Mandatory Government paid little attention to either the Arabic or the Hebrew press. However, increasing communal tension and the riots of August, 1929, ended British indifference. A commission was set up to investigate the causes of the riots and recommend measures to limit communal tension. The commission's report noted the role played by the press in local politics and recommended tighter regulation. The Press Ordinance of 1933 provided for licensing of the printed media, governmental supervision, and regulation of the content of newspapers, and administrative or penal sanctions for newspapers that violated these provisions (Lahav, 1978).

Stricter controls on the local press did not produce the desired results. Communal tensions intensified, and in 1936, the Arabs again were in the streets. Because units of the British Army were engaged in curbing these disturbances, military censorship was introduced. September, 1939, found relations between the Jewish Community and the British Mandatory Government at an all time low, largely as the result of a White Paper announced a few months earlier, which severely restricted immigration and land purchases. The outbreak of World War II produced more stringent censorship regulations; for example, references to the dangers facing Jews in Europe were banned as subversive attempts to undermine official policy on immigration (Canaan, 1969). News about the war and the theatres of battle was provided by official British communiques.

In response to these conditions, in 1942 the chief editors of the Hebrew papers and the editor of the *Palestine Post* (the precursor of the *Jerusalem Post*) formed the Reaction Committee to coordinate editorial policies and devise tactics to cope with restrictive British regulations (Goren, 1975). The committee was ad hoc; it lacked formal sanctions, and its members agreed that all decisions should be taken unanimously. In 1943, the editors decided that the committee should become permanent and informed the Executive Committee of the Jewish agency, the governing body of the Zionist movement, as follows:

> We hope that the supreme institutions will view the Reaction Committee as a suitable and welcome instrument to influence public opinion within the prevalent spirit of Zionist Policy. The Hebrew press is today the only voice, not only of the Yishuv (the Jewish Community in Palestine) but of the Hebrew nation as such, both in relation to history and to the rest of the world. It is therefore necessary that it (the press) should have a continuing and closer relationship with the factors determining our policy at this time. Such a relationship can be made possible with the help of the Reaction Committee, a small, select group made up of personalities who are influential in the press. We therefore beg you to make available to the committee all the necessary information, even when it is of such a nature that it cannot be made public. We should also like to suggest that members of the committee be invited to closed sessions of the Zionist Executive, or to lectures by important visitors from abroad, access to which is limited, and in general to make it possible for them to partake in whatever deliberations are necessary, so that they can better fulfill their task of guiding public opinion. We are certain that such cooperation between the supreme institutions and the Hebrew press will be very beneficial and help both sides to better fulfill their tasks in these fateful times . . . (Goren, 1975, pp. 123-24).

The editors were a select group; they belonged to the political elite and could be trusted with confidential information. Their commitment to the furtherance of the struggle for independence was beyond doubt, and guiding public opinion was a major contribution to this effort. The possibility that sharing the secrets of the leadership could compromise their editorial freedom of action was never considered. The editors were in a unique position—they were able to combine feelings of intense antagonism toward the British government, which imposed stringent restrictions on the press, with a position of dedicated patriotism, implying close cooperation with their own political leaders on matters of military and foreign policy.

The pattern of relations outlined in the letter set the terms of cooperation between the editors and the political leadership. The effects of these understandings would be felt long after the termination of the British Mandate. In June, 1948, the Reaction Committee was renamed the Editors' Committee and its primary function became mediation between the government and the media. The success of these efforts at mediation provided a context which made resort to legal measures superfluous.

However, the establishment of an independent government changed the relationship between the political leadership and the editors. The habits of cooperation, carried over from the struggle for independence, were reinforced by the constant military threat, but the government of Israel assumed the repressive power hitherto vested in the British. The case of military censorship, an issue fraught with misunderstandings, is one example of the new complexity of the relationship.

During the last months of the British Mandate, the Arabs launched a full scale armed campaign against the Jewish population of Palestine and the situation deteriorated rapidly. The Hagana High Command (the underground military force) became concerned lest the Hebrew papers inadvertently print information helpful to the Arabs. They put the problem to the Reaction Committee, which agreed to submit their copy to press censors designated by the High Command. The editors cooperated with this form of voluntary censorship, even as they strongly resisted the tight control of the British military censor to which they were still subject.

After independence, the editors continued to submit their copy to the same censors, under the mistaken belief that the arrangement was still voluntary. They soon discovered that the military censor was now operating under the provisions of the Defense Regulations (Emergency), 1945, which empowered the military censor to prohibit the publication of any material "likely to endanger the defense of the state or the public safety and order." The censor also had the authority to review any material intended for publication. The editors strongly objected to their government's continuation of the same repressive measures which they had fought under the British rule. However, they did not question the need for the exercise of prior military censorship.

During the War of Independence, controversies were resolved on an ad hoc basis, and misunderstandings were frequent. After the war, in 1950, an agreement was negotiated between the general staff of the Army and the Editors' Committee regulating the exercise of military censorship. The government's Legal Counselor and the experts of the Ministry of Justice strongly objected to the arrangement which they defined as "illegal" (Goren, 1975, p. 186), but the agreement went into effect.

The agreement regulated the actual exercise of military censorship: the military would not insist on compliance with the regulations, and every journalistic piece need not be submitted for review. Instead, a list of excluded subjects and a list of sensitive subjects was compiled to guide the press. The exclusion of certain subjects from the purview of the press did not generate controversy. The need for military security was so clear that it provided sufficient justification. However, the agreement did not end misunderstandings. Although censorship did not apply to political matters, some power over questions of public morale was retained. This ambiguity created grey areas, and in these areas, the press pushed its claims.

Eventually, in 1966, the agreement was revised and the censor's sphere of activity was more clearly defined. "Censorship does not apply to political matters, opinions or comment, or anything except for security information liable to help the enemy or harm national defense" (Rothenstreich, 1968). The revised agreement continues to shape government/media relations. The stipulation in the revised agreement that neither party will resort to legal sanctions or bring their disputes to court suggests the possibility of a two-tier relationship. The legal relationship is stringent and defined but of little practical consequence. The voluntary relationship, exemplified by the agreement, is flexible and ambiguous. In legal terms, the censor has the power to review all articles before publication; in fact, the censor is bound by the agreement and does not review articles treating strategic doctrine. In other words, the agreement effectively circumvents the law and illustrates how formal arrangements are supplemented or modified by informal ones.

The agreement applies only to those papers with representation on the Editor's Committee and to the Broadcast Authority which has the status of associate member. Its day-to-day implementation is supervised by a committee composed of representatives of the press and the military. Under the terms of the agreement, journalists are not liable to legal sanction for submitting material that is deleted by the censor, and journalistic protests of the censor's decision to delete are not uncommon. The relative obligations of the parties are defined by the agreement, not by law, for it is at the level of the voluntary relationship that the operative adjustments and constraints are found.

The exception is the foreign press; the censor's control of stories filed by foreign correspondents stationed in Israel does not come under the terms of the agreement. However foreign correspondents are as ready as Israeli journalists to recognize the existence of a national emergency (Goren, Cohen, & Caspi, 1975, p. 205). The censor's objective— avoidance of the publication of security information liable to help the enemy or harm the state—is accepted as legitimate. The censor, for the most part, stays within the limits of this mandate, although changing military and political circumstances may influence the stringency with which his rulings are applied.

If the censor appears to act outside legitimate security concerns, both foreign and local journalists are likely to challenge such decisions. On many occasions, friction has been intense, and at times, the censor has been accused of using his power to protect the military establishment. However, only a small segment of the media's output is affected by such controversies. For this reason, censorship has a relatively marginal effect on the performance of the Israeli press.

The second element in Israel's legal framework is composed of judicial decisions which affirm the claims of free speech and limit application of the Press Ordinance, 1933. In the early 1950s, shifting policy vis-à-vis the Soviet Union and the United States provoked intense controversy and criticism, especially from the newspapers of the extreme left. *Kol Haam,* the paper of the Communist party, was in the forefront of the critics, and in 1953, the Minister of the Interior closed the newspaper, invoking the Press Ordinance, 1933, as justification. The paper challenged the closure before the Supreme Court. The Court upheld the newspaper, declaring that Israel's Declaration of Independence was a commitment to the liberal tradition and made the principle of free expression an integral part of Israel's legal system. Prior restraint was more dangerous than subsequent punishment and was prohibited, "except in situations of unusual danger" (Lahav, 1976). The antipathy to prior restraint was reaffirmed in subsequent decisions; consequently judicial support for freedom of expression has modified the consequences of stringent legal sanctions.

The third element consists of laws enacted after independence, and here again formal arrangements are altered by informal understandings. Israel has several laws regarding secrecy which declare that everything official is secret unless disclosure is specifically permitted. The Penal Revision Law (State Security), 1957, deals with espionage, treason and damage to the state's security and foreign affairs and forbids disclosure of official information by civil servants. It also forbids the disclosure of information about issues that the Cabinet, with the approval of the Knesset (Parliament) Defense and Foreign Affairs Committee, declares secret, and provides sanctions for noncompliance. Section 28 of the Basic Law: Government, 1968, gives the Cabinet discretion to restrict publication of its decisions regarding state security, foreign affairs, and other subjects vital to the state.

The only portion of this legislation which is regularly utilized is the section of the Penal Revision Law (State Security) which makes it possible to forbid the disclosure of information about issues declared secret by the Cabinet. The Cabinet, however, needs the approval of the Knesset's Defense and Foreign Affairs Committee for any such decision, which makes it difficult to use this power for political reasons. Among the matters that can be declared secret under this section, the most important concerns the deliberations of the Cabinet when it is in session as the "Ministerial Committee on Security." In this case, no communique is issued at the end of the cabinet meeting. In the case of regular sessions, a rather brief communique is issued by the Cabinet Secretary. However such communiques are regularly elaborated in the press by "inside" stories of Cabinet deliberations. There are complaints that the Cabinet is incapable of guarding vital secrets, and it sometimes appears that the "state apparatus not only leaks, but actually resembles a sieve" (Galnoor, 1977, p. 176). The needs of politicians in coalition governments take precedence over twinges of conscience about noncompliance and leaks are an integral part of government/media relations in Israel.

The reasons for leaks as well as the political consequences of leaking will be discussed below. Here it is sufficient to note that an elaborate, albeit informal exchange system effectively guts the force of legal provisions restricting the dissemination of official information.

Coverage of Foreign Policy Issues

We have chosen to discuss coverage of foreign policy issues because this area illustrates government impact on the media and suggests the media potential for influencing the formation of policy. Stories on foreign policy often spark controversy. They can affect individual and party fortunes, relations with foreign countries, and ultimately the question of war or peace, but military censorship does not apply. The demarcation between security and political considerations is difficult to specify and attempts to balance the competing pressures, the impetus for greater openness, and the need for secrecy, at times produce paradoxical results. Moreover, the balance between competing pressures at any given moment is affected by the activities and stories of foreign correspondents, which though published abroad are readily available in Israel.

Although the first Foreign Minister, Moshe Sharett, was extremely sensitive to the treatment of Israel in the world press, he neglected the local press. Israeli political correspondence was in its infancy, and most reporters had few sources outside the Foreign Ministry spokesman. Editors adhered to the cooperative procedures developed during the struggle for independence and Sharett could shape coverage by briefing the members of the Editors' Committee. His main efforts were directed at keeping certain matters out of print. For example, when the Kremlin rejected Israel's candidate for ambassador in the early 1950s, the story was not covered in the Hebrew press, although it made headlines in the world press. News stories which were deemed capable of damaging Israel's efforts to expand its network of diplomatic relations were weeded out at the request of the Foreign Ministry spokesman. The press was asked to refrain from reporting on immigration from Arab countries and contacts with countries which did not maintain diplomatic relations with Israel (Goren, 1971).

However, foreign policy decisions, unlike matters pertaining to the security of the state, were not supported by a national consensus and there were sharp disagreements over some issues. To the extent that security considerations were entangled in foreign policy issues, the press was more or less prepared to follow the Foreign Ministry's direction. When security considerations were not present, coverage was open and controversies were aired. In the early 1950s, the question of Israel's relations with the Soviet Union and the United States provoked considerable controversy. The alleged pro-Western orientation of Israeli policy was strongly criticized by the newspapers of the left. The government attempted to curtail this criticism by using its powers under the Press Ordinance, 1933, to close Kol Haam, the newspaper of the Communist party. As discussed above, the effort resulted in the Supreme Court decision asserting the priority of freedom of expression.

A second foreign policy issue which caused bitter dissension was the question of relations with West Germany. The Reparations Agreement, signed in 1952, was vehemently opposed by political parties of the right and left. On one occasion, the Minister of the Interior tried to use his powers under the Press Ordinance, 1933, to prevent the official organ of Herut (an opposition party of the right) from attacking the government's policy. After issuing an initial warning to the editor, the minister did not carry out the threat (*Herut*, December 3, 1952). The first Prime Minister, Ben Gurion, who strongly supported the policy of building relations with Germany, tried over the next several years to keep the issue out of the public eye. In the late 1950s, this policy led to a showdown within his Cabinet in which the press played an important part (Goren, 1975).

In December, 1957, Ben Gurion planned to send Moshe Dayan, who had concluded his term as Chief of Staff to West Germany, to negotiate an arms deal. The Cabinet was not informed of the decision, but one of its members, representing Mapam, a small, socialist party, read of the decision in a German newsmagazine. The member brought the matter up in a Cabinet meeting, Ben Gurion called for a vote and his policy was narrowly approved despite the opposition of ministers from Mapam and Ahdut Ha'avoda, two of the smaller parties in the government coalition.

Next day, the Ahdut Ha'avoda newspaper, *Lamerhav*, carried a front-page story, headlined, "Ahdut Ha'avoda demands an urgent Cabinet meeting to cancel a grave decision." The article did not mention the nature of the decision but asserted that parliamentary representatives of the party were shocked. *Davar* (at that time closely allied with Mapai, the largest of the Labor parties) partially disclosed the content of the decision when it wrote that Ben Gurion cancelled the defense mission to Germany because Ahdut Ha'avoda leaked the story to further its electoral interests.

The incident sparked a government crisis. Ben Gurion demanded the resignation of the Ahdut Ha'avoda ministers. When they refused to resign, he resigned. Under Israeli law, the Prime Minister's resignation automatically results in the resignation of the entire Cabinet. Ben Gurion refused to form a new government until he secured a promise that legislative steps would be taken forthwith to tighten secrecy procedures to prevent leaks from Cabinet meetings. Eventually, some 10 years later, the pledge was redeemed with passage of Section 28 of the Basic Law: Government, 1968, but by this time "leaks" were an integral part of government/media relations.

It is ironic that the eventual resolution was new legislation since the precipitating incident occurred after the enactment of the Israel Penal Revision Law (State Security), 1957. This type of incident was rare during the Ben Gurion era, which partially explains his vehement response. On matters of consequence, Ben Gurion usually made his decision before the matter was brought to the Cabinet. For example, the decision to ally with the French and the British for the Suez campaign of 1956 was presented to the full Cabinet only at the last stage before implementation. Under these circumstances, it was not feasible strategy for a minister, who opposed a policy, to leak information to the press in hope of influencing that policy.

The situation changed when Ben Gurion left office and under his successors, Levi Eshkol, Golda Meir, and Yitzhak Rabin (Menahem Begin's premiership is too new to evaluate), leaking became increasingly functional. Not only was the Cabinet based on a coalition of parties, the largest labor party, Mapai, was split into several factions and factional leaders were represented in the Cabinet. Divisions among the latter were the product of substantive differences on military and foreign policy as well as personal and political disagreements. For this generation of politicians, it was good strategy to publicize disagreements in order to maximize support in the party and with the general public. Calculated leaks serve this purpose well (Tunstall, 1970).

As journalistic "scoops" became more frequent, political correspondents acquired a new prominence which produced a measure of autonomy and increased their leverage vis-à-vis government officials. Although leaks typically focused attention on personal rather than substantive aspects of policy disagreements, their cumulative effect increased the amount of information in circulation. Israeli officials and journalists remain constrained in their use of leaks by the consensus which urges caution in publishing information that might prove harmful to the state. However, the gradual increase of information in circulation may undermine that consensus, as greater awareness of alternative policy options alters perception of the problem.

The foreign press also plays a role in enlarging the quantity of information in circulation. Israel has been an important newsbeat since 1948 and its importance increased after the Six Day and Yom Kippur Wars. All the major news organizations of the world, with the exception of the Soviet Bloc countries who do not have diplomatic relations with Israel, have permanent representatives stationed in Israel. When dramatic events occur, such as an outbreak of fighting or more recently, President Sadat's visit to Jerusalem, hundreds of journalists flock to the country.

Foreign press coverage of sensitive subjects provides opportunities for expanded coverage of these subjects in the Hebrew press. Western newspapers are readily available in Israel. The major Israeli news media subscribe to the principal news agencies and also to the news services maintained by the *New York Times* and other prestige papers. References to matters concerning Israel in the foreign media are relayed home by Israeli corespondents stationed in most of the world. Censorship regulations prevent the publication of some stories about military matters in the Israeli press under an Israeli dateline, but are not applicable to stories that contain the same information but are quoted from a reliable foreign source. These transfers provide another example of the complicated information exchange system which flourishes in Israel and typically functions to circumvent stringent legal sanctions.

Government Information Systems

The government of Israel has created, in piecemeal fashion, an official network for the dissemination of information. The patchwork character is attributable, in large part, to the ambivalence of officials and the informed public about the propagandistic implications of establishing and operating such a network. Disagreements about the purposes and effectiveness of the network also influence its operation. And, as might be expected, the operation of the network is infiltrated with political considerations and the interests of various government officials and ministries.

A Government Press Office (GPO) was inherited from the mandatory government. Its primary function is the provision of technical services to correspondents. For example, foreign correspondents must apply to the GPO for accreditation. The office also distributes communiques composed by the various ministries to local and foreign correspondents and provides translation services for the latter. It has no policy function, but in gathering and providing material from all ministries, it has a small integrative function.

Controversy has surrounded the formulation of information policy. The focus of conflict has been the need for and the difficulty of preparing and presenting a unified position to the outside world. There has been less controversy concerning policy for the domestic audience, whose information needs, for the most part, were ignored during the first years of statehood. A brief account of the various attempts to formulate information policy and establish a central information office illuminates the political constellations which hindered the realization of a unified policy.

In the prestate period, a number of Zionist leaders devoted great efforts to winning the support of important public and journalistic figures for their cause. However, David Ben Gurion rarely participated in these efforts and did not appear to share these concerns. In 1949, Gershon Agron, an American-educated journalist and editor of the *Palestine Post,* was appointed to organize the informations services of the new state. His responsibilities included news for both home and foreign consumption. Agron was uniquely qualified for the position and determined to make a success of the job. He described his aims as follows: "arousing the country and its citizens by providing them with authoritative information . . . (and) collecting the springs of goodwill into the stream of national endeavor" (Agron, 1964). Although the objectives were lofty, the path was strewn with political obstacles. After a brief tenure, Agron resigned as Director of Government Information Services, when it became clear that Ben Gurion was indifferent to and would not support these efforts. Agron's plans to provide news services for both domestic and foreign audiences were never implemented. The parts of the organizational structure which were already in operation (radio was a department in the Prime Minister's Office and the Government Press Office) continued their separate existences. No liason or coordinating bodies survived this first attempt.

Until 1958, only the Army and the Foreign Ministry had full-time spokesmen. During the first months after the establishment of the state, both roles were filled by one individual. At the suggestion of Moshe Sharett, Moshe Perlman, a British-born journalist, upon his arrival in Israel in June, 1948, became the spokesman for the Army and the Foreign Ministry. Perlman, at the time, did not speak Hebrew, and his appointment suggested that the needs of foreign rather than local correspondents had priority. Shortly thereafter, Perlman was appointed to succeed Agron as Director of Government Information Services, and his twin functions as spokesmen of the Army and Foreign Ministry were separated. The irregularity and improvised nature of the early arrangements offer clues about the kind of obstacles that would constrain later attempts to coordinate the information services.

Other government ministries were not equipped with a full-time spokesman until 1958. On the rare occasions when a ministry wanted to acquaint the public with its activities, a press release was sent to the Government Press Office for distribution to various newspapers. Each minister handled his own press relations, usually through a member of his personal staff, who conducted these matters in ways which furthered the minister's interests and those of his party.

In 1957, the Penal Law Revision (State Security) was enacted. The relations of government officials at all levels with nonofficials were restricted. The Civil Service Commissioner published regulations to implement this legislation and interpreted the regulations to mean that journalists could have legitimate access only to the official ministry spokesman. If circumstances warranted, other officials could speak to the press but only with the permission of the spokesman and in his presence. The press was vehemently opposed to these regulations, and the Editors' Committee went so far as to petition Ben Gurion, asking the removal of the Civil Service Commissioner. No formal action was taken, the furor quieted down, and the dissemination of information followed well-established rather than legal routes (Goren, 1971). The only immediate result of the new law was that ministries which did not have a spokesman quickly acquired one. The position was designated as a civil service position, candidates were chosen according to qualifications and, once appointed, were eligible for tenure. As a result, the spokesman was no longer associated politically with the minister, and his usefulness to the minister declined accordingly. The spokesman's usefulness to the press then declined which in turn further reduced the utility of the position for the ministry.

For these reasons, it is impossible to generalize about the performance of ministry spokesman. The more influential spokesmen include those for Defense, the Foreign Ministry and the Army, whose material commands the attention of the foreign as well as the local press. The Spokesman of the Ministry of Finance commands the attention of the local press and attracts some attention from the foreign press. An additional factor in relative influence is the competence of the spokesman—some have had journalistic experience, others have had neither training in journalistic techniques nor previous experience with the media.

Spokesmen primarily provide formal services; they supply data and arrange interviews with the minister or the director general (the chief administrator) of their ministries. They also may be able to notify journalists of pending developments. Reporters make use of these services, but do not rely only or primarily on official spokesmen for information. Notwithstanding the legal prohibitions, most reporters develop and cultivate their own network of sources within the ministry.

With a single exception, no civil servant has been prosecuted under the terms of the 1957 regulations (Goren, 1975).

The spokesmen who deal with the foreign press offer similar kinds of formal services. The Spokesman of the Foreign Ministry meets with local and foreign correspondents on a regular basis. Because diplomatic usage assigns definite connotations to his formal statements, many of these briefings are background or "not for attribution." Such designations tend to increase rather than lessen the attraction of these briefings.

The Spokesman of the Ministry of Defense functions along much the same lines, although his relations with the press are of a less regular nature. In some circumstances, the spokesman functions as a trouble-shooter for the minister. Calls from reporters alert him to potential crises. A call or a query to the appropriate sector of the ministry initiates the attempt to defuse the situation (Rothman, 1978). The Spokesman for Defense handles policy matters while the Army spokesman deals with matters which concern the functioning of the Israel Defense Forces (IDF). Before 1967, the Army spokesman handled both subjects. The separation probably reflects the new pressures that were generated by the increased interest of the world press.

As a consequence of the 1967 war, Israel has become increasingly important as a newsbeat for the foreign media, and the organization of the Army spokesman has expanded accordingly. The Army spokesman's staff is much larger than the staff of any other information department. He and his aides handle both the local and the foreign press, providing "on" and "off the record" briefings. The Army spokesman is also in charge of issuing formal military communiques in the event of war or other armed occurrences. As discussed above, he commands the reserve unit to which military correspondents and other journalists belong (Schiff, 1969). The Army spokesman occupies a central position in the distribution of military information; but his influence is limited to this sphere by the apolitical tradition of the military.

Despite the obvious need to coordinate information emanating from the locus of government, the dissemination of information from the Prime Minister's Office has been handled on an ad hoc basis. When Yitzhak Rabin served as Prime Minister, he appointed Dan Patir as the Prime Minister's Counselor for Media Relations. When Menachem Begin assumed the office, Patir was asked to continue in the position and he accepted. Although it is too soon to evaluate the effectiveness or the uses of the office, appointment of a counselor is, at the least, a recognition of the importance of the function and perhaps the beginnings of a more formal system for the distribution of information.

A second gap in the information structure is the absence of a Cabinet or government spokesman. Except for a short period after the Yom Kippur War, when the Ministry of Information was operative, the Cabinet Secretary, in addition to his other duties, served as Cabinet spokesman. The secretary performed the task in prefunctory fashion; a tersely phrased communique was issued at the end of the Cabinet's weekly meeting. Reporters soon learned to rely on their own contacts among the ministers, the indispensability of the calculated leak was reinforced, and the practice flourished (Golan, 1972).

The creation of a Ministry of Information usually is attributed to the malfunctioning of the information services during and immediately after the Yom Kippur War, yet it can be viewed also as the culmination of sporadic attempts at reform. There have been demands for coordination of information services since the War of Independence and these demands rose to a crescendo whenever tensions mounted on the diplomatic or military scene. The new world interest in Israel after the Six Day War added impetus to the demands, but reforms were not initiated. There is some ambivalence about the creation of a Ministry of Information, the nuances sound totalitarian or at least propagandistic, and the need was not as obvious in 1968 as it was in 1973. In addition, the Foreign Ministry considers the task of coordinating Israel's information efforts abroad as one of its most important functions and was unwilling to surrender or share its prerogatives. In the interim between 1967 and 1973, the Israeli press became critical of the government's information policies and called for the establishment of a coordinated policy on information dissemination.

When the Yom Kippur War began, no single authority was responsible for information. The chaos of the first days of the war produced an improvised solution; the staff of the Army spokesman organized a National Information Forum, headed by General Aharon Yariv, a former Chief of Army Intelligence. The forum included the military spokesman, officers representing the chief censor and Army Intelligence, representatives from the Prime Minister's Office and the Foreign Ministry, and the news directors of radio and television. A number of academic experts were co-opted on an individual basis. Publication policy, during the critical days of the war, was determined by this ad hoc committee. The forum based its decisions on reports received from the battlefields, feedback from the world media, and considerations of military and civilian morale. Directives outlining policy were sent to the officers responsible for preparation of the communiques of the Army spokesman and to the censors who were reviewing press and broadcast reports. The forum also provided the Editors' Committee with background information. Its directives were not binding, since the forum lacked formal powers; but, for the most part, they were observed. However, the forum did not have sufficient authority to ensure overall coordination of the various information efforts. The primary obstacle was that major political and military figures, such as Prime Minister Meir, Defense Minister Dayan, and the Chief of Staff, failed to heed the directives of the forum in their frequent appearances on TV or when they briefed the members of the Editors' Committee. The divergent statements served to increase confusion and further undermined the credibility of the government and the Army.

Shortly after the war ended, without either press or public debate, the government decided to establish a Ministry of Information. Following the elections of 1973, Mrs. Meir was asked to form a new government. She presented her Cabinet several weeks later and announced that Shimon Peres would serve as the first Minister of Information. The logic behind the decision was clear. The Yom Kippur War demonstrated the need for coordination of information services and power had to be placed in civilian hands. Public loss of confidence in the ruling party's conduct of the war provided additional impetus for the decision.

Shimon Peres held the post of Minister of Information until May, 1974. During his short tenure, he assumed the role of Cabinet spokesman. He was in constant touch with journalists and attracted much attention both in the local and the foreign media. Peres is a prominent Labor party politician (who became the leader of the Labor party after the resignation of Yitzhak Rabin), and reporters were pleased to have easy access to such a high-level source. However, as a consequence of his political involvement, Peres assigned low priority to organizing the ministry. The ministry was to be composed of existing units (for example, the Government Press Office and the Information Center, which serves the domestic audience) and was to have overall responsibility for the Broadcasting Authority. Under the terms of the Broadcasting Law, however, the new ministry could not control broadcasting operations. Peres also did not take measures to oppose the Foreign Ministry's claim to have sole responsibility for informational work abroad. When his short tenure ended, there was still much that needed to be done.

There was no established organizational structure, and the political position of the new ministry was insecure.

Mrs. Meir's government resigned in May, 1974, and Yitzhak Rabin formed the new Cabinet. Peres became Minister of Defense, and Aharon Yariv was appointed Minister of Information. Yariv was new to politics. He had spent his life in the Army and for 10 years headed the Army's intelligence branch. He lacked the knowledge of an "insider" and the "street" wisdom of an apprenticeship in a rough and tumble political environment. While he acted as Cabinet spokesman, he was not part of the inner decision-making nucleus and sometimes saw his pronouncements contradicted by the pronouncements of the Foreign Minister.

Yariv tackled the task of organizing the ministry with enthusiasm, but the effort was soon frustrated by the lack of funds and the resistance of the Foreign Ministry. Yariv stayed on as Information Minister for approximately seven months, resigning in February, 1975, following a controversy over a public statement outlining his views on the Palestinian question which had not been cleared by the Cabinet. No replacement was named, and in a few months, the Ministry of Information quietly disintegrated. Its various departments returned to the ministries where they were originally located. Israel's experiment with a Ministry of Information ended as quietly as it had begun. Despite the obvious need for coordination, the ministry failed to generate sufficient political support to secure its position as the hub of communications or to alter the patterns of information dissemination.

Conclusion

From the beginning, situational factors, history, Arab hostility, military considerations, size, media centralization, and foreign interest in Israel have shaped and slanted the framework of government/media relations. Given the continuing threat to national existence, it is not surprising that there are stringent provisions to safeguard security. What is surprising is the ease with which these sanctions are circumvented, when their application appears dubious. Long-standing adherence to the consensus on preservation of the state inhibits full or strongly critical coverage of government decisions and official actions, but intra- and interparty competition functions to expand the quantity of information in circulation. As Galnoor noted, "government affairs are formally very secretive, yet a great deal of confidential information gets into circulation, occasionally concerning sensitive matters of security and foreign relations and quite regularly concerning internal deliberations on domestic issues" (1977, p. 176).

The shock of the first days of the Yom Kippur War dramatically lessened the government's credibility and shook the foundations of government/media relations. The Egyptian crossing of the Suez, the simultaneous attack from Syria, the heavy casualties and the confused and conflicting reports from the battlefields created public confusion and affected civilian morale. Later, some reports of some of the details of the initial days of the war began to appear. Although the reports were neither wholly accurate nor reliable, the public's perception of the leadership was affected. There were protests about the handling of the war. Early in 1974, when the reserve military forces were demobilized, soldiers organized a spontaneous protest movement which forcefully expressed the demand for changes in leadership.

In this unsettled period, the press also began to question its role and rethink its responsibility. Leading correspondents publicly regretted their former willingness to accept the government's view of defense and military matters at face value. The President of the Association of Israeli Journalists, during meetings of the Israeli Press Council, claimed:

> It seems to me that we were unduly ready to stand to attention whenever the word "security" was uttered. . . . We accepted official assessments of the situation without question because in the defense sphere, we did not develop norms for criticism and the exercise of independent judgement. We automatically agreed that there were people on whom we could rely with our eyes shut. (Report of the Israeli Press Council Debate, January 4, 11, and 18, 1974)

Protest and intense rhetoric failed to generate substantive alterations in the framework of government/media relations. The task of reconciling legitimate security needs with the commitment to a free press and frank and open coverage of governmental policy and actions remains as formidable as ever. The patterns of the past—the constraints, the expedient balancing of situational factors, and the improvised compromises for specific crises—remain in effect. The core of the relationship turns on the continued willingness of the press and the government to maintain democratic values in a society that, since its inception, has been at war with its neighbors.

References

Agron, G. *A Prisoner of Loyalty* (S. Shapira, Ed.). Tel Aviv: M. Neuman, 1964 (Hebrew).

Canaan, H. *The Struggle of the Press*. Jerusalem: The Zionist Library, 1969 (Hebrew).

Galnoor, Y. "Israel." In Y. Galnoor (Ed.), *Government Secrecy in Democracies*. New York: Harper and Row, 1977.

Golan, M. "Relations Between the Press and the Establishment." In *Yearbook of the Association of Israeli Journalists*. Tel Aviv: 1972, 6-33 (Hebrew).

Goren, D. *The Press and National Security*. Unpublished doctoral dissertation, Hebrew University, Jerusalem, 1971 (Hebrew).

Goren, D. *Freedom of the Press and National Security*. Jerusalem: The Magnes Press, 1975 (Hebrew).

Goren, D. *Secrecy and the Right to Know*. Tel Aviv: Turtledove Press, 1979.

Goren, D., Cohen, A., & Caspi, D. "Reporting the Yom Kippur War." *Journalism Quarterly*, Summer 1975.

Katz, K. "The Hagana, the Army and the Hebrew Press." In *Yearbook of the Association of Israeli Journalists*. Tel Aviv: 1948, 256-258 (Hebrew).

Kressel, G. *A History of the Hebrew Press in Eretz Yisrael*. Jerusalem: The Zionist Library, 1964 (Hebrew).

Lahav, P. "Freedom of Expression in the Decisions of the Supreme Court." *Mishpatim* 375, 1977 (Hebrew).

Lahav, P. "Political Censorship: Some Reflections on its Validity in Israel's Constitutional Law." *Israel Law Review*, 1976, 11, 339.

Lahav P. "Governmental Regulation of the Press: A Study of Israel's Press Ordinance." *Israel Law Review*, 1978, 13, 230.

Moshayov, D. "The Press in Israel." Jerusalem: Government Press Office, 1977.

"Report of the Israeli Press Council Debate, January 4, 11, and 18, 1974." In *Yearbook of the Association of Israeli Journalists*. Tel Aviv: 1974 (Hebrew).

Rothenstreich, J. "The Legal Position of the Israeli Press." In *Yearbook of the Association of Israeli Journalists*. Tel Aviv: 1968 (Hebrew).

Rothman, R. "Domestic Politics and Israel's Information Policy." Paper presented at the Annual Convention of the Midwest Political Science Association, Chicago, April 20-22, 1978.

Schiff, Z. "The Military Spokesman Announces." In *Yearbook of the Association of Israeli Journalists*. Tel Aviv: 1969 (Hebrew).

Tunstall, J. *The Westminister Lobby Correspondents*. London: Routledge, Kegan and Paul, 1970.

Yardeni, G. *The Hebrew Press in Eretz Yisrael, 1863-1904*. Tel Aviv: Tel Aviv University Press, 1969 (Hebrew).

Official Documents

Laws
The Press Ordinance. *Laws of Palestine,* Vol. II, Ch. 116, 1933.
Defense Regulations (Emergency), 1945.
Revision of the Penal Law (State Security), 1957. *Laws of Israel,* 255.
Broadcasting Authority Law, 1965.
Basic Law: The Government, 1968. *Laws of Israel,* 540.

Judgements of the Supreme Court
Kol Haam v. the Minister of the Interior, 73/53 - 83/53. *Piskei Din,* Vol. 7 at 871.
Ulpanei Hastrata Be Israel v. Levi Geri and the Film Control Board, Ministry of Interior, 243/62. *Piskei Din,* Vol. 16 at 2410.

Statistical Publications
Educational Statistics, August, 1977, No. 80. Central Bureau of Statistics and the Ministry of Education.

XI.
Government and the News Media in Japan: A Focus Upon Political Reporters and Public Officials*

Young C. Kim

This paper is concerned with the orientations (cognitive, evaluative, and affective) which the political reporter and the public official in Japan have about selected aspects of their relationship. The orientations are assumed to be significantly related to behavior. Before an analysis of their orientations is presented, however, a brief discussion of several factors that condition the process of newsgathering and reporting in the Japanese setting is in order.

The Context of Government—News Media Relations

THE CONSTITUTIONAL SETTING

One must begin with a fact of obvious but fundamental importance, namely, that Japanese reporters work in a society where the freedom of expression is guaranteed in law and practice. The freedoms of assembly and association—as well as speech, press, and all other forms of expressions provided for in the Constitution—are regarded as inviolate, fundamental human rights, and their guarantee is accepted as a basic principle of democratic government in Japan, although the Japanese Supreme Court has held that restrictions may be imposed to protect the public welfare. Furthermore, it is generally accepted by constitutional scholars that freedom of reporting is included under the protection of the freedom of expression stipulated in Article 21, although the Constitution does not make specific reference to the freedom of reporting. There are legal restraints on the freedom of reporting such as those designed to insure fair trial, fair election, the right to honor and privacy,

*This is part of a larger study, supported by the Social Science Research Council, Earhart Foundation, and the Institute of Sino-Soviet Studies, George Washington University. The author gratefully acknowledges their financial support.

and national security. Controversy, however, still surrounds the status of "the freedom of newsgathering"; any statement that such freedom is guaranteed by the Constitution would be defended by some, but challenged by others as unwarranted. There is no law explicitly protecting the "right" to protect news sources or refusal to turn over material evidence. Yet, the freedom of newsgathering is considered as worthy of respect, at least in the spirit of Article 21. There are virtually no legal impediments to newsgathering and reporting in Japan. This is not to deny the operation of nonlegal restraints. The reporters have occasionally exercised "self-restraint" on reporting for political or commercial reasons.

Constitutional provisions and court decisions apart, freedom of the press is well grounded in the dominant system of values of the postwar period and sustained by the presence of significant political forces ever sensitive to any signs of infringement on the freedom of expression.

THE COMPETITIVE SETTING

Japanese newspaper organizations operate in a society where the rate of newspaper diffusion (population per copy) is one of the highest in the world. In 1975 the figure was one copy for every 2.74 persons. In total circulation of newspapers Japan ranks third, following the U.S.S.R. and the U.S.A. Japan ranks second in diffusion rate.

The five national papers jointly account for more than half of the total newspaper circulation in Japan. By convention, daily newspapers in Japan are classified into three broad categories: general, sports, and specialized. General papers in turn are divided into national papers and local papers. The national papers refer specifically to the following five papers: The *Asahi, Mainichi, Yomiuri, Sankei,* and *Nihon Keizai.* These national papers, with editorial offices and printing plants maintained in two to five different cities, enjoy nationwide circulation. There is a strong tendency for the papers to shun alienating any significant segment of the public. Thus, injection of overtly partisan attitudes is avoided. Each paper exerts constant effort to enhance its visibility and prestige, and its involvement in other business activities is in part related to this consideration. Each paper must try to appeal to the broadest spectrum of the population and must cover a wide range of interests, needs, tastes, and preferences of the present and potential readership.

Most newspapers rely for their capital on money invested in the company by its management and the employees. The peculiarly small size of internal capital of a typical major daily—all the more surprising in view of the mammoth scale of its operations—makes the daily at least potentially and theoretically vulnerable to the exercise of influence of financial and business interests. The substantial share of advertisement revenues relative to sales revenues (one-half of all revenues are from advertising) reinforces its potential susceptibility.

PATHS OF RECRUITMENT AND PROMOTION

The process of recruitment of reporters and the patterns of their placement and promotions affect newsgathering and processing. Japanese reporters are recruited through a formal systematized means of selection. The system of a highly competitive, rigorous examination geared to college graduates has contributed to the development of professionalism. Many seek a career in journalism because the job is perceived to be free, unfettered, dynamic, and socially significant, a job that provides the opportunity for demonstrating one's individuality and ability.

Newspaper organizations are staffed with graduates of diverse universities, though certain universities contribute a disproportionate share to the world of journalism. The absence of a preponderance of Tokyo University graduates contrasts sharply with the central government bureaucracy. Another feature of interest is that a preponderant number of reporters have a background in humanistic studies.

The case of lateral entry into news organizations is practically nonexistent, i.e., there is no mobility between newspaper organizations. The rate of resignation is extremely low and virtually all reporters work for the same firm until their retirement. The sense of job security and the weight of seniority consideration contributes to the intense loyalty and sense of identification with "my own company." That reporters enter the profession in their early 20s is also significant in that they are exposed to the same subculture and tradition of a particular news company.

It is also relevant that a sense of hierarchical relationships pervade the production and processing of news. Personnel are hierarchically organized, both effectively and meaningfully, by age and year of entry. Reporters who actually interact with government officials in newsgathering are normally in their 20s and 30s. Older reporters are elevated to managerial posts progressively removed from newsgathering, writing, and even processing. Under these circumstances a columnist of great stature, comparable to those in the American press, cannot be expected to emerge. Clear generational gaps exist between the young reporters and their sources of news (government bureaucrats, politicians, and leaders of other social groups) and between managerial personnel and front-line reporters.

ORGANIZATIONAL FACTORS

Organizational/bureaucratic requirements and the standard operating procedure of newspaper organizations have an important impact on newsgathering and processing. Each of the major dailies in this study is sensitive to the contents of other rival papers, kinds of items selected as news, and values assigned. In addition to the institutionalized practice of a formal review comparing the pages of the major papers, rival papers as well as one's own are carefully read by the newspapermen at various levels of the organizational hierarchy. The sensitivity to the pages of rival papers, sustained by intense competition for a larger share of readership, reinforces the desire to be the first with a news item and the tendency to resort to sensationalism. It also leads to mutual emulation. In a sense, these papers collectively direct national attention to the events they treat as being newsworthy and important. The function of these papers is thus agenda-setting and the creation of reality by influencing the salience of issues and shaping the cognitive world of the readers.

An overview of the entire process involved in the preparation of a newspaper indicates the immense time pressure under which the newspapermen operate. the requirement of speed pervades newsgathering and processing, making adherence to the norm of accuracy and a preparation a well-rounded, or in-depth analysis of news items difficult. Each of the major papers considered in this study is a "set paper," publishing both morning and evening papers, each with multiple editions. The pressure of time magnifies the operation of preconceptions and prejudices of individual newsmen throughout the entire process of gathering and editing news.

A reporters' club is found at each governmental agency and at major social, political, and economic organizations. About 50 to 100 reporters of various news organizations frequent a club. At any one time around 15 or 20 news organizations are represented at the reporters' club of a governmental agency. Some companies assign a multiple number of reporters to a club. This system of reporters' clubs provides an effective and useful channel of newsgathering. But it also imposes constraints on newsgathering and tends to diminish incentives for outstanding individual performance. Individual initiatives and activities outside the framework of the system tend to be neglected or discouraged. The virtual absence of by-line articles in Japanese newspapers contributes to diffusion of responsibility and stultification of individual initiatives. The club system serves as a common defense mechanism against maverick reporters who might otherwise exhibit individualized behavior. It also provides a justification for self-censorship by way of agreement among the members not to report certain news items. So long as the club system is the main channel of newsgathering and the clubs are intimately related to government agencies, susceptibility to government manipulation is likely. What is more, the club system predisposes the reporters to view and assess matters from the perspective of that agency to which they are assigned. The opportunity for specialization in the news sources is made difficult due to the relatively short period of time a reporter is assigned to a government agency.

Reference should be made to night attack, the practice where a reporter visits a news source at his home late at night to elicit information. The targets of night attacks by political affairs reporters are most frequently the Cabinet secretary, Cabinet ministers, major leaders of the ruling and opposition parties, and ranking officials of government ministries. Reporters from various newspapers flock to the private residence of the target at night, especially when major developments are taking place, around 10:00 to 11:00 p.m. The practice of night attack in part attests to extraordinary zeal and dedication that Japanese reporters bring to their work. But at the same time it occasionally gives rise to "factional reporters" (with attendant corruptive practices) and to difficulty in a more rational use of manpower.

Newsgathering and processing is also affected by the distribution of power or responsibility within the news organization and the relations among the beat reporters, desks, and higher officials of those organizations. The desks hold the most important responsibility for the composition of pages. For example, in the *Yomiuri* office alone, more than 1,000 reporters are assigned to diverse news sources and to cover news on a round-the-clock basis. News collected and manuscripts prepared by these reporters are sent to the Home Office. All incoming manuscripts are scrutinized by the desk, deputy head of a subject matter department, say, political affairs. The desk makes judgments on the news value of a story, sometimes correcting commentaries. The revised manuscript is sent to the makeup department where judgments are made on the value of news item; decisions are made about how big a treatment to give it; and appropriate heads and subheads are prepared.

The beat reporters may be said to be front-line gatekeepers, for they are the first to screen a multitude of facts coming their way. The desks participate in this process of first-stage screening to the extent that the reporters are sensitive to the preferences of desks and to the extent that desks provide guidance and instructions to the beat reporters. Desks then add their value judgment on the stories provided by the beat reporters, thus constituting the second-stage gatekeepers. Inasmuch as the desks consult and are sensitive to the desires of superiors (department head, director and deputy director of the Editorial Bureau), the latter comprise the second tier of gatekeepers. These high-ranking officials at the same time constitute the third line of gatekeepers, at least to the extent that they maintain their own contacts with news sources, make judgments on news values, and communicate their views to their subordinates. The question of to what extent consensus exists among them on role orientations will be explored in the following section.

On the whole, the desks of each substantive department are the linchpin of newspapermaking, and they carry the heaviest responsibility for page composition. The responsibility of makeup desks is equally heavy, given the impact of heads and subheads—which, in turn, reflect value judgments—on the reader. The desks of substantive and makeup departments serve as the bulwark of conscience and the ethos of the newspaper company. Their political orientations have profound influence on the newspaper pages. True, their views are influenced and can be contradicted by their superiors, but newsgathering and processing is such that their role is crucial. Moreover, to the extent that the desks' views coincide with and are supported by the beat reporters, they exert tremendous and decisive impact on newspapermaking.

The Reporter's Orientations

What is the normative conception reporters themselves hold of their jobs? What orientations do they hold about the various aspects in the performance of their jobs? What orientations do they bring to bear upon interactions with government officials? These are some of the questions examined here in an effort to delineate the reporter's orientations and, as data permit, to identify correlates of orientations. The major underlying assumption is that the individual's overt behavior is significantly shaped by his orientations. In the section to follow, the orientations held by government officials will be presented.

Data used in the present section come largely from interviews which the author conducted with a purposive sample of 44 Japanese reporters—11 selected from each of the 4 newspaper organizations (the *Asahi, Mainichi, Yomiuri,* and *Sankei*). The following categories of respondents were interviewed:

TABLE 1

Categories of Reporters Interviewed

Home Office Reporters	
Editorial writer	4
Director or deputy director of Editorial Bureau	4
Department head	8
Deputy department head (desk).............................	8
Beat Reporters	
Reporters assigned to the Foreign Ministry, Ministry of International Trade and Industry, and Diet.................	20
Total	44

Interviews with personnel departments heads centered on their work and did not cover the whole range of questions used in other interviews. Consequently, the number of respondents for most categories presented here is 40. Interviews were conducted in Japanese by the author and, in most cases, lasted from two to three hours.

In addition to the Japanese data, comparable data on American and German reporters will be introduced when pertinent. One source is William Chittick's data on a sample of 40 American reporters covering the Department of State (1970). Another source is unpublished data collected by John Starrels in the summer of 1973 in West Germany specifically for this research. Ten interviews with German reporters representing *Suddeutsche Zeitung, Die Welt,* and *Frankfurter Allgemeine* were completed. They cover the Ministries of External Affairs, Finance, and Economics. A third source is the unpublished data David Nickels gathered in 1972 from 10 American correspondents covering the Department of State. In view of the small size of samples involved, the data presented here must be interpreted with caution. The data collected by Starrels and Nickels will be used only for making a crude comparison. Their data will be displayed when a predominant pattern emerges, especially in a direction opposite to that found in Japan.

Analysis of Japanese data offered here should also be regarded as suggestive.

Three specific working hypotheses guided the construction of a portion of an interview schedule administered to the Japanese journalists used to gather and analyze data for this section:

1. The nature of the work of a government agency is significantly related to variations in the reporters' orientations. Thus, orientations held by the reporters covering the Foreign Ministry (FM) will differ from those held by reporters who cover the Ministry of International Trade and Industry (MITI).

2. The nature of the responsibility of an individual or a class of reporters is significantly related to orientations. Thus, orientations held by the beat reporters, assigned to a ministry, differ from those held by "the managerial group" of reporters at home (desk, i.e., deputy head, head of Department of Political Affairs, deputy director and director of the Editorial Bureau, and editorial writers).

3. The four newspapers studied differ in the set of orientations held by their respective reporters, i.e., reporters from the *Asahi* would subscribe to orientations different from those of the *Sankei*.

Data were analyzed in terms of these hypotheses, and unless specifically noted, no additional patterns of response were observable.

THE REPORTER'S ROLE

Two questions were used to identify the reporters' normative conceptions about their job—"How would you describe the job of being a reporter? What are the most important things you should do?" Answers varied, but the single modal response, constituting about a half of the sample, concerned the way a reporter should transmit information: "accurately," "fairly," "impartially," or "objectively." The remainder focused on the goal of a reporter's activity; about 15 percent mentioned "search for truth;" about 10 percent named "pursuit of social justice." The remainder shared the following categories more or less equally: the enlightenment of the public, guidance of the public, reflection of public opinion in government policy, service as a "pipeline" or conduit between the government and the public, and service as an opinion leader.

It is significant that with a single exception, every respondent said that he saw his role as expressing and shaping public opinion in addition to informing the public. The question was: "Do you see a role for yourself as expressing and shaping public opinion in addition to informing the public?" There was also near unanimity among the respondents that they did not see their roles as participants in government policymaking. This was in response to the question: "Do you see a role for yourself as a participant in government policymaking?" Even the several reporters who responded affirmatively spoke in terms of the indirect effect which they believed their activities had on government policymaking. German respondents showed an opposite pattern to that of Japan. With the exception of two reporters, both from *Suddeutsche Zeitung*, the remaining eight reporters responded affirmatively, i.e., they saw their role as participant. A reporter from *Frankfurter Allgemeine Zeitung* qualified his affirmative answer by, "This is not the most important role of a journalist. My first goal is to instruct the readers about an event. I do not pose as their guardian."

Ignoring, for the moment, the kinds and amount of news released by government agencies, the decision to write a given story lies largely with individual reporters assigned to the ministries. When questioned as to "who determines what stories to write," most reporters interviewed declared instantly, "myself—sometimes in consultation with the captain and/or the desk." Generally speaking, the degree of autonomy of reporters increases with experience but inversely with the importance of issues. A captain, who heads the group of reporters from the same newspaper at a ministry, is consulted by his junior colleagues, and in turn, he consults, or is in touch, with the desk. On important matters, the head of the Political Affairs Department and, in some cases, the deputy director or even the director of the Editorial Bureau (managing editor) are consulted. A captain said, "Routine matters are taken care of by the reporters themselves. About 80 percent of the work is handled by us. On important matters, we consult the desk." Another reporter stated that he alone decides on the overwhelming majority of cases. Sometimes, he added, he gets advice regarding angles from the desk. "Seventy percent of the work was by myself and the rest in consultation with the desk," was another response. Another said, "We decide through discussion among our reporters at the ministry."

In some cases, the instructions to prepare a given story originate from the Editorial Office, especially in connection with special feature stories that are planned for future use. It should be noted that the reporters who cover the ministries usually return to their home office in the evening and have an opportunity to discuss ideas informally with the desk and department head.

NEWS CRITERIA

The respondents were asked to identify the criteria they use in determining or selecting stories to write and publish on a certain day: "How do you determine what stories to write and print? What criteria are used?" I was impressed with the general difficulty, or inability, of the Japanese respondents to articulate these criteria. A long pause preceded most of the responses, and the question elicited a wide variety of responses. For some respondents, the importance of a particular piece of information was easily determined by their training and experience. A few swiftly identified as criteria those items of information judged to have major impact on politics or upon life of the people. A few mentioned topicality as a consideration in major issues, and this was determined by the trends of the time. A few mentioned the prominence of news sources, i.e., other things being equal, preference would be given to more prominent personalities as newsmakers. Some mentioned newness, novelty, or unexpectedness of news items as of primary importance and, secondly, "follow up items," to maintain continuity in the news.

In response to the question as to what they consider to be the characteristics of a *good* news story, the single, most frequently mentioned was "accuracy." A reporter said a good story is one in which the news source can be clearly identified. Other characteristics mentioned are "objectivity," "comprehensiveness of treatment," "the use of proper angle," and "the degree of usefulness to the reader." Several reporters referred to content, saying that the content must be "rich," "interesting," "unambiguous," "easy to understand," and "deep in background analysis."

There is no perceived difference between what the reporters like and what they think the desk prefers. "What do the editors and ranking members of your department consider a good news story?" The reporters generally conceded difficulty in ascertaining what the public desires to read, pointing to the broad range of their readers. "What kind of stories do you think your readers like to read about most?" A few commented that pages devoted to social affairs, shocking news, or human interest stories appeal most to the reader. Most news stories written by respondents are considered hard reading material, and they strive to make this material easier to comprehend. Other than this general concern, the public or readership does not appear to loom large in the minds of reporters.

Decision to print is further influenced by practical considerations. The supply and demand in relation to available space is a determinant. Therefore, a news item may be buried if more newsworthy developments occur on the same day. For example, the news of President Nixon's proposed trip to China outweighed less important news items of the day. Another factor is the desire to provide more accurate information by delaying a day. This competes with the desire to achieve a scoop at the risk of some inaccuracy of details. Another factor may be a serious question about "angle" or contents of a story, especially on a matter of acute political sensitivity. For example, a reporter pointed out editorial decisions not to "play up" certain news issues or their aspects, i.e., a decision not to give extensive coverage to pro-Taiwan activities.

Our respondents were asked if a majority of the news items they write are printed. The responses were an emphatic "yes," and their estimates of the proportion printed ranged from "80 percent," "90 percent," to "all items." No respondent was able to specify any particular kinds of stories that were difficult to get printed. Reasons generally cited for nonprint were space limitations, poor writing, poor timing, and incomplete contents.

With a single exception, all respondents conceded that at times their stories were revised at the editorial office. Most respondents denied, however, the tampering of content. A few conceded that sometimes rewriting was necessary on a topic of great importance. For example, a reporter's original assessment of the prospect of Yen revaluation was revised in consultation with the editor's office (including the director). Another respondent recalled a case of an unbalanced article and the use of the improper angle which resulted in revision. Prior to revision, the writers were consulted. Every respondent insisted, however, that wording, expression, punctuation, or style occasion revision in most cases.

SOURCES

On what sources of information do they rely most heavily for their news stories? Choices available to our respondents were: press conference, background conference, news release, interviews with line officials, interviews with information officials, and talk with fellow newsmen. Every reporter singled out interviews with policy officials and politicians as being the most important source. In a typical account, background briefings given by the minister or vice-minister provided the reporter with some hints, and he then tries to develop a story by interviewing policy officials (chiefs of bureaus and/or sections). The reporters prefer private interviews, and in this connection, they occasionally practice "morning run" and "night attack." Morning run refers to a practice whereby the individual reporter tries to conduct interviews with officials early in the morning at the official's home or en route to his office. News releases and press conferences outweigh other sources for the reporters, but for the development of their own stories they rely most heavily on private conversations with policy officials.

GOVERNMENT-PRESS RELATIONS

How do the Japanese reporters perceive the press-government relations? A remarkably skewed answer was obtained to the following questions: "Do you feel the government press relations are basically conflicting or basically harmonious? How would you describe this relationship?"

Over 90 percent of Japanese respondents characterized government-press relations as basically conflicting. The remainder saw them as basically harmonious. A few of the first group would prefer the expression "tense relationship" to "conflicting relationship," and some qualified their responses variously by saying their posture should really be one of watchdog, offering constructive criticism, or that it need not be conflicting. For most respondents the question brought a swift response: "conflicting; so it should be, and so it is." The distribution of responses shows that *Sankei,* not *Asahi,* showed a greater tendency toward a "conflicting" posture. Contrary to my initial expectation, not all economic affairs reporters assigned to MITI showed a moderate posture toward MITI officials (one out of four did). No association exists between the perceived nature of relationship and individual characteristics of reporters such as age and amount of professional experience.

The American pattern is striking in its contrast. Of the 40 American reporters (Chittick, 1970) about 38 percent described their relations with department policy officers as either "usually cooperative" or "more cooperative"; 35 percent perceived the relations to be either "usually antagonistic" or "more antagonistic." Approximately 23 percent of the sample characterized relations as "both cooperative and antagonistic." The pattern of response showed by the German reporters is similar. Virtually every respondent described government-press relationships as "tension-filled" and "not harmonious."

I attempted to probe the reporters' perceptions of the ways and to what extent the press influences government policy by asking: "In what ways do you think the press shapes or influences government policy? Could you give some examples? And to what extent?" The responses vary considerably, but they can be grouped into three categories. The first category of response emphasized government uses of the press. One response was that the government uses the press for "trial balloon" purposes to gauge public reaction; another response was that the government needs the support of the press to implement policies. In the second category, the press was said to change the direction or modify the content of government policy or to promote the adoption of a particular policy. The press is also said to politicize an issue which otherwise might not become political. As one reporter put it, the press keeps a "watchful eye" on the activities of the government. First and second category responses are similar in one fundamental aspect. That is, the influence of the press is presumed to operate through the press' capacity to shape "public opinion." The third category of the responses concerned the press as a source of information for government bureaucrats. For example, MITI officials often learn about the views of the Foreign Ministry through the press. The press also provides information through the reporters' participation in numerous government commissions.

Every reporter interviewed characterized the degree of press influence on government policymaking as "considerable" or "very much." The responses reveal no meaningful variations among reporters except that the first group of responses came from the reporters assigned to the MITI. This is indicative of relatively closer relations between the reporters and economy-related government agencies. Several respondents qualified their assessment by saying that the influence of the press is indirect, not direct. The press campaign for government legislation on campaign financing was cited as ineffective.

Chittick (1970) provides no comparable data, but the American correspondents interviewed by Nickels (1972) ascribe "medium" to "slightly high" influence to the press. The German reporters (Starrels, 1973) indicate a low rating. One person replied "a lot," but six reporters said variously, "measurably small," "in small degree," "strictly limited," "not very much," "very conditional," or "hardly any at all." The German reporters' perception of the path of influence is primarily indirect. Press generates publicity which, in turn, influences the government to either modify policy or take into account their views.

The perceived high degree of press influence on Japanese government policy is related to the perception of the degree to which officials care about what reporters write and the officials' opinion of reporters. The reporters' unanimous view is that officials fear reporters and regard them as a nuisance. One reporter covering the Foreign Ministry puts it, "Those fellows at the Foreign Ministry operate as though they are under the injunction: *kisha o mitara dorobō to omoe*," literally translated as "When you see a reporter, regard him as a thief." Some respondents, however, added that the degree of personal friendship between a reporter and an official makes some difference. The perceived sense of distrust and "conflicting" relations is more intense and pervasive among reporters who cover the Foreign Ministry than their colleagues at the MITI.

Several questions were designed to elicit the reporters' views concerning the role of public opinion as criteria for information transmission. The respondents were unanimous in accepting the view that public opinion should influence government policy. At the same time, there was near unanimity in rejecting a notion that government officials do in fact base their decisions on public opinion. All respondents shared the belief that government officials are obligated to inform the public of their activities to the maximum extent possible. The expressions used by the respondents included "everything," "to the greatest extent possible," "as much as possible," or "in principle, everything." About a third of the respondents qualified their remarks by adding, "with some exceptions in the area of foreign policy." Two gave an unqualified affirmative response, saying the public needs to be informed of "the whole thing." Nearly all the respondents are convinced that officials do not share this belief.

The reporters were asked to establish general criteria for releasing or withholding information: "To what extent do you feel that government officials should or should not do the following?":

1) Release information selectively because it may strengthen the government negotiating position,
2) Release information because it may promote domestic political support for official policies,
3) Release information because the public has a right to know,
4) Withhold information because it may endanger national security.

With regard to Item 1, about one-third of the respondents said that government should not; 20 percent thought the government should; and the remainder gave qualified approval by saying either, "it can't be helped," or "it is permissible." A great proportion of American reporters approve such a practice. Three-fourths of the Chittick (1970) sample of

40 thought the State Department officers should. The German reporters' responses (Starrels, 1973) were similar to the Americans, with six respondents affirmative, two negative.

Concerning Item 2, about half of the Japanese respondents thought this should not be done, whereas 15 percent thought the government should do so. About one-third of the sample thought it cannot be helped or is permissible. Of the American sample (Chittick, 1970), almost three-fourths approved the practice and one-third opposed it. The German responses (Starrels, 1973) were closer to those of the United States. Six gave affirmative answers while two were negative. Again, the greater proportion of the Japanese reporters were opposed to the practice.

Item 3 brought a resounding "of course" or "definitely yes" from every Japanese reporter. This criterion finds enthusiastic support in the United States (Chittick, 1970). Virtually every American reporter accepted the proposition that the State Department should release information because the public has a right to know: 16, said absolutely must; 9, preferably should; 13, should unless the situation precludes it; one, may or may not; one, no answer. All the German reporters who responded (eight) gave affirmative replies (Starrels, 1973). Regarding Item 4, about three-fourths of the Japanese sample accepted the proposition with varying degrees of reluctance. About the same proportion of American reporters agreed with the statement but with greater willingness (Chittick, 1970). Of the eight German respondents (Starrels, 1973), seven were affirmative, and one said that the practice is admissible. In comparison with American counterparts, the Japanese reporters appeared least willing to approve this criterion as justifiable for withholding information. It should be kept in mind that the American data were collected prior to the 1970s controversies over the Pentagon Papers and Watergate. American attitudes may have moved closer to the Japanese pattern in recent years. It is interesting to note that Nickel's data collected in Spring 1972 show that four out of nine correspondents thought the officials should not, with the remainder indicating mild approval, saying either "preferably should" or "may do so."

Returning to the Japanese reporters, the distribution of answers for Items 1, 3, and 4 reveals no meaningful patterns. On Item 2, however, nearly all *Asahi* reporters responded negatively, while a much smaller proportion of reporters of other newspapers expressed a negative attitude. This may be indicative of relatively greater critical attitude on the part of the *Asahi* toward the government.

The respondents were also asked, "To what extent should reporters do or not do the following?":

1) Report the facts without any interpretation,
2) Write without regard for the editorial guidelines of their news organization,
3) Attempt to influence government policies,
4) Act in the role of opposition or watchdog.

With regard to Item 1, about three-fourths of the Japanese reporters said there was no question that an interpretation or a commentary should accompany news reports. The remainder said that there were some cases where an interpretation might not be necessary, but they too felt that news reports should be accompanied by an interpretation. Of the nine American reporters interviewed by Nickels (1972), five disagreed with the statement. Three thought that the reporters might or might not do so, and one agreed with the statement. The German pattern was conspicuous, diverging from the Japanese response pattern. Of the nine German reporters who responded (Starrels, 1973), eight said that the reporters absolutely must do so, i.e., reporters should report the facts without any interpretation, and one person saying the reporter may not.

On Item 2, practically every Japanese reporter thought that he should try to stay within the editorial policy guidelines of his news organization. However, several reporters added that they were not always conscious of the guidelines.

In probing their responses, it became clear that policy guidelines were perceived to be too broad as to impose restrictions. When a supplementary question concerning editorials was asked, the responses varied somewhat: several reporters, all of the *Mainichi*, felt that they should write without regard for editorial views of their papers, but they added that it would be desirable that their writings be consistent with editorial views. The rest accepted that there should be compatibility between editorial views and their own articles. The *Asahi* reporters were more sensitive to and felt obligated to follow editorial views more than did the reporters of other papers. The *Mainichi* reporters mentioned above proudly recalled several incidents when such incompatibility occurred.

American responses offer a sharp contrast. Virtually every American reporter of the Chittick sample (1970) thought the reporter should write without regard for the editorial views of their news organizations. The German data were closer to the American's with five accepting and two rejecting the proposition (Starrels, 1973).

Item 3 revealed a near unanimity of the view among the Japanese reporters that the reporter should attempt to influence government policy. Of those who agreed with the proposition, about 50 percent gave unqualified approval with the remainder qualifying their approval by adding that it is permissible to do so "to a certain extent," "sometimes," or "depending on circumstances." Only two respondents disagreed with the statement. At any rate, this response is interesting in view of their earlier statement that they did not see a role for themselves as participants in government policy making. Evidently, to the Japanese, an attempt to influence government policy does not constitute participation in policymaking.

The overwhelming majority of the American reporters (30 out of 40) thought the reporters should not "attempt to influence policy officers" (Chittick, 1970). In the case of the Japanese data, the wording was "to attempt to influence government policy." In the United States, the conscious desire to influence government policy did not appear to be pervasive. However, the Nickels data (1972) were based on the identical phrase as the Japanese version. Eight out of nine reporters stated emphatically that the reporter should not. In this regard, the German data were closer to the Japanese. Eight of 10 reporters responded affirmatively (Starrels, 1973).

With regard to Item 4, nearly every Japanese reporter felt that he should act as an opposition element or watchdog vis-à-vis the government. Two thought they should not. Of those who gave affirmative replies, everyone gave a swift and unqualified response with the exception of two who qualified by saying "only to a certain extent or depending on circumstances." As for the German sample, six reporters thought the reporter absolutely must do so, with another respondent saying the reporter may do so. The Nickels study (1972) of American reporters indicated a tendency opposite to that in Japan and Germany. Six American reporters gave negative answers, whereas three were affirmative.

To reject the proposition that the reporter should act in the opposition role is not to deny the presence of the norm of a critical attitude on the part of American reporters. However, as compared with their American counterparts, the Japanese reporters are more likely to feel that they ought to influence government policy and to act in the role of opposition or watchdog. Again, the Pentagon Papers and the Watergate affair may have brought about a change in this orientation.

Each respondent was asked whether he was satisfied with the work of others with whom he interacts within his organization. Most reporters who cover the ministries in fact grouped the desk and other superiors at the Bureau as one group. Home Office personnel, too, make such a distinction. Most of the respondents at the Home Office (desks, department heads, etc.) said they were satisfied with the way the reporters were doing the work. On the other hand, most beat reporters indicated their dissatisfaction with the way editorial personnel at home offices were carrying out their work. The source of dissatisfaction on the part of beat reporters was that editorial personnel were preoccupied with administrative work, devoting little time to the proper work of newspaper making. These reporters-turned-"bureaucrats" were thought to be deficient in news sense and out of touch with reality. They were perceived as lacking the capacity to provide leadership in molding the opinion within the newspaper organization. This line of criticism was directed primarily toward those who were above the desk. The respondents were asked whether there had been disagreement or conflict between the desk and reporters regarding gathering and processing news. About two-thirds of the respondents said such conflict occurred occasionally, while the rest denied it.

The Official's Orientations

This section approaches press-government interactions primarily from the perspective of the officials. What are the normative conceptions that the officials hold regarding the role of the reporter? Do they perceive any advantages in their interactions with the reporter? What orientations do they hold concerning various aspects of these interactions? The underlying assumption is that the activities of the officials, especially their news-transmitting activities vis-à-vis the reporter, are conditioned by these orientations. From the perspective of the reporter, the officials—with such orientations as they hold—constitute a target area or an environment in which he must operate. The reporter must cope with the officials' orientations, and his activity (the nature, pattern, and degree of his access to the officials included) is affected by them.

Data used here come primarily from interviews the author conducted with a sample of 26 officials from the Foreign Ministry (FM), the Ministry of International Trade and Industry (MITI), and the members of the Diet. Nine officials, who hold the rank of section chief and above, were selected from among the FM officials. They represent two geographic bureaus and a functional one (Bureau of Information and Cultural

Affairs). Eight officials of the MITI are of comparable rank to the FM sample and represent two policy bureaus and the Information Section of the Minister's Secretariat.

Nine members of the Diet were chosen; two each from the Liberal Democratic party, the Komei party, the Japan Socialist party, and one each from the Japan Communist party and the Democratic Socialist party. In the case of the first three parties, one member is from the House of Representatives, the other from the House of Councillors. One is a member of the Foreign Affairs Committee; the other is of the Committee on Commerce and Industry. In the case of the remaining two parties, the members interviewed have membership in the Foreign Affairs Committee in the House of Representatives. Interviews, conducted in Japanese, lasted from one to two hours in most cases.

Several working hypotheses guided the structure of the questions and the analysis of the data. The orientations which the officials hold:

(1) differ from those of the reporters.
(2) vary with the nature of the work of the ministry. Thus, the orientations held by the Foreign Ministry officials differ from those of MITI officials, and the orientations held by the legislators differ from the administrative officials.
(3) are influenced by the nature of the work of individual officials, i.e., the orientations of policy officials differ from those of information officials.
(4) vary with the ranks of officials, i.e., the higher the rank of the official, the more sensitive and favorably disposed toward the press he is apt to be and the more likely to ascribe influence to it.
(5) vary with the perceived prestige of the newspapers which reporters represent. Officials have a more favorable attitude toward, show greater sensitivity to, and ascribe greater influence to prestigious newspapers.

THE REPORTER'S ROLE

The normative conception the officials hold of the role of reporters will be considered first. The question employed was "How would you describe the job of being a reporter? In other words, what do you think are the most important things a reporter should do?" The responses came swiftly and were unanimous: "reporting of facts," though a few respondents added phrases such as "to provide material for judgment," "to identify problems," and "to provide responsible commentaries." About half of the interviewees proceeded to specify what may be proper reporting by adding such adjectives as "accurate," "faithful," "fair," and "objective." It should be noted that this conception is quite congruent with the normative conception the reporter himself holds in respect to his job. Some excerpts from the officials' responses follow:

> The most important thing is to report facts accurately. If the reporters want to evaluate policies, they should give fair assessment. They should try to contribute to the shaping of public opinion from a fair standpoint. (MITI)
> The most important thing is to report truth. It is necessary for the press to play the role of fair critic, but it should not oppose things just for opposition sake. (MITI)
> Accurate reporting. At the same time, there should be more back-ground information. Everything has a reason. No amount of hysteric writing about the rising prices would stop it. What is often lacking is a commentary explaining the whys of rising prices. My dissatisfaction is that even if we explain the government's positions on the matter written about in the paper, our explanation does not get printed. (FM)
> There is clearly anti-American bias on the part of most Japanese major papers. They seem particularly interested in printing stories which would embarrass the government. (FM)
> The most important thing is to write fair articles. One's beliefs and values necessarily enter into a story, but a story should show high objectivity. (Komeito Dietman)
> To provide reportage with objective and accurate judgments. Gener-ally speaking, I consider the editorials of major dailies to be valid. The problem of the press is that it tends to emphasize current, immediate problems, particularly those of human interest stories, instead of dealing with long-range problems. (Socialist Dietman)
> I hope the newspapers report the truth. The papers are edited errone-ously and with subjectivity. I am very much dissatisfied. There is too much subjectivity in reporting. The press suffers from commercialism. The reporters write stories that would sell. Often the stories reflect ideological tendencies. (Liberal Democrat Dietman)
> The most important job for a reporter is to inform the public of the facts about everything accurately. I think the reporters are too much concerned with a big play their stories would get in the paper. (Democratic Socialist Dietman)
> The most important thing is to report truth. The state of public opinion is reported erroneously. The reporters are too sensitive to the left wing opinion and are sympathetic to the latter's views. The most conspicuous example is their belief in Marxism and Leninist theory. To them, social-ism equals peace and capitalism, war. Japanese reports about China are often inaccurate. The Japanese reporters do not have moral courage to criticize China. They were responsible for the major disturbance over the Security Treaty. (Liberal Democrat Dietman)

All the interviewees expressed some degree of dissatisfaction with the activities of the reporters. The sources of such dissatisfaction varied, although the following received frequent mention: (1) lack of objectivity, (2) dearth of factual reporting, (3) partial and unfair reporting, (4) tendency to concentrate on stories which embarrass the government, (5) abundance of speculative and inaccurate reporting, and (6) anti-American bias. The sense of dissatisfaction is especially strong among the FM officials. MITI interviewees generally articulated similar dissatisfaction, but with less intensity, and their dissatisfaction was directed largely toward reporters from the Social Affairs Department of newspapers, as distinct from those from the Economic Affairs Department. It will be recalled that economic affairs reporters on their part characterized their relationship with the officials in more satisfactory terms than did their colleagues from the Social Affairs Department.

The dissatisfaction felt by the officials toward the reportage is related to their perception of the criteria which the reporter applies in news selection. They are sharply critical of what they perceive to be dominant criteria. A question designed to identify these criteria yielded several responses. For some officials, an "antigovernment stance" (usually combined with anti-American) constitutes the major criterion. Some others mention "appeal to the mass public or human interest." Several point to the reporter's perception about a story likely to be accepted by the desk and, when pressed, named an antigovernment posture to be the criterion. A few mentioned novelty of news and a major change in hitherto pursued policy. Still others thought the sensational character of a news item was a determinant. On the whole, the perceived criterion of an antigovernment stance looms large in the minds of the officials. It is noteworthy that only a few officials mentioned other criteria, such as novelty and major policy change, which the reporters themselves identified as being their criteria for news selection. There is then much dissatisfaction and resentment on the part of the executive officials and members of the ruling party toward the reporters.

Distrust toward the press is revealed in response to what role the officials expect the press to play. About one-third of the respondents called on the press to eliminate antigovernment bias and to refrain from the "act of opposition for opposition's sake." About one-fifth repeated its call for accurate and/or fair reporting of facts. These two categories constituted about half of the respondents. Another third of the sample expressed a desire that the press more adequately reflect, rather than manufacture, public opinion. The remainder expressed a hope that newspapers would provide material reflecting diverse viewpoints so as to facilitate the reader's judgment. A few respondents deplored what was thought to be the practically identical manner in which the issues are treated in various major dailies.

Nearly every official stated that the views of the press are not equivalent to, nor do they constitute, the whole of public opinion. One official put it, "the press does not certainly represent the view of the silent majority." Most respondents, however, conceded the difficulty in gauging "true public opinion."

HOW OFFICIALS USE THE PRESS

In spite of the sense of distrust toward the press, the officials are not wholly negative toward interactions with the reporters. Not only are they resigned to the need for dealing with the reporter in a democratic polity, but they are also conscious of resulting advantages. Only one official declared flatly that he derives no advantage whatsoever. About half of the executive officials see the principal advantage lies in being able to gauge the mood of the public. While some of them appear to be interested in public moods, primarily from a manipulative standpoint, the remainder state that such information is occasionally "instructive as it represents the viewpoint of the ruled." Other officials see the chief utility as being able to learn of the attitudes and evolving policies of rival ministries on given issues. For others, the press is seen as a useful instrument in "educating and sensitizing the public" on a particular issue along the line their ministry is advocating. Several interviewees mentioned a "trial balloon" function. When reminded, most of the respondents stated that a manipulation of the press for such purposes is difficult to manage.

During probes, officials said that they found it useful when they obtained through the press information on an overseas development before an official cable reached them. When asked if they ever thought news commentaries were useful or enlightening, the response was generally negative. As most officials see it, reportage or commentary is superficial, rarely going beyond a common-sense treatment. This assessment is related to the officials' evaluation of the attributes of the reporters. Except for a few reporters, both in the FM and MITI, thought to have a good command of the subject matter they are covering, most reporters are regarded by the officials as suffering from a deficiency in technical knowledge. We shall later return to the question of the officials' evaluation of the reporters with regard to other attributes. In general, the legislators have more positive attitudes than administrative officials toward contact with reporters. All the legislators stated that interactions with reporters provide them with valuable information on the activities of other parties, the government, factional politics, and the Diet. One legislator added that sometimes he obtains hints from reading newspapers about questions to be used at committee meetings.

The officials betray a high degree of sensitivity to press reportage. Most officials interviewed say they are sensitive to material written about their agency or themselves, while only a handful of officials profess to care little about it. This is consistent with the reporters' perception in this regard. About half of those officials who conceded their sensitivity recalled that they have communicated their reactions to reporters and/or editors. Occasions for such action arise under two circumstances—in the case of inaccurate information and the reporting of security leaks. Protest or complaint is generally communicated to the reporters assigned to the ministry, but in serious cases the department head and even the chief of the Editorial Bureau may be contacted. Matters involving interpretation are usually ignored as they presumably represent differences of judgment and protesting them would prove futile.

RELEASING INFORMATION TO THE PRESS

From the standpoint of government officials, the methods of communication most useful are press conferences and informal contacts with reporters. These two means are considered superior to other means such as press releases and formal briefings. It will be recalled that the reporters say they rely most heavily on interviews with policy officials. As was the case of reporters, the same set of questions were used to elicit the officials' attitude about the transmission of information. Nearly every executive official interviewed agreed with a statement that information may be selectively released in order to strengthen the government's negotiation position vis á vis foreign countries. About half of these were unqualified responses, whereas the remainder added such qualifiers as "to a certain extent," "should be done cautiously," "not toward an ally such as the United States," or "only in relation to the Soviet Union." Of seven Dietmen who responded, three were negative. Of the affirmative responses, one was unqualified while the rest were qualified. It will be recalled that about one-third of the reporters thought the government should not manipulate information in such a way. Of those officials who gave an affirmative response, a handful indicated that the government is involved in such a practice to a certain extent, the rest declaring that the government seldom practiced it. A few respondents added that such a practice is usually ineffective. As for the American sample, nearly every official thought the Department of State should release information if it is thought to serve to strengthen the government's negotiation position (Chittick, 1970).

Again with a few exceptions, all the administration interviewees agreed with the statement that the government official may release information so as to promote domestic political support for official policies. Four out of seven Dietmen gave negative responses, with the remainder giving a qualified yes. Most of those who agreed said that the government is actually doing so, with a few demurring that this occurrence is not frequent. It should be recalled that about half of the Japanese reporters thought this should not be done. Almost three-fourths of the American policy officers accepted the proposition that the Department should release information because it might promote domestic political support for Department policies (Chittick, 1970).

It is noteworthy that most Japanese officials do not feel that they "ought to release information because the public has the right to know." Only one official replied affirmatively without qualification. A few agreed with the statement, with the provision that diplomatic secrets be excepted. For most officials it is not so much a matter of the public's right to know, but rather, it is beneficial to release information since it would enable them to gauge public reaction and to provide public understanding for government policy. The response of the legislators was strikingly different. Everyone agreed with the statement in question, although the position of two LDP members was somewhat qualified. The reponses of the officials contrast sharply with those of the reporters who unanimously endorsed the statement that the government ought to release information because the public has a right to know. As for the American counterpart, virtually every State Department respondent accepted the proposition that the Department should release information because the public has a right to know. This feeling is, however, not intensely felt since responses of about half of the sample were that the Department may, rather than should, do so (Chittick, 1970).

Regarding the question of whether government officials should withhold information "because it may endanger national security," Japanese responses were resoundingly affirmative—"of course." A few officials saw fit to enter a qualification that strict interpretation should be made concerning what constitutes a danger to national security. All legislators agreed with the statement, albeit with varying degrees of conviction. Some added a qualifying statement such as "in principle," or "to a certain extent." One legislator put his reservation more explicitly when he said, "In principle, I agree. The problem is how to stop its abuse. The trouble with our government is that it tends to hide anything inconvenient or embarrassing to the government under the cloak of national security." When asked this same question, it will be recalled, three-fourths of the Japanese reporters responded affirmatively with the remainder opposed. Almost without exception, American officials felt strongly that the Department should withhold information which might endanger national security (Chittick, 1970).

GOVERNMENT-PRESS RELATIONS

Given the overall sense of distrust toward the reporter described earlier, it is remarkable that all the Japanese officials interviewed claimed that their press relationship was "good." A few of them said further that they "would not call their relationship cooperative, though it is not bad," but most went on to describe their relationship as either "usually cooperative" or "always cooperative." Various reasons were cited for the existing relationship. A few thought their candor in dealing with the reporter explains it. Some declared it is "because I don't lie." Others ascribed it to the lack of prejudice, their openness to the reporter, their willingness to spare time to hear the reporter out, or of not deliberately misleading the reporter. The common theme underlying all these reasons is the candor and accessibility granted to the reporters.

In general, U.S. State Department policy officials described their relationship with reporters in favorable terms (Chittick, 1970). About 30 percent characterized the relationship as being both cooperative and at the same time antagonistic; about 43 percent of the sample described it as "more cooperative" or "usually cooperative" and 15 percent said "more antagonistic" or "usually antagonistic." (The remainder gave no response.)

The American data also indicated that the reporter's perceptions of relations with Department policy officials bore remarkable resemblance to those of the policy officials themselves. The number of American policy officials perceiving antagonistic relations was indeed small. In Japan there was wide incongruity in the perceived interpersonal orientations so far as the cooperative-antagonistic dimensions were concerned. While every Japanese reporter perceived conflicting relations, nearly all Japanese officials characterized their relationship with reporters as cooperative.

There are some discernible differences between the MITI and the FM officials, which are not clearly revealed in the simple tabulation of responses presented above. What came through clearly is that, on the whole, the MITI officials reveal a strong awareness of an interdependent relationship with reporters and show little antagonism toward the press. This is not to deny the presence of resentment they feel toward some reporters from the Social Affairs Department. The MITI officials explain their good relationship with the reporters much the same way their FM counterparts do. However, some of them offered an additional explanation: "the nature of the work of our ministry is such that we can afford to be open and candid." This is, indeed, the crux of the matter.

Of course, the perceptions of the existing relationships are distinct from the normative conception. With the single exception, all FM interviewees declared that the relationship between officials and reporters should *not* be "basically conflicting" and deplored the perceived antagonistic or conflictual attitude of the reporters. This, of course, contrasts sharply with the reporters' orientations—their predominant orientation being that it should be conflicting and that it is.

REPORTERS' QUALITIES

Our respondents hold to a man a favorable evaluation with regard to the basic intelligence and trustworthiness of reporters with whom they interact. Their rating by administrative officials range from "poor" to "fairly high," with most responses falling within the category of fairly high. Some respondents used measures of their own. One official indicated the grade of B would be appropriate, another giving 70 points out of 100. Regarding the level of information deemed to be possessed by the reporter, the officials' rating is somewhat austere, ranging from "not much" to "fairly high" but with most responses still falling within the latter. There are no significant differences in the distribution of answers either in terms of the ministries or other factors. The only difference is that the rating given by the legislators of intelligence, trustworthiness, and the level of information is uniformly higher than those given by administrative officials. The pattern of distribution obtained in the United States by Chittick (1970) found that about three-fourths of Department policy officers rate reporters from "fairly high" on the qualities of "intelligent, informed, skilled, and helpful." The rating given by the information officers is somewhat higher, with three-fourths falling between the medium point to the highest.

The Japanese officials' perception of the social prestige of the reporters was somewhat more complex. Nearly all interviewees thought that the reporters' social standing was "good" or "fairly high" but was somewhat lower than that of other occupations such as medical doctors, lawyers, and bureaucrats. Only two executive officials deviated from the pattern; one indicating the reporters' social standing to be comparable to that of the other occupations listed and another declaring it to be higher than the latter. Of those who gave the lower occupational rating to reporters, several administrative officials observed that they would not give consent to their daughters' marriage to the reporters. One official went on to observe that the reporter is pampered and lacks decorum and a sense of propriety.

It should be noted here that the officials generally classify the reporters into two groups. One group consists of those whom they term representing first-rate or prestigious papers such as the *Asahi, Mainchi,* and *Yomiuri.* The other consists of the reporters of less prestigious papers. With regard to the officials' ratings of the reporters, both in terms of specific attributes and social prestige mentioned earlier, about a third of the respondents felt it necessary to preface their remarks by saying they were speaking of reporters of the first-rate newspapers. Their evaluation of the reporters of the second group, therefore, is lower. Another distinction the officials make about the newspapermen is between the beat reporters and those who serve as ranking members of the Editorial Bureau and editorial writers. The officials accord the latter much respect and prestige. In sum, the officials treat the reporters (at least those of the first-rate newspapers) with some respect, but they rate themselves higher than the reporters in terms of occupational prestige and level of expertise. How this sense of superiority affects their interactions with the reporter is difficult to ascertain.

INTERPRETATIVE REPORTING AND EDITORIALIZING

There were several additional aspects of the reporters' activities about which the officials' orientations were elicited. The officials are not prepared to exclude interpretation or commentary, as distinct from reporting of facts, from press activity. Thus the administrative officials interviewed feel that it is "permissible" for an interpretation to accompany the reporting of facts. Their proviso was that the reporter's subjectivity be kept to a minimum. The legislators' attitude is more positive;

they feel it is natural and desirable for an interpretation to accompany
the presentation of facts. Some respondents added, however, that there
are some things which may not require interpretation. This contrasts
sharply with the American sample. Close to three-fourths of the American officials felt that reporters should be factual, avoiding any interpretation whatever (Chittick, 1970). Regarding the question as to whether
the reporters should write without regard for the editiorial views of
their newspapers, the predominant view among Japanese officials, both
executive and legislative, is that there need not be consistency between
the two. Most respondents thought such is the actual case. Several
officials, all from the FM, thought that there should be consistency
between the news stories and the editorials. Incidentally, the *Asahi* is
singled out by them as being fairly consistent in this regard. They
complained that editorials of Japanese papers are usually ambiguous,
making it difficult to ascertain the position of a newspaper on a given
issue. One of them suggested that editorials are deliberately made
ambiguous as an escape hatch or a shield against possible criticism,
while the contents of stories in the paper clearly are allowed to denote
antigovernment bias which advocates a definite policy action.

A perfect example, according to one official, is the issue of the United
States-Japan Security Treaty. The kind of headlines used and the
contents of stories are clearly anti-Security Treaty, while the editorial
views are ambiguous and demonstrate "good behavior" in the eyes of
the government. He condemned such practice as being improper. The
overwhelming majority (just over three-fourths) of U.S. State Department officials, both policy and information, felt strongly that the reporters' writings should disregard the editorial views of their news organizations (Chittick, 1970).

The overwhelming majority of the Japanese officials interviewed
thought it all right or permissible to attempt consciously to influence
the government's policy. Several officials gave their negative response
without qualification. Most of those who gave affirmative answers
qualified their responses by adding such phrases as "to a certain
extent," "there should be a limit," or "it shouldn't be done excessively."
The one official who disagreed stated that this would be permissible if
divergent viewpoints were expressed in the newspapers. He observed
that the Japanese newspapers take practically identical positions on
key issues, and hence the reporter should not. Another official, who
avoided a direct answer, said, "In any event, such is the result of the
reporter's activity." The near consensus on the proposition may indi-

cate a resignation to the de facto situation or a grudging acceptance of the principle rather than an accurate expression of internalized value. About half of the sample thought that the reporters are actually engaged in a conscious attempt to influence government policy. The other half declared that little of such an attempt is observable. The reason cited for the latter is that the reporters are driven by a search for a "scoop" and simply do not have the time to study policy questions thoroughly.

There appears to be no discrepancy between the reporters' orientations and that of the officials. It will be recalled that on their part most reporters felt in varying degrees that they should attempt to influence government policy. True, to say something is "permissible", as in the case of the official, is different from saying one should, but the officials' responses are interesting. Comparable American data show that a majority of policy officers and about three-fourths of reporters accept the proposition that reporters should attempt to influence policy officers (Chittick, 1970).

With regard to the propriety of assuming the role of the opposition, nearly every official conceded that it is either "necessary to some extent" or "permissible" for the reporters to act as oppositionists. A few executive officials added a proviso that this should be done "fairly," "selectively," or "with due recognition that such is not a sole function of the press." Two executive respondents stated that the reporter should not act in the opposition role. For them it is wrong for a reporter to assume such a posture, for the reporter should evaluate government policies on the basis of the merits of the issues.

As for the legislators, with a single unqualified rejection, all of them thought it necessary or permissible although qualified by such phrases as "depending on the case," "to a certain extent," "if there is an objective validity to the opposition." Some gave more elaborate responses: "Well, it depends on the nature of issues. . . . It is all right for a reporter to present logical, rational arguments so as to make the government proceed on the right course. However, he should not adopt antigovernment postures on everything." Despite some reservations expressed about the role of opposition, no respondent objected to a reporter assuming the role of watchdog.

Here again the MITI officials are more relaxed in attitude toward this than their FM counterparts. Several MITI officials remarked that very seldom have they experienced situations in which the press played the role of opposition to the MITI. On the other hand, the FM officials' stand on this issue is ambivalent. It will be recalled that nearly every reporter felt that he should act as the opposition element or watchdog vis-à-vis the government. In the abstract, nearly every official subscribed to a statement that the reporters may try to act in the role of opposition. However, the officials demonstrated considerable disapproval and resentment. Their verbal acceptance of the proposition appears merely to indicate a sense of resignation to a reality, unpalatable as it may be.

As for the perception which government officials have concerning the influence of the press, the responses of MITI interviewees are generally more positive as compared with those of their FM counterparts. Several MITI officials went so far as to acknowledge considerable direct influence of the press on their ministry's policies, while every FM official denied the presence of direct influence, insisting that influence is at most indirect. Those MITI officials who perceived indirect influence were prepared to say that they take into account the views of the press. As for the FM officials, about half say that it pays attention to the views of the press, while others say it does not take into account but merely takes note of them!

Direct influence is understood to occur when government officials, conscious of the views of the press, allow them to shape policy output. A MITI official recalled that when the press gave good coverage to the boycott against the high price of color TV sets conducted by the League of Housewives, the MITI felt compelled to intervene. Likewise, newspaper reports about hoarding or dumping by a trade company led to MITI investigations.

Summary and Interpretation

It is noteworthy that a high degree of consensus exists among the reporters on the wide range of orientations examined in this paper. This is particularly true of normative aspects of the orientations about the reporter's role, appropriate news criteria, the nature of government-press relations, and the propriety of acting as a watchdog/opposition. A consensus extends to other objects of orientations as well, such as the weight editorial guidelines should carry and the appropriateness of interpretation accompanying news.

Some divergences are observable in relation to the orientations that the reporters hold about the work of officials. The reporter's orientations regarding what general criteria the public official ought to apply in releasing information is a case in point. Of several correlates of the orientations examined, the nature of the work of a government agency is most meaningfully associated with the variations in the reporter's orientations. Thus, the reporters assigned to the Ministry of International Trade and Industry hold orientations that are different from those of their colleagues covering the Foreign Ministry.

Data do not support the assumption that there are significant differences among the reporters of different newspapers, particularly between Sankei reporters and the rest. Likewise, few significant differences exist between the front-line reporters and those who work at the editorial office. This is not to deny occasional disagreements between them about the processing of news.

Also noteworthy is the high degree of consensus that is present on officials' orientations on a wide range of subjects, particularly about the role of the reporter. There is, for example, a near unanimity among the public officials' normative conceptions about what the reporter ought to be doing and what news criteria ought to be applied. Some differences observable pertain to the degree of distrust and antagonism felt toward the reporter, the perceived influence of the newspaper on policy-making, and the perceived value of contact with the reporter. For example, as compared with MITI officials, FM officials show a greater degree of distrust and antagonism.

It is significant that a high degree of congruity exists between the reporter's reflexive orientations and the official's interpersonal orientations. Thus, with few exceptions, the public officials hold essentially the same normative conceptions about many aspects of the reporter's work as the reporters themselves. However, the officials voice considerable criticism and dissatisfaction with the actual performance of the reporters in fulfilling these norms.

The fundamental assumption underlying the study is that orientations are significantly related to overt behavior. Since no data on actual behavior have been introduced in this paper, it would be inappropriate to make substantive comments. However, based on a preliminary analysis of the data on the interaction between a reporter and an official, and on other factors shaping newsgathering and processing, the following observations seem warranted:

The reporters do in fact—with varying degrees of consciousness— attempt to adhere to and actualize the orientations delineated in this paper, especially the normative orientations. At the same time, these orientations constitute the criteria by which the public officials and others can judge the performance of the reporters. To the extent that a certain set of orientations function as working norms on the part of both parties to interaction, they constitute an effective motivating force with behavioral consequences.

References

Chittick, W. *State Department, Press, and Pressure Groups.* New York: John Wiley & Sons, 1970.

Nickels, D. Untitled and unpublished manuscript, 1972.

Starrels, J. Untitled and unpublished manuscript, 1973.

ABOUT THE AUTHORS AND EDITORS

MARVIN ALISKY, professor of political science, Arizona State University. His research interests are in the political and communication processes of Latin America. His books include *Political Forces in Latin America: Dimensions of the Quest for Stability* and *Latin American Media: Guidance and Censorship.* He has contributed two hundred articles to numerous journals.

FRANCIS BALLE, is the director of Institut Francais De Presse Et Des Sciences De L'Informattion at the Université De Droit D'Economie Et De Sciences Sociales De Paris. He is co-editor of the *French Review of Communication.*

GEORGE BOYCE, is a lecturer in the department of political theory and government, University College of Swansea, England. He has authored *Englishmen and Irish Troubles: British Public Opinion and the Making of Irish Policy, 1918-1922* and *Newspaper History: From the 17th Century to the Present Day.* He has published articles in numerous academic journals.

ALLAN BROWN, was a Ph.D. candidate at the economics department, University of Queensland, Australia, at the time his contribution to this book was written. His research work relates to the structure, regulation, and economics of the Australian media.

JEAN-MARIE COTTERET, professor of political science, Sorbonne, is a co-editor of the *French Review of Communication.* Among his publications is "Televised Debates in France," in Political Communication Review.

CARMAN CUMMING, a former parliamentary editor and correspondent for The Canadian Press, is now an associate professor of Journalism at Carleton University. He has been an editor with CP in Toronto and served as CP's United Nations correspondent. His current research interests are press-government relations in Canada.

DELMER D. DUNN, is professor of political science, University of Georgia, and director of the Institute of Government. Among his books are *Financing Presidential Campaigns* and *Public Officials and the Press.* He has written widely on the media and politics.

DINA GOREN, is senior lecturer in the Communications Institute of Hebrew University, Jerusalem, Israel. She is the author of several books and articles on government and media relations. She was a visiting scholar at Yale University at the time this chapter was written.

YOUNG C. KIM, professor of political science, George Washington University. His publications include *Future of the Korean Peninsula* and *Japanese Journalists and Their World*.

MICHAEL W. MANSFIELD, is associate professor of political science at Baylor University. He is co-editor of *Drama in Life: The Uses of Communication in Society* and contributor to books and journals concerning communication and methodology.

DAN NIMMO, has joint appointments as professor of political science, Department of Political Science, and professor of journalism, College of Communications, University of Tennessee. Among his many books are *Newsgathering in Washington*, *The Political Persuaders*, *Popular Images and Politics*, *Political Communication and Public Opinion in America*, and *Subliminal Politics*. He is co-author of *Candidates and their Images* and editor of *Communication Yearbook 3* and *Communication Yearbook 4*.

ROBERTO PETROGNANI, member of the Institute of Political Science of the University of Florence. He is interested in the theory and empirical study of communications in general and of political communications in particular. Author of various articles on political communications and the theory of information. He is co-author of *Cinema Industriale e Societa Italiano* and co-founder of the review *Quaderni di Sociologia della Communicazione*.

ROZANN ROTHMAN, gathered the data for her chapter while a Fellow of the Leonard Davis Institute for International Studies at Herbrew University, Jerusalem. She is the author of several articles on government and media relations, the symbolic uses of communications, and Israeli government and politics.

ANTHONY WESTELL, professor of journalism, Carleton University, Ottawa, and editorial page columnist for the *Toronto Star*. He has served as chief editorial writer and Ottawa Bureau Chief for *The Globe and Mail*. He has published *Paradox—Trudeau as Prime Minister* and *The New Society*.

JOHN WESTERN, is professor of sociology at the University of Queensland. He had published extensively in the area of the mass media in Australia.

OSMO A. WIIO, professor, chairman of Communication Department, University of Helsinki. He has served as a member of the Finnish Parliament, assistant to the Finnish Prime Minister, and on numerous commissions and boards on communication and broadcasting policy.